D0044854

Global
Investing

Global Investing

The Professional's Guide to the World Capital Markets

Roger G. Ibbotson
Gary P. Brinson

McGraw-Hill, Inc.
New York   St. Louis   San Francisco   Auckland   Bogotá
Caracas   Lisbon   London   Madrid   Mexico   Milan
Montreal   New Delhi   Paris   San Juan   São Paulo
Singapore   Sydney   Tokyo   Toronto

Library of Congress Cataloging-in-Publication Data

Ibbotson, Roger G.
   Global investing : the professional's guide to the world capital
markets / Roger G. Ibbotson, Gary P. Brinson.
   p.   cm.
   Includes index.
   ISBN 0-07-031683-X
   1. Investments, Foreign.   2. Portfolio management.   I. Brinson,
Gary P.   II. Title.
   HG4538.I464   1993
   332.6'73—dc20   92–34241
                                                                 CIP

        6 7 8 9 0   DOC/DOC   9 8 7 6 5

ISBN 0-07-031683-X

*The sponsoring editor for this book was Betsy N. Brown, the editing supervisor was
Barbara B. Toniolo, and the production supervisor was Pamela A. Pelton. It was set in
Baskerville by Caliber/Phoenix Color Corp.*

Printed and bound by R.R. Donnelley & Sons Company.

Table 15.1, "Summary of Generally Accepted Accounting Principles for Major
Industrialized Countries" from *Financial Accounting: An Introduction to Concepts,
Methods, and Uses,* Sixth Edition, by Clyde P. Stickney, Roman L. Weil, and
Sidney Davidson, copyright © 1991 by Harcourt Brace Jovanovich, Inc.,
reprinted by permission of the publisher.

Contents

Part 6. Conclusion

Preface

Five years ago, when we wrote *Investment Markets*, the stock markets of the world were experiencing one of the greatest expansions in their history. High inflation rates were a recent and vivid memory. Bonds were recovering so vigorously from their lows of a few years earlier that they frequently outpaced the booming stock market. In the political arena, China appeared to be leading a retreat from communism, while relations with the Soviet Union were thawing from one of the bitterest periods of the Cold War as its new leader, Mikhail Gorbachev, made an opening to the free world.

It has been an eventful half-decade. As we write this, the republics of the former Soviet Union search for political structures more suitable than the deposed communist regime that somehow lasted more than 70 years. With the June 4, 1989 massacre in Tiananmen Square, China took a giant step backward toward central political control, although its primitive economy has remained stable. The Berlin Wall fell later in 1989, and the formerly communist states of central and eastern Europe are slowly emerging as capitalist democracies.

Equities crashed on October 19, 1987, in what proved to be the first truly global capital market event. A day later, no stock exchange, not even the gravity-defying Tokyo market, had escaped severe damage. Equity markets later went on to establish new highs, but the vigor of the middle 1980s was not recaptured. The New York Stock Exchange yielded first place to Tokyo in market capitalization, then regained it when Japanese stock prices fell by nearly half in 1990.

New types of financial instruments were created by the score while others, such as junk bonds, lost favor. In the United States, a declining real estate market and regulatory failures combined to undermine the entire financial services sector. The savings and loan industry was the first casualty, and banks and insurance companies threatened to follow. As we write this, the general economic recession has entered its second year.

Capital markets have, like other markets, become increasingly global over the last 5 years. International investing is well-established in the United States, where it was almost unheard of a generation ago. All of the factors of production not bolted to the ground—people, goods, and capital—are beginning to flow across national borders as borders lose their relevance.

This phenomenon has motivated us to write a second book, focused more clearly on the global character of capital markets. Once again, we seek to treat all assets more or less equally, but with an emphasis on those held by institutional investors and those for which reliable data are obtainable. The focus of this book is on the institutional market, necessitating a slightly more technical treatment of some topics. Nevertheless, we believe there is much here to benefit the well-informed general reader.

This book is divided into six sections, each concentrating on one aspect of global investing. Part 1 provides an overview of the issues. The current state of the world is portrayed in terms of population, economic activity, and capital markets. Because exchange rates and other capital asset prices are the topics of greatest concern to global investors, we discuss the leading theories that provide a paradigm for investigation of these issues.

Part 2 highlights the importance of the asset allocation decision and discusses alternative methods of portfolio management.

The next three sections are devoted to particular asset classes. Part 3 analyzes the world equity markets, both past and present, while Part 4 does the same with the world fixed-income market. Part 5 covers a potpourri of other assets, and includes a study of inflation around the world.

Part 6 concludes the book with some speculations about what the future holds and its implications for investors.

Acknowledgments

This book could not have been written without the dedication, patience, and talent of many colleagues over a period of years. Brinson Partners, Inc. and Ibbotson Associates, Inc. both provided considerable financial support.

At Ibbotson Associates, Mark W. Riepe was involved with every aspect of the manuscript from start to finish, including the initial conceptualization and ongoing exposition of ideas, writing, data analysis, exhibit preparation, and editing. Laurence B. Siegel crafted the outline and provided the organizational structure, coordinating the efforts of the others named here, as well as contributing a substantial body of his own material and editing the entire book with great care. Paul D. Kaplan made a major contribution to Chapters 2 and 3, and his mastery of conceptual and theoretical issues enabled us to write the rest of the book with the comfort that most of the ideas expressed are correct. Julie Lubeck and David M. Montgomery fulfilled data requests and answered a blizzard of questions with accuracy, grace, and good humor.

At Brinson Partners, Brian P. Singer coordinated the efforts of his colleagues, made substantial editorial modifications to the entire book, and collaborated with the authors on Chapters 4 and 5. Denis S. Karnosky read the manuscript with red pencil always in hand, catching our mistakes and making an irreplaceable intellectual contribution. We are particularly indebted to Bart A. Holaday, who not only supplied the research necessary to write Chapter 15, but provided a draft of the text that required almost no change.

Professor William N. Goetzmann of Columbia University provided much of the research used in Chapter 14 and the section on art within Chapter 16. Some of his ideas and words were used with only minor modification. The clarity of the books and articles by Professor Bruno Solnik of

Centre HEC-ISA is, we hope, reflected in Chapters 2 and 3, which cover some of the material for which he has gained fame. Other members of the academic financial community, too numerous to mention individually, answered questions and clarified subtle points in a timely and helpful manner.

Katie B. Weigel at the Frank Russell Company was particularly helpful in providing and explaining the Salomon-Russell indices. Without the efforts of Kate Jonas and Carla Dearing at Morgan Stanley Capital International, our detailed treatment of the historical returns on non-U.S. equities would not have been possible. At Goldman Sachs, Barbara Mueller contributed the indices her firm developed with the *Financial Times*. Bryan Allworthy at Barclays de Zoete Wedd provided the study, which he co-authored, of historical returns in the United Kingdom. Brian R. Bruce of State Street Bank and Trust Company supplied helpful commentary on international equity markets. Judy Otterman and Rosario Benavides of Salomon Brothers graciously provided the data on world bond market capitalization. Peter Tropper and Peter Wall of the International Finance Corporation did the same for the emerging equity markets data. Yasushi Hamao of Columbia University compiled much of the data on Japanese small stocks. To the many others who contributed their expertise, we offer our thanks.

Roger G. Ibbotson
Gary P. Brinson

PART 1
The Global Marketplace

1

The World: People, Production, and Capital Markets

The global market for investments operates in the context of the world and its people. While the rest of this book focuses on capital markets, this chapter examines the social and economic framework that encompasses them. We begin by asking how a global economy capable of sustainable growth came to exist. We then portray the world in terms of demography and economic activity. We close by examining the basic structure and returns of the capital markets in which investors have the opportunity to participate.

Toward a Borderless World

It was not that Nature herself had become more generous. On the contrary, as the famous Law of Diminishing Returns made clear, Nature yielded up her wealth more grudgingly as she was more intensely cultivated. The secret to economic growth lay in the fact that each generation attacked Nature not only with its own energies and resources, but with the heritage of equipment accumulated by its forebears. And as that heritage grew—as each generation added its quota of new knowledge, factories, tools, and techniques to the wealth of the past—human productivity increased with astonishing rapidity. A factory worker in the 1960s in the United States turned out over *five times* as much goods in an hour's toil as a worker at the time of the Civil War—not because he worked harder . . . but because he worked with technological powers that made him a superman compared with his Civil War predecessor.[1]

[1]Robert L. Heilbroner, *The Worldly Philosophers: The Lives, Times and Ideas of the Great Economic Thinkers*, 6th edition, Simon & Schuster, New York, 1986.

For the first time in history, most of the world's people have the opportunity, if not the fact, of living at a standard above subsistence. In the wealthiest countries this state of affairs is scarcely 2 centuries old; in the poorest countries the creation of wealth is just beginning.

Why now? Roughly 55 centuries of recorded history encompass scores of examples of wealth accumulation. When wealth and power have been combined with knowledge, remarkable achievements were observed. Ancient Greece and Rome are outstanding examples. But these flourishings of wealth and culture were followed by collapses of a magnitude far greater than any modern economic depression. The civilizations ceased to exist. Why should the present moment, the civilization we live in, be fundamentally different?

The reason is that *human capital*—the stock of ideas and information possessed by human beings—is mobile to an unprecedented degree and is the predominant form of capital in any civilization; Heilbroner's "technological powers" are composed of little else. Most of the capital embodied in the machines the worker needs to be productive is not in the physical essence of the machines, but in the knowledge of how to build and use them. The world of today is unlike that of any other historical period because fast and cheap communication enables this human capital to migrate to the places where the market most values it. Moreover, with fast and cheap transportation, people themselves (carrying their human capital with them) face lower barriers to physical migration. These combined circumstances permit the world stock of human capital to grow quickly and efficiently.

The natural barriers of high communication and transportation costs that prevented local knowledge and wealth from being spread around the globe in past times, then, are essentially gone. The only significant barriers left are those erected intentionally. These, too, are crumbling as people, acting in their own interest, expend great effort to render them ineffective.

Of course, no person or nation is immune from difficulties that can loom large in the short span of a human life. The catastrophic economic depression during the years 1929–1933 undid the previous two decades of growth in the United States; the prosperity of 1929 was not seen again until after World War II. What is important, however, is that the Great Depression did not end a civilization, nor did it undo the growth of 2 centuries. We survived and later prospered.

This rosy picture of the period since the industrial revolution,[2] and its suggestion that the future is even rosier, requires some tempering. The tra-

---

[2] The term *industrial revolution* is usually associated with the introduction of power-driven machinery in manufacturing. This occurred in northwestern Europe (most notably the United Kingdom) and in the United States over the period 1750–1830. We regard this period of transition as the *first* industrial revolution of modern times. The second, spanning the

ditional scourges of humankind—war, pestilence, tyranny, and famine—are still with us. The twentieth century has been a relatively warlike one. On net, pestilence and tyranny are both in retreat, although the exceptions are spectacular and tragic. Famine is far less widespread than it was even a generation ago, but the economic problem is still perceived by many persons as the hard reality of "how to survive," not the economist's generality of "how to allocate scarce resources among unlimited wants." While some societies enjoy an extended boom punctuated only by minor setbacks, other societies—sometimes geographically next door—seem unable to develop at all. As judged by the ideals of our own time and place, the world is a mess.

All this understood, the wealth of the world and of its individuals is greater today than it has ever been before, both in totality and per capita. The long-run outlook is for more growth—a great deal of it, especially for those who have experienced less of it. Environmental considerations will cause the costs of growth to be more carefully accounted for, but they will not impose strict limits to growth as some persons have suggested.

The remaining chapters of this book, as well as the final parts of this chapter, focus on the implications of these ideas for the investor in capital markets. First, however, in the belief that documentation of the basic structure of the world fosters comprehension, we examine the distribution of the world's population. Then, in the same spirit, we examine the world economy at this unique juncture in its development, as it converges gradually but forcefully on the eventual reality of a borderless world.

Where the People Are

As we noted, the principal capital asset of the world is its people. To put the distribution of people in perspective, we have drawn the odd-looking map shown in Figure 1-1. Unlike most maps, which show land masses in proportion to their shape and area, this map shows principal countries and regions of the world in proportion to their population. (Some semblance of the shape is preserved so that the places are recognizable.)

This map is dominated by China and India. Although the Americas, Europe, Africa, and the Pacific rim of Asia all have substantial populations, they sum to little more than half the world's total. The United States, Japan,

---

period 1870–1920, was characterized by the use of electricity and encompassed the age of invention, in which the basic tools of contemporary life—the telephone, automobile, airplane, and basic radio communication—were introduced. The third, which is still ongoing, saw the introduction of computers and other semiconductor-based electronic devices as additional basic tools of living.

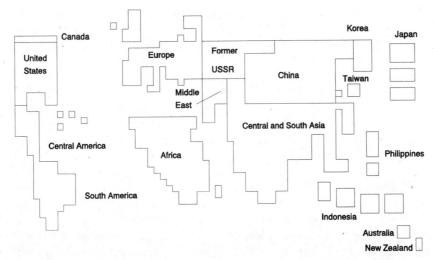

Figure 1-1. Where the people are: countries and regions drawn in approximate proportion to population. *(Source: Ibbotson Associates, Inc., using data from* World Development Report 1992: The Challenge of Development. *Copyright © 1992 by the International Bank for Reconstruction and Development/The World Bank. Reprinted by permission of Oxford University Press, Inc.;* The World Book Encyclopedia *(Taiwan and USSR), World Book, Inc., Chicago, 1990.)*

and the rich countries of western Europe look unexceptional—neither large nor small—on the population map.

Population and world influence have been closely related throughout history. The population map shows why China, despite its poverty, is often perceived as a global power. Europe, on the other hand, reached its peak of influence around the beginning of the twentieth century, when it also reached its peak of relative population. In 1900 one-third of humanity was European; today the ratio is just over one in ten. The map suggests that the power of India as well as China has yet to be fully realized.

Another remarkable observation prompted by the population map is that much of the land area of the world is empty space. This empty space is disproportionately contained within the richer countries, making Australia, Canada, Greenland, the United States, and the republics of the former Soviet Union much larger on a conventional map than they are here.

This does not mean that spaciousness makes for wealth, or crowding for poverty. The world's greatest accumulations of wealth are in the fabulously crowded cities of New York, London, Paris, and Tokyo; these cities provide a bewildering array of opportunities and enticements. The opportunities to exchange ideas and make money attract the poor, so that many cities seem to be full of poor people. But cities do not create poverty, they dispel it. Great centers of population enable the matching of human skills to economic needs to take place efficiently and creatively.

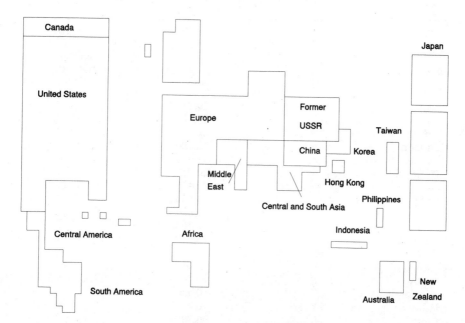

Figure 1-2. Where the money is: countries and regions drawn in approximate proportion to GNP. *(Source: Ibbotson Associates, Inc., using data from* World Development Report 1992: The Challenge of Development. *Copyright © 1992 by the International Bank for Reconstruction and Development/The World Bank. Reprinted by permission of Oxford University Press, Inc.;* The World Book Encyclopedia *(Taiwan and USSR), World Book, Inc., Chicago, 1990.)*

Where the Money Is

Like the population map, the map in Figure 1-2 has an unusual appearance. In this second map, each country or region is drawn in proportion to its gross national product (GNP). In dramatic contrast to the population map, the wealth map shows the United States as the largest single country in the world. Japan is also huge, about half as large as the United States. The United Kingdom is larger than either India or the entire continent of Africa.

Comparison of the population and GNP maps brings political and economic conflicts into focus. The population map shows why the leaders of the former Soviet Union felt political rivalry with its huge neighbor China. Similarly, the GNP map helps explain China's rivalry with Russia, and more pointedly, with its economically powerful capitalist neighbor Japan.

Population, per capita GNP, and the real (inflation-adjusted) growth rate of GNP from 1965 to 1989 are shown for selected countries in Table 1-1. We classify countries according to their per capita GNPs, considering this statistic to be a reasonable proxy for relative wealth. We use the classification

Table 1-1. Basic Indicators of World Income and Growth, by Country (1989 Data)

Country	Population (millions)	Per capita GNP ($)	Real growth rate of per capita GNP (%) (1965–1989)
High-Income Economies			
Switzerland	6.6	29,880	4.6
Japan	123.1	23,810	4.3
Norway	4.2	22,290	3.4
Finland	5.0	22,120	3.2
Sweden	8.5	21,570	1.8
United States	248.8	20,910	1.6
Germany	62.0	20,440	2.4
Canada	26.2	19,030	4.0
France	56.2	17,820	2.3
Austria	7.6	17,300	2.9
Netherlands	14.8	15,920	1.8
Italy	57.5	15,120	3.0
United Kingdom	57.2	14,610	2.0
Australia	16.8	14,360	1.7
Singapore	2.7	10,450	7.0
Hong Kong	5.7	10,350	6.3
Israel	4.5	9,790	2.7
Spain	38.8	9,330	2.4
Ireland	3.5	8,710	2.1
Saudi Arabia	14.4	6,020	2.6
Upper-Middle-Income Economies			
Greece	10.0	5,350	2.9
Korea (South)	42.4	4,400	7.0
Portugal	10.3	4,250	3.0
Czechoslovakia	15.6	3,450	n/a
Iran	53.3	3,200	0.5
Hungary	10.6	2,590	n/a
Brazil	147.3	2,540	3.5
South Africa	35.0	2,470	0.8
Taiwan	20.4	n/a	n/a
Republics of former U.S.S.R.	288.2	n/a	n/a
Lower-Middle-Income Economies			
Algeria	24.4	2,230	2.5
Malaysia	17.4	2,160	4.0
Argentina	31.9	2,160	−0.1
Mexico	84.6	2,010	3.0
Poland	37.9	1,790	n/a
Chile	13.0	1,770	0.3
Turkey	55.0	1,370	2.6
Thailand	55.4	1,220	4.2

(Continued)

Table 1-1. Basic Indicators of World Income and Growth, by Country
(Continued)

Country	Population (millions)	Per capita GNP ($)	Real growth rate of per capita GNP (%) (1965–1989)
Lower-Middle-Income Economies (Continued)			
Colombia	32.3	1,200	2.3
Ecuador	10.3	1,020	3.0
Peru	21.2	1,010	−0.2
Morocco	24.5	880	2.3
Ivory Coast	11.7	790	0.8
Philippines	60.0	710	1.6
Zimbabwe	9.5	650	1.2
Egypt	51.0	640	4.2
Low-Income Economies			
Indonesia	178.2	500	4.4
Sri Lanka	16.8	430	3.0
Pakistan	109.9	370	2.5
Kenya	23.5	360	2.0
China	1,113.9	350	5.7
India	832.5	340	1.8
Zaire	34.5	260	−2.0
Nigeria	113.8	250	0.2
Nepal	18.4	180	0.6
Bangladesh	110.7	180	0.4
Tanzania	23.8	130	−0.1
Mozambique	15.3	80	n/a
Myanmar (Burma)	40.8	n/a	n/a
Sudan	24.5	n/a	n/a
Vietnam	64.8	n/a	n/a

NOTES: All countries with large populations are shown, even if economic data are not available (marked n/a). Countries with no available economic data are listed at the bottom of the group in which it is believed they would fit; no implication that they would be ranked at the bottom of the group is intended. All data for Germany are for the former Federal Republic of Germany (West Germany) only.

SOURCES: *World Development Report 1992: The Challenge of Development*, pp. 204–205. Copyright ©1992 by the International Bank for Reconstruction and Development/The World Bank. Reprinted by permission of Oxford University Press, Inc.; *The World Book Encyclopedia* (Taiwan and U.S.S.R), World Book, Inc., Chicago, 1990.

scheme set forth by the World Bank, which identifies economies by four levels of income—high, upper middle, lower middle, and low.

Per capita GNP has some shortcomings as a measure of the monetary wealth of a country's people. First, GNP is not adjusted for the varying costs of living in different countries. For example, it is more expensive to live in Switzerland, Japan, and the Scandinavian countries than it is to live in the United States; a recent study that adjusts for living costs ranks the United States as the wealthiest country in the world. Second, countries have richer and poorer regions within them. Third, per capita GNP is only an average across individuals; the character of an economy is defined by the degree of income inequality as well as the average income. With similar average incomes, Brazil and Hungary are examples: Brazil is a place of abject misery and sudden fortune, whereas Hungary does not have much of either.[3]

Of course, the money income of a person, even if correctly estimated, is not an ideal measure of that person's wealth. Wealth is the extent to which an individual has the means to enjoy living. Many kinds of wealth differences—in climate, natural beauty, public health, cultural amenities, freedom—are masked by this measure. Of the many components of wealth, however, money incomes are the most readily measurable. Consequently, we use concepts such as GNP, the market value of publicly traded securities, and other money amounts as measures of the wealth of a person, a community, a nation, or the world.

We do not make the traditional distinction between the developed capitalist first world, the formerly communist second world, and the developing or undeveloped third world because that taxonomy is increasingly meaningless. Instead, we believe that a purely economic, rather than geopolitical, classification scheme—such as that used by the World Bank and represented in Table 1-1—is the simplest and most effective way of organizing information about the world's nations. For example, the republics of the former Soviet Union are upper-middle-income economies, and are classified with various other upper-middle-income countries which were never subject to communist rule. China has the political form of a communist country but shares many economic characteristics with noncommunist, low-income, rapidly developing economies. Table 1-2 provides summary data of world population, production, and growth rates with countries grouped according to this economic classification scheme.

The Geographic Distribution of Wealth

Nearly a billion people live in high-income countries—as many people as lived on the entire earth 2 centuries ago—but they account for only one-sixth of the world's population today. Almost all of the high-income countries are in Europe, in North America, and along an arc of the western Pacific stretching from Japan to New Zealand. The largest geographic con-

---

[3]Data for Hungary are prerevolutionary (1989) and may be unreliable.

Table 1-2. Basic Indicators of World Income and Growth:
Aggregations by Income Category
(1989 Data)

Category	Population (millions)	Percent of world population	Per capita GNP ($)	Real growth rate of per capita GNP (%) (1965–1989)
Total high income	855	16.4	18,330	2.4
Total middle income	1,399	26.9	2,040	2.3
Upper middle income	714	13.7	3,150	2.6
Lower middle income	685	13.2	1,360	2.0
Total low income	2,952	56.7	330	2.9
China and India	1,946	37.4	350	3.6
Other low income	1,006	19.3	300	1.4
World total	5,206	100.0	3,980	1.6

NOTES: Totals include countries not shown separately in Table 1-1. Countries with no available economic data are included in population totals but not in economic totals.

SOURCE: *World Development Report 1992: The Challenge of Development,* pp. 204–205. Copyright © 1992 by the International Bank for Reconstruction and Development/The World Bank. Reprinted by permission of Oxford University Press, Inc.

centration of wealth is in western and central Europe; the United States and Canada together form the other great concentration.

With three-fifths of the world's population, Asia has the widest disparities of wealth found on any continent. Japan, itself a casualty of war 50 years ago, has the second highest per capita GNP in the world, while the countries of Indochina, casualties of a more recent war as well as communism, have among the lowest. China and India, by far the world's largest countries in population, have experienced rapid growth but started from such a low point that both countries still rank among the poorest in terms of per capita GNP. As one might expect, development of these continent-sized countries has been geographically uneven, with India's growth concentrated in the north and west and China's in the south.

Sub-Saharan Africa is the poorest part of the world. The tiny oil-exporting nation of Gabon and the moderately industrialized and resource-rich Republic of South Africa are the only upper-middle-income countries in the region.

The experience of Latin America has been heterogeneous and puzzling. The economist Walt W. Rostow has called Argentina the first formerly developed country; in the early 1900s it was a credible rival of the United States. Neighboring Uruguay has followed the same path. The large countries of the region, Brazil and Mexico, have had turbulent growth, with some of the most exuberant booms and severest depressions ever observed.

The World's New Middle Class

Americans are accustomed to thinking that the middle class is the most likely place for a person to be. This way of thinking is an artifact of the remarkable growth of the United States economy over the last two centuries. Through most of world history, the paradigm of economic distribution was a pyramid, with the vast majority of people at the bottom. As one moved up on the pyramid, one found fewer and fewer people. At the top were a few very wealthy chiefs, kings, and captains of industry.

While low-income countries still account for a plurality of the world's population, economic growth has created a global middle class in which most people are relatively far from the precariousness of subsistence living and also far from the luxury of wealth. Of course, the standard of living of these people in the middle would strike most Americans as quite poor. If one leaves out China and India, middle-income countries (including lower middle and upper middle) have a plurality of the population today; the wealth distribution pyramid is transformed into a rhomboid, with a thick middle and thinner top and bottom.

Where the Capital
Markets Are

Equities

Of the many forms of capital that are traded in markets, the stock market is the most sensitive to the ups and downs of the economy. This is because stock price changes reflect changes in the value of the corporate sector of the economy *on the margin*. Stated another way, stock markets show changes in economic performance, and differences among economies, through a magnifying glass.

In Figure 1-3, the size of each country is drawn in proportion to the capitalization (price times number of shares outstanding) of its equity market. A few countries have no stock market at all. Many more, including developing countries where considerable wealth has been accumulated, have small markets. The large stock markets of the world are concentrated, even more so than overall wealth, in the high-income countries of North America, western and central Europe, and the Pacific rim, which is dominated by Japan.

Over the few decades for which market capitalization data are available, the United States was dominant until recently. In 1960, non-U.S. stocks made up only about 30 percent of world equity capitalization. For the next 3 decades, non-U.S. stocks (European as well as Asian) grew in capitalization

Figure 1-3. Where the equity capital is: countries and regions drawn in approximate proportion to equity market capitalization. (*Source: Batterymarch Financial Management.*)

**MARKET CAPITALIZATION
IN MILLIONS US$**

0 - 5,000

5,001 - 25,000

25,001 - 100,000

100,001 - 200,000

200,000 - 1,000,000

Over 1,000,000

at a rate consistently faster than U.S. issues.[4] In 1960 Japan's stock market made up just over 3 percent of world market value; by year-end 1989 it represented 40.5 percent. (The United States had 29.9 percent of world market value on the same date.) The bear market in Japan that began in 1990 has made the United States once again the largest market, but not a dominant one. At this time, the North American, European, and Pacific Rim markets are roughly equal in size.

The equity market capitalization that is *available* to investors outside one's home country typically differs from the total capitalization represented in Figure 1-3. The Salomon-Russell indexes of available capitalization are calculated by adjusting total capitalization for corporate crossholdings (one company owning shares of another), government holdings of shares, large private positions such as family holdings, and restrictions on foreign ownership.[5] These factors each figure differently in the adjustments made for different countries. The net result of these adjustments is to increase the importance of U.S. and British equities, which have the fewest encumbrances, in the world market. (See Table 6-1.)

Financial Wealth of the World

While the stock market is the most vivid indicator of changes in wealth, it makes up only a minority of the financial capital of the world economy. Figure 1-4 illustrates the division of financial wealth between the various asset markets. For the purpose of this exhibit, financial assets are considered to include real estate, even though most real estate is held privately in a relatively illiquid market. Likewise, total rather than available capitalization is used for all categories of assets.

Using these broadbrush estimates, the financial wealth of the world was $44.4 trillion as of year-end 1990, or $8529 per capita. Real estate outside the United States is the largest asset class, with an estimated value of $21.5 trillion. Non-U.S. assets dominate U.S. assets, making up 67 percent of the total. Bond markets are larger than equity markets, making up about 27 and 19 percent of world financial wealth, respectively.

---

[4]The growth rate of equity market capitalization is the combined effect of net new issues and increase in the market value of existing issues. Net new issues consist of new issues (including privatization of state-owned businesses) minus retirement of issues (due to bankruptcy, certain kinds of buyouts, companies going private, and nationalizations).

[5]The Salomon-Russell Global Equity indices are jointly compiled by Salomon Brothers Inc., New York, and the Frank Russell Company, Tacoma, Wash.

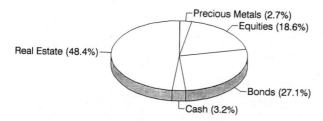

Figure 1-4. Financial wealth of the world 1990: $44,425 billion. *(Source: I/IDEAS World Capital Markets/Equity and World Capital Markets/Fixed Income data modules, Ibbotson Associates, Inc., Chicago, 1991.)*

Human Capital

The economist Simon Kuznets has demonstrated that the income from ownership of assets other than human capital (including all financial assets shown in Figure 1-4 plus other physical assets such as consumer durable goods) is roughly 20 percent of all income.[6] Income from human capital—that is, paid to employees—represents about 80 percent of all income. This ratio appears to be stable across long time periods and a wide variety of countries. Using this information, and assuming that the ratio of total wealth to financial and physical wealth is the same as the ratio of total income to financial and physical asset income, we estimate the total wealth (including human capital) of the high-income countries to be approximately $222 trillion.

Using the population and GNP data from Table 1-2, it is possible to estimate the wealth of the entire world. The GNP (in total, not per capita) of the middle- and low-income countries amounts to 18.4 percent of world GNP. Assuming that the wealth of each category of countries is proportionate to GNP, the wealth of the world amounts to approximately $272 trillion.

Investable Wealth

The wealth of the world that is accessible to investors is drastically smaller than the aggregate wealth of the world. Human capital is not investable, and real estate outside one's home country is typically difficult to obtain. Consumer durables and other private holdings are likewise excluded from investable wealth.

---

[6]See Simon Kuznets, *Modern Economic Growth*, Yale University Press, New Haven, 1966, pp. 168–170. Kuznets's estimate of income from ownership of assets includes income from certain nonfinancial assets such as consumer durable goods.

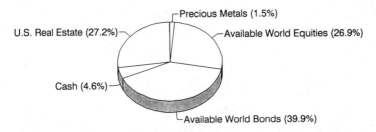

Figure 1-5. Financial wealth of the world available to U.S. investors: 1990—$22,417 billion. *(Source: I/IDEAS World Capital Markets/Equity and World Capital Markets/Fixed Income data modules, Ibbotson Associates, Inc., Chicago, 1991; Salomon-Russell Global Equity Indices; and authors' estimates.)*

Figure 1-5 indicates the investable wealth of the world from the standpoint of a U.S. investor. At year-end 1990, investable wealth for a U.S. investor amounted to $22.4 trillion. Of this amount, about one quarter is U.S. real estate, which is dominated by single-family homes. Although institutional investors do not typically hold such residential properties, they should be counted in a broadbrush estimate of investable wealth because they make up a large part of most asset owners' portfolios.

Mirroring the proportions found for world assets, U.S. bonds exceed U.S. stocks in market capitalization. As noted earlier, the capitalization of non-U.S stocks and bonds that are available to the U.S. investor is considerably smaller than the total capitalization of these markets.

Returns on the World Market Portfolio

The most important characteristic of any asset class is its total return. Figure 1-6 shows an index of the total returns on each of the principal financial assets of the world, where the index is initialized at $1 at the end of 1959. For comparability across countries, all returns are denominated in U.S. dollars. Here, only global aggregations of asset classes are reported; country-by-country asset class returns are reported elsewhere in this book.

The return experienced by holders of each asset class is related to the risk they took. Equities, the financial asset class with the most variable returns, had the best results: a dollar invested at year-end 1959 in the global stock market grew to $23.25 by the end of 1990. This value, which assumes unhedged returns and reinvestment of dividends and ignores taxes and transaction costs, represents a compound annual growth rate of 10.7 percent.

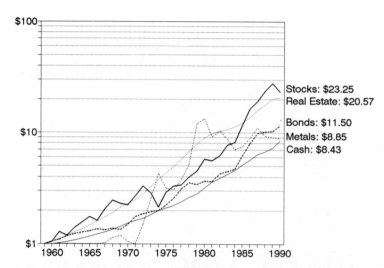

Figure 1-6. Growth of $1 invested in world asset classes (year-end 1959 = $1). *(Source: Morgan Stanley Capital International, I/IDEAS U.S. Capital Markets, World Capital Markets/Equity, and World Capital Markets/Fixed Income data modules, Ibbotson Associates, Inc., Chicago, 1991; Roger G. Ibbotson, Laurence B. Siegel, and Kathryn S. Love, "World Wealth: U.S. and Foreign Market Values and Returns," The Journal of Portfolio Management, Fall 1985. This copyrighted material is reprinted with permission from Institutional Investor.)*

We do not report global real estate returns because high-quality data for such returns are scarce outside the United States. Real estate in the United States had returns just below those of global stocks, with a dollar invested in 1959 growing to $20.57. Although the real estate return series appears smooth, we believe that there are hidden risks which the return data do not reveal. (See Chapter 13.) Investors require and, over the long run, receive compensation for these hidden risks. In addition, the period studied was unusually favorable to real estate because of its high inflation rates and, until the last decade, high tax rates.

A dollar invested in global bonds grew to $11.50 over the 31-year period studied, representing an 8.2 percent compound annual return. Cash equivalents grew to $8.43 over the same period, returning 7.1 percent annually. Monetary metals (gold and silver) had almost exactly the same return as cash equivalents over this long period, which is unsurprising since both assets tend to track inflation. (See Chapter 15.) The volatility of returns on gold and silver, however, was the highest of all the asset classes shown in Figure 1-6.

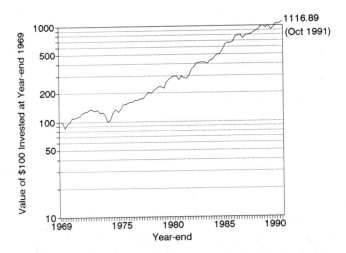

Figure 1-7. Returns on world investable wealth: the Multiple Markets Index. *(Source: Brinson Partners, Inc.)*

The Multiple Markets Index

To condense the returns on global assets available to the U.S. investor to a single benchmark, Brinson Partners' Multiple Markets Index (MMI) was created.[7] The benchmark is intended as an alternative to traditional multiasset benchmarks for U.S. pension plans, which over the last 30 years have held an average of 60 percent in equities and equitylike securities, and 40 percent in fixed-income securities. Rather than build a market capitalization-weighted portfolio of available assets, the constructors of the MMI used optimization techniques to identify the portfolio mix of available global asset classes that matched the risk level of a typical U.S. pension plan. (For this reason non-U.S. equities, for example, are underrepresented relative to market capitalization weights.) The optimization results were rounded to obtain the final MMI weights, shown in Table 1-3. (The weight of cash equivalents rounds to zero.) The weights are highly stable over time, and the index is rebalanced to the policy weights quarterly.

Figure 1-7 shows the performance of the MMI since its inception at year-end 1969. An investment of $100 in the index grew to $1116.89 by the end of October 1991, for a compound annual return of 11.7 percent. The most remarkable feature of Figure 1-7 is the steady rise of the index. For this diversified portfolio, the only major downturn over the 22-year period was

---

[7]The Multiple Markets Index is described in Gary P. Brinson, Jeffrey J. Diermeier, and Gary G. Schlarbaum, "A Composite Portfolio Benchmark for Pension Plans," *Financial Analysts Journal*, March/April 1986.

Table 1-3. Composition of the Multiple Markets Index
(In Percent)

Asset class	January 1, 1970 to June 30, 1987	July 1, 1987 to June 30, 1991	July 1, 1991 to present
Equities			
U.S. large capitalization	30	28	28
U.S. small and midcapitalization	15	12	12
All other countries	10	15	15
Venture capital	5	5	5
Fixed income			
U.S. domestic investment grade	15	18	18
U.S. domestic high yield	0	0	3
International dollar bonds	4	2	2
Nondollar bonds	6	5	5
U.S. real estate	15	15	12
Cash equivalents	0	0	0
Total	100	100	100

SOURCE: Brinson Partners, Inc.

that of the 1973–1974 period when both the stock and bond markets fell in most countries. Smaller global declines are visible in 1970 and 1990. The period from early 1981 to mid-1982, containing a mixture of up and down returns, represented a substantial decline in real (inflation-adjusted) terms because of the high inflation rates of that period. The stock market crash of October 1987 shows up as a negative return, but it is greatly mitigated by the strong bond market and by the large weight of Japan, where the stock market fell less than in other countries.

2

Currency Markets and Exchange Rates

To understand the global marketplace for capital assets, which are denominated in various monetary units, or currencies, it is necessary first to understand the terminology, history, and behavior of currencies. First, we describe the basic properties and terminology of currencies and their relative prices (exchange rates). Second, we recount the recent history of exchange rate regimes that led up to the floating rate system now prevailing. Finally, we describe some hypotheses that have been proposed as characterizing the behavior of exchange rates and indicate to what extent these hypotheses have been successful.

Money and Exchange Rates

On Yap Island, gigantic circular stones are money.[1] In most of the rest of the world, notes issued by a central bank or governmental authority are money. The notes bear no interest and are redeemable only for more notes. Neither the stones nor the paper currency have any value in use. The obvious conclusion is that money is whatever people accept as payment for real economic goods and services.

Since people around the world seem willing to accept bank notes as money, the probing observer might ask why the world does not adopt a single currency, avoiding the many costs, risks, and general confusion of multiple currencies. The reason is that sovereign governments wish to maintain

[1] More exactly, the stones form the basis of the monetary system. Ownership interests in portions of the stones are exchanged for goods and services.

21

control of the supply of their domestic currency and use the money supply as a source of revenue.

Examples of the importance of controlling one's money supply abound. France in the 1920s was prone to devaluing the franc as a means to boost French exports. Many countries have hyperinflated their currencies to finance their massive government deficits. The United States Federal Reserve has increased the money supply in times of economic slowdown while restricting it at other times to restrain inflation. In short, diverse currencies exist because governments want to retain them as tools for achieving domestic objectives.

Exchange rates are the mechanism by which these currencies are tied together in the global economy, providing the price of one currency in terms of another. Exchange rate risk is the possibility that one's holding of foreign currency will change in purchasing power when converted back to one's home currency. Through most of history, governments have attempted to control this risk by maintaining fixed exchange rates. For example, under the gold standard, currencies were defined as a certain weight of gold. The rate of exchange between two currencies was simply the ratio of the weights of gold defining the currencies. The risk to a foreign currency holder was official revaluation.[2]

Since about 1970, the world's currencies have become decoupled from gold. Their value has been set by the interaction of the policies of central banks (which control the money supply within a country) and free market forces (which set the exchange rates between countries' currencies). Agreements between governments to restrain these market forces have been somewhat effective, and these agreements are reviewed later in this chapter. Nevertheless, under the current floating-rate system, the movement of exchange rates is an important component of the return on an investment denominated in a foreign currency.

Exchange rate risk is important in today's markets for several reasons. The growth in international trade means that all companies, not just multinational and import-export sensitive companies, are exposed to exchange rate risk. A hypothetical French car manufacturer that sells only in France is nonetheless exposed to exchange rate risk because the relative strength of the French franc will influence the price of its competition, cars imported into France.

---

[2] Under the gold standard, revaluation is an officially sanctioned change in the gold-weight definition of the currency. The term revaluation is sometimes used to denote only an increase in the gold weight per unit of currency; a decrease is then called a devaluation.

Under a fiat money standard, revaluation is the revision of an official exchange rate into other currencies.

For the investor holding a capital asset denominated in a currency other than the one in which he consumes, exchange rate risk has a special importance. To such a cross-border investor, exchange rate fluctuations are a direct source of substantial risk in the short run, and possibly also in the long run. To control exchange rate risk, investors may hedge—that is, place currency bets that offset those implicit in their asset holdings. Whether or not to hedge is an important issue in global investing and is covered in Chapter 5.

Terminology of Exchange Rates

An exchange rate is a price, specifically the relative price of two currencies. For example, the sterling deutschemark exchange rate is the price of a deutschemark expressed in pounds sterling. In practice, two types of exchange rates are most commonly quoted: the spot rate and the forward rate. The *spot rate* is the relative price between two currencies for immediate delivery. The *forward rate* is the relative price of two currencies for delivery at some specified point in the future. For example, on July 23, 1992, the spot delivery price for the Japanese yen was quoted at 126.80 yen per dollar and the 30-day forward rate for yen was 132.48 yen per dollar. Entering into a forward rate contract on that day creates a long position in yen, committing the long side to receive 132.48 yen per dollar 30 days later (on August 22, 1992), regardless of the spot price at that time. The party taking the long side of this transaction is considered to be long in yen. The counterparty, who commits to deliver yen at 132.48 per dollar on August 22, 1992, is considered to be long dollars and short in yen.

Eurocurrency rates are the interest rates earned by bank deposits denominated in a currency other than the currency of the country in which the bank is located.[3] For example, deposits in non-U.S. banks that are denominated in dollars are called Eurodollar deposits. On July 23, 1992, the interest rate on a 3-month Eurodollar deposit was quoted at 3.375 percent. This was higher than the 3.16 percent interest rate on a 3-month U.S. Treasury bill, which is a virtually riskless form of deposit. This spread, called the Treasury-Eurodollar or TED spread, reflects the credit risk of the banks

---

[3] There is nothing uniquely European about "Euro" deposits, interest rates, and so forth. The U.S. Interest Equalization Tax of 1963 placed a tax on foreign securities sold in the United States. U.S. citizens and firms could legally avoid this tax by depositing dollars in foreign—at that time, typically European—banks. Because of other advantages of the Eurocurrency market, it continued to flourish after the tax was repealed. For a fuller discussion of these markets see Chapter 11.

holding the Eurodollar deposits and the sovereign risk, which is the possibility that the foreign country will impede or prohibit investors from retrieving their deposits in dollars.

Structure of the Currency Market

In terms of volume, the currency market is the largest financial marketplace in the world, with daily volume totaling an estimated $650 billion.[4] Normal commercial and financial transactions dominate this highly efficient market. Liquidity is provided by market makers and speculators who can influence exchange rates in the short term. But the long-term value of one currency in terms of another is dominated by the fundamental economic relationships among nations.

Foreign exchange market makers stand ready to buy and sell at any time, at posted quantities and prices. The motivation is to earn the spread between bid and offering (asking) prices, while avoiding overexposure to any one currency. Hedgers are exposed to currency risk from operating a line of business and take positions in the currency market to offset that risk. For example, a Japanese car manufacturer selling in the United States receives dollars and uses the currency markets to lock in a yen-dollar exchange rate. The speculator has an opinion on the direction of exchange rates and comes to the currency market to make that bet.

The currency market is predominantly an "interbank" market where a decentralized collection of banks, nonbank financial institutions, and foreign exchange brokers canvass each other by telephone or telex, looking for the best prices. Now, computer links allow subscribers to enter prices at which they are willing to transact. These prices are summarized on a single screen so that, at a glance, other traders can see with whom it is most advantageous to execute a trade.

The efficiency of the currency market is astounding. Communications technology allows executed trades, bids and offers, and news of events affecting exchange rates to be transmitted instantaneously throughout the world, 24 hours a day. The result is a market which is very price-efficient (exchange rates incorporate available information) as well as cost-efficient, with paper-thin bid-offer spreads.

---

[4] *The Wall Street Journal,* August 28, 1991.

The Historical Development of Today's Currency Market

The history of the currency market is fraught with controversy about how each country's money ought to be backed—by gold reserves, the "full faith and credit" of a government (that is, a fiat money standard), or some other arrangement. In addition, controversy arises over the best means to achieve a given monetary or exchange rate goal. The interaction of these decisions has produced a complex array of exchange rate regimes, some arrived at by international agreement and others by market forces. Figure 2-1 shows some of the outcomes of these forces. The graph shows the changing value of the U.S. dollar in terms of yen, deutschemarks, and pounds sterling from 1960 to 1991.[5] Over this period, the U.S. dollar depreciated (fell in value) at a 3.27 percent annual rate against the yen and at a 3.11 percent annual rate against the deutschemark. The dollar appreciated (gained in value) at a 1.27 percent annual rate against the pound sterling.

The Collapse of the Worldwide Gold Standard

Prior to World War I, exchange rates were determined by a country's stock of gold. The gold standard was scrapped during the war, but the German and other hyperinflations of the 1920s convinced many countries that the gold standard was the best method for controlling the growth of a country's money supply. In practice, however, many countries began to devalue their currency relative to gold, attempting to make their exports more attractive. In addition, lack of confidence in various countries' ability or willingness to redeem their currency in gold at official rates resulted in gold bullion, rather than gold-backed currencies, serving as acceptable payment for international trade. By 1934 the only currency that was officially convertible into gold was the U.S. dollar.

---

[5] The dollar prices of each foreign currency unit are normalized so that year-end 1959 = 1. This allows a direct comparison between the dollar-denominated performance of the three nondollar currencies. Exchange rates are typically quoted in the *less* valuable of the two currencies. Employing that convention, the exchange rates in January 1960 were: 361.777¥/$; 4.1705 DM/$; 2.8025 $/£. As of December 31, 1991, they were: 124.8 ¥/$; 1.515 DM/$; 1.8695 $/£. Exchange rates can also be quoted on a foreign currency per U.S. dollar basis; thus, the December 31, 1991, exchange rate of 124.8 ¥/$ is equivalent to 0.008013 $/¥.

Figure 2-1. Value of U.S. dollar in terms of foreign currencies, 1960–1991 (1959 = 1). *(Source: pre-1988 data from*
International Financial Statistics, *various issues, published by
the International Monetary Fund; data since 1988 are from*
The Wall Street Journal.*)*

The Bretton Woods Era

In 1944, representatives of the Allied governments met in Bretton Woods,
New Hampshire, to establish an exchange rate system that would correct
the failings of the prior gold standard. The new system sought to discourage
countries from aggressively manipulating the convertibility ratio between
their currencies and gold as they had under the old system. Devaluations
and revaluations of more than 10 percent were to require International
Monetary Fund permission.

Under the Bretton Woods agreement, the U.S. dollar would be convertible into gold at $35 per ounce,[6] and that the prices (exchange rates) for
other currencies would be fixed in dollars. If a country's currency began to
diverge from the stated rate, the country was required to intervene by transacting in order to push the market rate back to the stated rate.

---

[6] The federal government offered to convert dollars to gold only for foreigners. U.S. citizens were prohibited from holding more than $100 in gold.

Excessive monetary expansion and accelerating inflation in the United States led to the massive conversion of dollars into gold beginning in the late 1960s. This occurred because the intrinsic dollar value of gold was higher than the stated conversion price. The conversions proceeded at such a rapid pace that by August 1971 the United States suspended the convertibility of the dollar. Major trading nations met at the Smithsonian Institution in Washington, D.C., in December to address the situation. The resulting Smithsonian agreement revalued currencies with respect to the dollar and allowed for a wider band of fluctuation before intervention was required.

The Free Float

The new agreement did not save the fixed exchange rate system, however, as the various nations continued with divergent domestic economic policies. In 1972, the European Monetary Union or "Snake"[7] was formed, establishing a narrow band of exchange rate fluctuation between member currencies but a wide band of fluctuation against the U.S. dollar. By 1973, a free float against the U.S. dollar was approved by the European Monetary Union.

In 1979 the European Monetary System was established. The EMS placed tighter bands around member currencies with respect to each other, while the free float for member currencies against the U.S. dollar was retained.

The Dirty Float

By 1985 the United States was running enormous trade deficits. Blame was placed on the record high value of the dollar, which made U.S. exports uncompetitive in foreign markets. The so-called Group of Five (G-5) met at the Plaza Hotel in New York.[8] The resulting "Plaza Accord" committed participants to coordinate their policies in an effort to reduce the value of the dollar. In 1987, the G-7 countries met at the Louvre in Paris and agreed to the "Louvre Accord."[9] Member countries agreed to continue cooperation on exchange rate matters with the purpose of reducing the variability of exchange rates. The term "dirty float" refers to a system where the market determines exchange rates, but governments will intervene and attempt to slow the speed with which exchange rate adjustments take place. As of this writing the dirty float is in effect in all of the principal industrialized nations.

---

[7] The "Snake" refers to the shape of a graph of European currencies plotted in price per dollar, normalized so that each had the same beginning value. The nondollar currencies moved with each other but separately from the dollar, producing a snakelike graph.

[8] The G-5 consisted of the United States, United Kingdom, Japan, Germany, and France.

[9] The Group of Seven, or G-7, is comprised of the G-5 countries plus Canada and Italy.

The Behavior of Currency Markets

We now briefly discuss attempts by theorists to explain and predict exchange rate movements. Some of the theories do not hold up under empirical scrutiny, but they are included because their failings provide insight into the currency market.

Purchasing Power Parity

The law of one price, a basic economic principle, says that in the absence of information and transaction costs, identical goods should be priced identically no matter where they are sold. For example, if a newspaper is selling for 35 cents on one corner and 40 cents on another corner, arbitrageurs will buy on the cheap corner (raising the price) and sell on the dear corner (lowering the price) until the prices are equalized. In practice, arbitrage is costly, and the law of one price must be modified to state that with free trade opportunities, the prices for identical tradeable goods in different places will differ only by the cost of moving the goods from one place to the other.

The theory of purchasing power parity (PPP) applies to international markets and is derived from the law of one price. PPP states that, in the absence of trade restraints, prices of identical goods, when priced in a common currency, will be the same in every country. This implies that as prices for goods in country A rise relative to country B, then A's currency will depreciate by the full amount of the A's relative price increase. For example, if the Canadian annual inflation rate is 10 percent and the U.S. annual inflation rate is 6 percent, then the spot rate of Canadian dollars would decline by about 4 percent per year. If it does not, then Canadian exports to the United States will be overpriced and U.S. exports to Canada underpriced. The demand for U.S. dollars to purchase U.S. goods for import into Canada will cause the dollar to appreciate until the competitive disadvantage is removed.

PPP is a powerful statement. If it holds across all assets, then the real return on assets with identical risk characteristics would be the same everywhere. Thus, exchange rates would be of no importance in determining an asset's returns because they would only reflect inflation differentials between countries.

The PPP relation between exchange rates and inflation is summarized by the following equation:

$$\frac{S_1}{S_0} = \frac{1 + I_f}{1 + I_d} \qquad (2.1)$$

where
  S_1 = amount of foreign currency for a given amount of domestic currency one period from now (the future spot rate)
  S_0 = amount of foreign currency for a given amount of domestic currency in the current period (the current spot rate)
  I_f = foreign inflation rate
  I_d = domestic inflation rate

The percentage change in the spot rate over time can be approximated as the difference between the foreign and domestic nominal inflation rates. That is,

$$\frac{S_1}{S_0} - 1 \approx I_f - I_d \qquad (2.2)$$

Empirically, PPP has virtually no explanatory power for short-term exchange rate movements. Its performance is particularly poor for monthly changes in the spot rate and only slightly better for yearly changes.

PPP fails as a short-term forecasting device for several reasons. Most importantly, one of the assumptions underlying PPP, that consumption baskets are identical across countries and across time, is quite unrealistic.[10] Moreover, the transaction costs of conducting international arbitrage in the goods market are so large that effective arbitrage can take place only over the longer run. Most importantly, common measures of inflation, such as the consumer price index, reflect only current prices of goods, ignoring the futures prices that are implicit in asset markets. The effect of resource flows in response to differences in asset prices among nations appears to be unrelated to current goods prices. In short, PPP in the short term requires the elusive "true" inflation measure.

The Fisherian Relations for Closed and Open Economies

Early in the twentieth century, Irving Fisher, the noted Yale University economist, pointed out that the interest rate that we observe is composed of two parts, the expected inflation rate and the real interest rate:

$$1 + i = (1 + r)(1 + E[I]) \qquad (2.3)$$

---

[10] This assumption underlies PPP because inflation rates within a country, and relative inflation rates across countries, are determined by comparing the prices of a consumption basket of goods across time and across countries. For such a comparison to be meaningful the basket must be unvarying in both dimensions.

where

      i = nominal interest rate
      r = real interest rate
      $E[I]$ = expected inflation rate

This relation is known as the Fisherian relation in a closed (one-currency) economy, or "Fisher closed" for short. The nominal rate can be approximated as the sum of the real interest rate and the expected inflation. That is,

$$i \approx r + E[I] \tag{2.4}$$

By allowing for an open economy (multiple currencies), it follows that differences in nominal interest rates between countries will be linked to differences both in real interest rates and inflation rates. This is known as the "Fisher open" relation. Specifically, it is:

$$\frac{1+i_f}{1+i_d} = \left(\frac{1+r_f}{1+r_d}\right)\left(\frac{1+E[I_f]}{1+E[I_d]}\right) \tag{2.5}$$

where

      $E[I_f]$ = expected foreign inflation rate
      $E[I_d]$ = expected domestic inflation rate
      i_f = foreign nominal interest rate
      i_d = domestic nominal interest rate
      r_f = foreign real interest rate
      r_d = domestic real interest rate

This identity implies that if real rates of return are equal for two countries, then any difference in their nominal rates can be explained solely by differences in expected inflation between the two countries. Real returns should be equal across countries because, in the absence of restrictions on capital movement, investors will allocate funds to those countries which offer the highest expected (risk-adjusted) real return. This arbitrage will continue until real returns are equalized. The linear approximation of Fisher open is:

$$i_f - i_d \approx r_f - r_d + E[I_f] - E[I_d] \tag{2.6}$$

The evidence on the equality of real interest rates is mixed: in some periods it is a better model of reality than in others. Investors in countries without well-developed capital markets find it difficult to move funds to exploit real interest rate differentials. This significant transaction cost makes the hypothesis of equal real interest rates suspect for some currencies. Also, for the same reasons as PPP, it is better used to describe long-term relations than as a short-term forecasting tool.

Expectations of Exchange Rates

The expectations hypothesis of exchange rates states that the expected spot rate as of one period from now is equal to today's forward rate for delivery one period from now:

$$E[S_1] = F_1 \qquad (2.7)$$

where
    $E[S_1]$ = expected spot rate one period from now
    F_1 = today's forward rate for delivery one period from now

If an investor expects that in 30 days the yen-dollar spot rate will be 135 (that is, $E[S_1]=135$) and today the 30-day forward rate is 136 (that is, $F_1=136$), a perceived opportunity exists. To capture the opportunity, buy yen forward at 136; in 30 days sell the same amount of yen on the spot market at 135. This transaction results in a 1 yen profit per dollar invested. Such trades would continue until selling pressure forced the 30-day forward rate to the expected future spot rate.

    The percentage deviation between the forward and current spot rate is called the *forward premium, f:*[11]

$$f = \frac{F_1}{S_0} - 1 \qquad (2.8)$$

where
    S_0 = today's spot rate
    F_1 = today's forward rate for delivery at time 1

Empirical tests of expectations are difficult in that the expectations of the market are not directly observable. To circumvent this, researchers have compared forward rates to the resulting spot rates. The results have shown forward rates to have virtually no power for forecasting spot rates.

---

[11] If the spot rate exceeds the forward (a negative premium), the deviation is instead called a *discount.*

Interest Rate Parity

Interest rate parity is the condition in which interest rates in different countries must be equal when denominated in a common currency. This condition is the law of one price applied to the market for borrowed funds. The condition comes in two forms, uncovered and covered. The uncovered interest rate parity theorem asserts that the difference in nominal rates equals the expected future spot rate over the current spot rate. In application, this implies that the forward rate is an unbiased predictor of the future spot rate. We have already seen that this cannot occur in the presence of uncertainty. We will thus investigate only the covered interest parity condition, which asserts that interest rates denominated in a common currency are equal only if one's foreign exchange exposure is fully hedged.

The equation describing covered interest parity contains no expectations terms and states:

$$\frac{1+i_f}{1+i_d} = \frac{F_1}{S_0} \tag{2.10}$$

where

i_f = foreign nominal interest rate
i_d = domestic nominal interest rate
S_0 = spot rate
F_1 = forward rate for delivery at time 1

The linear approximation of this is:

$$i_f - i_d \approx \frac{F_1}{S_0} - 1 \tag{2.11}$$

To see how arbitrage would be possible if covered interest rate parity did not hold, consider the individual who is able to transact at the Canadian dollar/U.S. dollar one year forward rate of 1.17 and a current spot rate of 1.16 and is able to borrow U.S. dollars (US\$) at a rate of 10 percent and earn 13 percent on an investment in Canadian dollars (C\$). Applying Equation 2.7 we find that:

$$\frac{1+0.13}{1+0.10} > \frac{1.17}{1.16} \text{ or } 1.027 > 1.009 \tag{2.12}$$

To exploit this arbitrage opportunity, the trader borrows (say) US\$100,000 at 10 percent for one year. The proceeds are converted into C\$ at the spot rate of 1.16 C\$/US\$, which yields C\$116,000. This is invested in a Canadian security that yields 13 percent for one year. This would be a riskless arbitrage if future exchange rates are known with certainty to be less than 1.1916, but they are not.[12] To hedge the uncertainty about the future C$/US$ exchange rate, and lock in a riskless profit, the trader would buy a forward contract that will, in one year, allow him to exchange C$131,080 for US$112,034.[13] At that time, he uses the proceeds from the Canadian investment (now converted back into U.S. dollars) to repay the US$100,000 originally borrowed plus the US$10,000 in accrued interest. The remaining US$2034 represents the riskless arbitrage profit.

Conducting this arbitrage depends on the ability to transact quickly, not only in the foreign exchange markets, but in the home-currency and foreign-currency credit markets. Such credit liquidity is greatest in the Eurocurrency markets where covered interest rate parity describes conditions very accurately. An example of the validity of covered interest rate parity is provided by checking actual dealer quotes on the morning of June 11, 1991:

Japanese yen spot rate: 141.15

6-month yen forward rate: 142.01

6-month Eurodollar rate: 6.4375%

6-month Euroyen rate: 7.71875%

Altering the formula by converting the annualized rates to six-month rates we get:

$$\frac{(1+0.0771875)^{1/2}}{(1+0.064375)^{1/2}} \approx \frac{142.01}{141.15}$$

$$\text{or } 1.0060 \approx 1.0061$$

The closeness confirms that covered interest rate parity holds because the arbitrage previously described would not yield any profits. In markets that are more regulated and less liquid, covered interest rate parity is less likely to hold.

Figure 2-2 is a schematic diagram that summarizes the interrelationships between PPP, Fisher open, and covered interest parity. The upper left box illustrates hypothetical expected inflation rates in the United States and U.K. Following the down arrow (to the lower left box) we see that the expected inflation differential, if realized (according to PPP), would cause

---

[12] That is, the Canadian dollar could depreciate during the subsequent year, eliminating the arbitrage profits; or the Canadian dollar could strengthen, providing additional profits.

[13] The Canadian dollar amount is given by: C$116,000 × 1.13 = C$131,080. The U.S. dollar amount is given by: C$131,080 ÷ 1.17= $112,034, where 1.17 is the C$/US$ forward exchange rate.

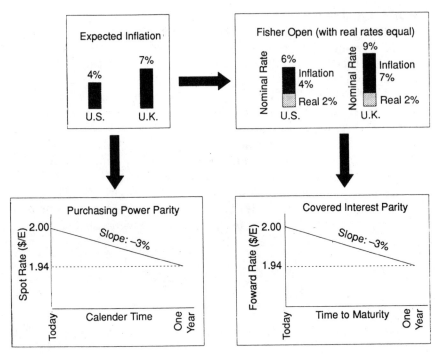

Figure 2-2. Currency, inflation, and real and nominal interest rate relations.

the pound to depreciate relative to the dollar at a rate equal to the inflation differential. Turning to the upper right box, the Fisher-open identity illustrates the contribution that the expected inflation differential makes to the nominal rate differential. If real rates are equal in both countries, the nominal rates differ by the expected inflation differential. Following the down arrow to the lower right box, we see that the covered interest parity arbitrage implies that the term structure of forward rates slopes downward at the same rate.

Equity Expectation Parity

Just as there are conditions under which the law of one price holds for borrowed funds (interest rate parity), there may be conditions under which it holds for investments in corporate equities. If all equities are priced in a single global market, and other arbitrage conditions hold, then the expected return on all equities in the world should be identical after controlling for their risk. This provocative proposition is explored in the context of the capital asset pricing model (CAPM), and, in particular, the variant known as the world CAPM, in Chapter 3.

Conclusion

This chapter has delineated a variety of views on exchange rate behavior and its implications. Purchasing power parity (PPP) implies that exchange rates are of no importance in determining an asset's real returns because they only reflect inflation differentials between countries. Empirically, while PPP has virtually no explanatory power for short-term exchange rate movements, it is quite robust in the long run. The evidence on the equality of real interest rates is mixed: in some periods differences in expected inflation between countries explain differences in nominal interest rates, whereas in other periods the two seem only loosely related. The expectations hypothesis of exchange rates, which proposes that forward rates are a forecast of spot rates, generally fails empirically. Covered interest parity asserts that interest rates stated in a common currency are equal only if one's foreign exchange exposure is fully hedged. In relatively unregulated and liquid markets, covered interest rate parity holds quite well. The more general assertion of uncovered interest rate parity, that real interest rates are everywhere equal before hedging, is not supported.

3

Capital Market Returns in Equilibrium

When the Duke of Wellington met Napoleon at the battle of Waterloo, the British financial markets were in a state of suspense. A British defeat would cause security prices to plummet while a victory would result in a price surge. Nathan Rothschild, the great international financier, quietly began buying. When official word of British victory reached London, prices soared and Rothschild multiplied his fortune many times. The wily Rothschild had beaten the market because his information source—carrier pigeons—had beaten the human messengers.

Investors today can still legally profit from access to information, skill in selecting and timing transactions, and careful analysis of market behavior. Even in the generally efficient stock markets of developed countries, financial economists have discovered many anomalies in which returns are substantially higher or lower than one would expect by looking exclusively at risk. One possible reason for the existence of anomalies is that there are hidden risks, or nonrisk factors such as information costs, that affect the equilibrium return on a stock. It is also possible that the market for various stocks, or the whole market, is in a state of disequilibrium.

To explain how capital markets function, economists often assume that such markets are in equilibrium. Many financial economists also believe that markets are efficient, which means that market prices of capital assets reflect all available information. In this chapter, the cases for and against efficient markets are explored. We then consider two major theories of capital market returns grounded in the concept of equilibrium: the capital asset pricing model (CAPM) and arbitrage pricing theory (APT). Finally, we call for a broader framework, loosely referred to as a new equilibrium theory (NET), in which nonrisk capital costs as well as various risks affect returns.

Characteristics of Efficient Markets

Efficient markets are those that immediately and fully reflect all available information in the price of every asset. A necessary condition for an efficient market is that there are no barriers preventing investors from using information and information-interpreting skills to trade. For example, if world capital markets are efficient, then an announced reduction in the flow of Middle Eastern oil causes each asset in the world to change price instantaneously, in accordance with the impact that the event is perceived to have on the asset's underlying value.

This hypothesis has profound implications for investor behavior. Prices would only change in response to unanticipated information. If an announcement or event is expected, then that information would already be incorporated into the price. All attempts to outperform market indexes would fail.

More specifically, any technique that beats the market would be, by definition, a form of information. As investors utilize such a technique, the under (over) valued assets are purchased (sold) until the opportunity for further arbitrage profit is exhausted. Thus, arbitrageurs seeking profit are the enforcement mechanism for an efficient market. The best strategy for investors in an efficient market is to buy and hold a diversified portfolio.

Why Markets Might Be Efficient

Are markets efficient? An intelligent case can be made for either a yes or no answer.

The observational case for efficient markets runs as follows. A multitude of analysts, backed by capital which causes prices to move, are continually looking for trading opportunities. The costs of transacting are low and continuing to fall. The most remarkable drop in costs has been in the cost of information. The universal use of the computer, combined with advances in communications, allow the dissemination of raw and interpreted data and news to investors worldwide. Where investment firms in fact commit substantial resources to profit from minute mispricings of or between assets, markets must be relatively efficient. A vivid case in point is the effort and expense spent to arbitrage price differentials between stock index futures contracts and their component stocks.

Why Markets Might Not Be Efficient

Despite the arguments presented above, investors persist in seeking profits by analyzing securities and carefully timing their transactions in the hope of earning above average returns. Such effort is only rational if these returns are perceived to be available in the markets—that is, if markets are not thought to be efficient. Here, we identify three lines of reasoning that lead to this conclusion.

The Costly Information Argument

Students, unburdened by efficient market orthodoxy, often point out a paradox concerning efficient markets: If every investor believed that markets were efficient, then the market would not be efficient because no one would analyze securities. Even upon first hearing the efficient market hypothesis, the students recognize the obvious justification for inefficient markets. Prices can only reflect what is knowable about underlying value if investors try to earn superior returns by ascertaining the underlying value. If investors abandoned such efforts, the efficiency of the market would diminish to naught.

The "student's proof" that markets are inefficient has been formalized by Sanford Grossman and Joseph Stiglitz,[1] who show that costless information is a necessary condition for a perfectly efficient market to exist. If information has a cost, and if information is purchased, then the information must have value. Marginal buyers of the information must believe they can at least break even after paying to obtain it. This means that assets will differ from their true value by an amount up to the cost of the information needed to determine their true value. Because of information costs, markets must be inefficient to a degree.

The Costly Arbitrage Argument

Inefficiencies may also arise because arbitrage is costly.[2] In practice, arbitrageurs must concentrate their holdings into undiversified portfolios, incur transaction costs, and often take leveraged and/or short positions. An investor would only be willing to behave in this way if the expected payoffs

---

[1] Sanford J. Grossman and Joseph E. Stiglitz, "On the Impossibility of Informationally Efficient Markets," *American Economic Review,* June 1980.

[2] Arbitrage may also be prohibited by law or regulations that apply unevenly across investor groups. Broadly speaking, such prohibitions may be regarded as costs.

were very large. Investors find that the borrowing and short selling needed for effective arbitrage are especially costly, since these financing techniques involve monitoring of collateral as well as the costs of obtaining credit. Because investors may not always be willing to bear arbitrage costs, they may not take advantage of all instances of mispricing resulting in a market that may inefficiently price various assets.

To clarify this point, consider an extreme example. The person best able to arbitrage would be someone with perfect foresight. Suppose you are given a copy of *The Wall Street Journal* dated one full year in the future, with accurate prices as of that future date. Clearly, you would make a fortune by correctly anticipating all of the price changes.

Yet even in this case, the infinite arbitrage needed to bring today's prices in line with those a year from now is next to impossible. Assuming that you could not show the *Journal* to anyone else (or that few people would believe you had an accurate forecast of the future), capital constraints would keep you from moving prices very much. Thus, even if you could know the future with certainty (which, of course, is impossible), your arbitrage activity would be unlikely to bring today's (or the intervening year's) prices in line with known future prices.

The Socratic Argument

The ancient Greek philosopher Socrates claimed to have special knowledge. Other Athenians were so threatened by his claim that they brought him to trial to ask just what special knowledge he had. He replied: "I know what I do not know."

Socrates's observation has importance for investors. If investors have differing abilities to analyze and act on information, markets may be inefficient because the smart will exploit the less smart. Some academics argue that markets can still be efficient if market participants have differing abilities; if less skilled investors have Socratic knowledge, and realize that they are at a disadvantage, they will drop out of the market, buy index funds, or hire talented investors to manage their portfolios. The talented investors would remain in the market and arbitrage away any mispricing.

However, if market participants are not knowledgeable in the Socratic sense, the unskilled will remain as active participants. These unskilled investors who lack Socratic knowledge will still be exploited by skilled investors, and markets may be inefficient.

If all unskilled investors dropped out, the market would dry up. The volume of trading, however, suggests that unskilled as well as talented investors stay in the market. This result can be seen by supposing that all investors knew what they did and did not know, thus perceiving their relative ranking. Investors in the lower half of the hierarchy would know that they are below average and drop out of the market. Once that group dropped out, the second quartile would become below average. Each successive group would drop out until only the top-ranked investor would be left—without trading partners.

Although investors are generally rational, they probably have inexact and unrealistically high perceptions of their relative rankings. Most, if not all, active investors believe themselves to be above average, although obviously not all can be. If investors have differing abilities and do not perceive these differences, then markets are inefficient. This argument is based on investors having bounded rationality, giving them biased perceptions of their relative rankings.

To sum up, markets should probably not be characterized as efficient or inefficient. Efficiency is not an "either or" proposition, but one of degree. All markets are efficient to a certain extent, some more than others. In markets with substantial impairments of efficiency, more knowledgeable investors can expect to outperform less knowledgeable ones. We recognize the existence of mispriced assets, but feel that most markets are largely efficient and bargains are the exception rather than the rule.

Asset Pricing in Equilibrium

While there may be good reasons to believe that markets are in some sense inefficient, financial thinkers have acted sensibly in assuming market efficiency for the purpose of developing formal asset pricing models. These models, while imperfect descriptions of reality, provide important insights into investor behavior. The principal asset pricing theories are the capital asset pricing model (CAPM) and arbitrage pricing theory (APT). Both identify the *expected return* from holding an asset. Since an asset's price is the market's assessment of the asset's future cash flows, discounted by the asset's cost of capital or expected return, a theory of expected return is also a theory of pricing.

The Capital Asset Pricing Model

The CAPM describes a market in equilibrium as discussed earlier. The theory is the product of the efforts of three Nobel laureates in economics (at two different times): Harry M. Markowitz, James Tobin, and William F. Sharpe. While Sharpe is well-known as the CAPM's formulator, both John

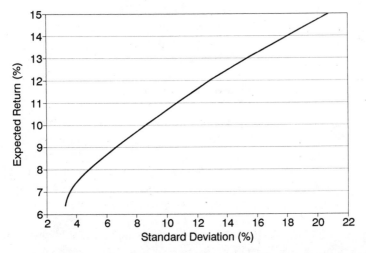

Figure 3-1. Efficient frontier for portfolio of U.S. stocks, bonds, and cash. *(Source: EnCorr/Optimizer, Ibbotson Associates, Inc., Chicago, 1991.)*

Lintner and Jack Treynor made important advances independently of Sharpe.[3] Even so, the work of all three benefitted from Markowitz and Tobin's pioneering work. In 1952, Markowitz demonstrated a method of portfolio construction that minimizes risk for each level of expected return.[4] The array of portfolios that minimize risk for given expected returns is called the *efficient frontier* and is illustrated in Figure 3-1. In 1958, Tobin drew on the work of nineteenth century neoclassical economists to use utility theory to describe investor behavior in the capital markets.[5]

CAPM Assumptions. The CAPM assumes that investors live in a single-period world[6] and behave as follows:

[3] John Lintner, "The Valuation of Risky Assets and the Selection of Risky Investments in Stock Portfolios and Capital Budgets," *Review of Economics and Statistics*, February 1965. William F. Sharpe, "Capital Asset Prices: A Theory of Market Equilibrium Under Conditions of Risk," *Journal of Finance*, September 1964. Jack L. Treynor, "Toward a Theory of Market Value of Risky Assets," unpublished, 1963.

[4] Harry M. Markowitz, "Portfolio Selection," *Journal of Finance*, March 1952.

[5] James Tobin, "Liquidity Preferences as Behavior Towards Risk," *Review of Economic Studies*, February 1958.

[6] Multiperiod, intertemporal CAPMs have been developed by Robert Merton, "An Intertemporal Capital Asset Pricing Model," *Econometrica*, 1973 and Robert E. Lucas, Jr., "Asset Prices in an Exchange Economy," *Econometrica*, 1978, among others.

- They seek to maximize the expected return and minimize the variance of returns on their investments.

- They have identical expectations concerning future return and risk for each asset.

- They pay no transaction costs or taxes.

- They can borrow and lend unlimited amounts of capital at the riskless rate.

- No single investor can control the price of an asset.

- Investors seek wealth in nominal, not real, terms (a hidden assumption uncovered by Bruno Solnik[7]).

Behavior of Investors in a CAPM World. In a CAPM world, investors evaluate every risky asset on the basis of its expected return and risk measured by variance, but because investors have identical expectations for a given asset, each investor chooses the same risky assets in identical proportions.

All assets in the market must be held. If all investors have the same portfolio of risky assets, that portfolio must be the market itself! Thus, in the CAPM, the risky portfolio that investors hold is the *market portfolio*, composed of all of the risky assets in the world. Each asset is held in proportion to its market capitalization. This market portfolio is the optimal portfolio of risky assets for every investor.

What is in the market portfolio? Because an economic good must be risky and return-generating (among other attributes) to be an asset in the sense of being addressable by asset pricing theories, assets do not include riskless securities, but include risky holdings such as human capital, real estate, and personal property, as well as more conventional portfolio components such as stocks and bonds. In practice, a portfolio of financial assets, or just the stock market, often is used to proxy the true (all-asset) market portfolio.

The CAPM assumes that there exists a single *riskless asset*, that is, an asset perceived by all investors as having no risk. Because the CAPM is a single-period model, a short-term Treasury bill is often used to proxy the riskless asset in applications of the CAPM. The *market risk premium* is the amount by which the expected return on the market portfolio exceeds the expected return on the riskless asset.

Because investors have different tolerances for risk, they do not put the same percentage of their wealth in the market portfolio. More risk-averse

---

[7] Bruno Solnik, *International Investments*, Addison-Wesley, Reading, Mass., 1988.

investors hold a higher percentage of their wealth in the riskless asset, while less risk-averse investors allocate a greater percentage of their wealth to the market portfolio.[8]

The CAPM predicts, then, that every investor will hold a portfolio (including short and long positions) constructed from just two funds: (1) the riskless asset and (2) the market portfolio. This principle is called the two-fund separation theorem.

CAPM Equation.   Given knowledge of the expected return on the riskless asset and the market risk premium, the CAPM describes the equilibrium expected return on every individual asset:

$$r_s = r_f + \beta_s \times rp \qquad (3.1)$$

where

   r_s = expected return on security s
   r_f = expected return of riskless asset
   β_s = beta of security s
   rp = expected market risk premium

The beta of an asset is given by:

$$\beta_s = \frac{\text{cov}(r_s, r_m)}{\text{var}(r_m)} \qquad (3.2)$$

where

   $\text{cov}(r_s, r_m)$ = expected covariance between return on security s and market return
   $\text{var}(r_m)$ = expected variance of market return
   r_m = return on market

The CAPM equation describes a line, called the *security market line*, shown in Figure 3-2. In a CAPM world, all assets lie on this line.[9]

---

[8] No one prefers risk since this would lead to gambler's ruin in an indefinitely long succession of gambles. The most risk-averse investor will hold his entire wealth in the riskless asset. The least risk-averse investor will borrow at the riskless rate and invest the proceeds in the market portfolio, in addition to investing all of his current wealth in the market portfolio.

[9] Beta is a measure of the systematic risk of an asset. An asset with a beta of 1 tends to rise and fall as much as the market portfolio, and in the same direction. An asset with a beta of 2 tends to rise twice as much in a rising market and fall twice as far in a falling market. An asset with a beta of 0.5 rises half as much as the market portfolio in a rising market and falls half as far in a falling market. An asset with a zero beta has returns unrelated to those of the market. Assets with negative betas move opposite the market.

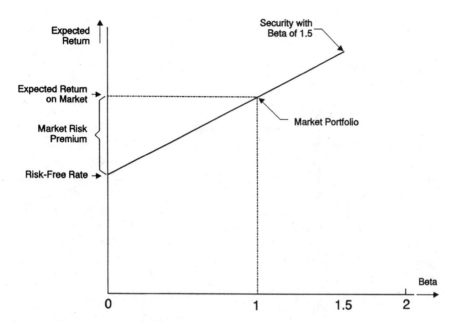

Figure 3-2. The security market line.

CAPM Conclusions. The logic of the CAPM leads to some startling conclusions. The risk of an asset is composed of two parts: systematic and unsystematic risk. Systematic risk is inherent in every risky security, and is measured by the security's beta. It represents the portion of total risk that cannot be avoided by diversifying among securities. Because systematic risk cannot be avoided, investors demand and, over the long run receive, compensation for bearing such risk in the form of an excess return (that is, an expected return in excess of the riskless rate). As Equation 3.1 indicates, the expected excess return on a security is proportional to its beta. Systematic risk is also referred to as undiversifiable risk, market risk, or beta risk.

Unsystematic risk is the risk unique to a particular asset. It is the portion of the total risk of an asset that is *not* captured by its beta. Investors can eliminate unsystematic risk from their portfolios by diversifying, and they are consequently not rewarded for taking this risk. Unsystematic risk is also referred to as diversifiable risk, nonmarket risk, or idiosyncratic risk.

A simple example draws the distinction between systematic and unsystematic risk. Shares of General Motors are subject to the risk that Toyota and Volkswagen will take market share away. This risk can be reduced by holding shares in all three automobile companies. A fall in the price of General Motors shares would tend to be offset by the rise in Toyota and Volkswagen share prices. Thus, this risk is diversifiable, or unsystematic, and investors should expect no reward for taking it.

General Motors shareholders also face the risk that the general level of demand for cars will fall, harming Toyota and Volkswagen also. This quite different kind of risk is undiversifiable, or systematic, and investors expect to be rewarded for taking it.

Toward a World CAPM. The CAPM is a general model of the consequences of investor behavior, and, as already noted, theoretically applies to every asset in the world. Because borders may interfere with integrated asset pricing, however, the CAPM is typically used to describe the way assets are priced within a single-country market. To apply CAPM to the actual world with more than one currency, a modification must be made to the model. In the 1970s, Bruno Solnik pointed out that in an integrated world capital market with exchange rate risk and purchasing power risk, the international investor constructs his or her portfolio from not two, but three funds.[10] This "three-fund separation theorem" depends on the additional assumption that future inflation rates can be anticipated, and it says that global investors hold:

- A riskless asset in their home currency
- A currency-hedged portfolio of worldwide risky assets
- A portfolio of riskless assets in each foreign country

This yields a CAPM equation that can be applied to all assets in a hypothetical fully integrated world market,

$$r_s = r_f + \beta_s(r_m - r_c) \tag{3.3}$$

where
r_s = expected return on security s
r_f = expected return on riskless asset in home country
β_s = beta of security s
r_m = expected return on hedged world market portfolio
r_c = expected return on portfolio of unhedged riskless assets in foreign currencies

Note that this "world CAPM" equation identifies the expected return on a security as a function of the expected return on three funds (r_f, r_m, and r_c), in contrast to the two funds identified in the Sharpe-Lintner CAPM. In practice the equation may be modified to eliminate the requirement of perfect integration.

---

[10]Bruno Solnik, "An Equilibrium Model of the International Capital Market," *Journal of Economic Theory*, July/August 1974.

Arbitrage Pricing Theory (APT)

The law of one price states that, in a competitive market, identical goods must sell for identical prices. This law is the basis for the arbitrage pricing theory (APT) developed by Stephen Ross.[11] The APT predicts that asset portfolios that are equivalent in risk will have equal expected returns. Risk-equivalent portfolios with different expected returns will attract arbitrageurs who will buy higher-returning portfolios and sell lower-returning portfolios until returns are equalized. The APT assumes that:

- Returns in the market are generated by a linear process in several dimensions.

- In equilibrium, portfolios with no systematic or unsystematic risk and no net investment must offer no return.

- Markets are perfectly competitive.

Note that in contrast to the CAPM, which forms conclusions about the market from first principles of behavior toward risk, the APT makes no assumptions about behavior. The APT uses assumptions about the market to draw conclusions about the market.

In the APT world, an asset's expected return is determined by adding the riskless rate to various risk premiums representing each of the factors that potentially influences an asset's return. A simple example posits two kinds of market risk, one described by responsiveness with industrial production and the other by responsiveness to inflation:

$$r_s = r_f + \gamma_1(IPRP) + \gamma_2(IRP) \tag{3.4}$$

where

r_s = expected return on security s
r_f = expected riskless rate
γ_1 = expected coefficient of sensitivity of security s to changes in industrial production
$IPRP$ = expected industrial production risk premium
γ_2 = expected coefficient of sensitivity of security s to changes in inflation
IRP = expected inflation risk premium

[11] Stephen A. Ross, "The Arbitrage Theory of Capital Asset Pricing," *Journal of Economic Theory*, December 1976.

Industrial production and inflation are just two of the many factors that could go into an APT formulation of an asset's expected return. The factors are assumed to be independent of each other, and each has an associated risk premium. The expected return on any asset or portfolio is a linear combination of the risk premiums. The general form of APT is:

$$r_s = r_f + \gamma_1\lambda_1 + \dots + \gamma_n\lambda_n \qquad (3.5)$$

where

r_s = expected return on security s
r_f = expected riskless rate
γ_1 = loading factor for variable 1
λ_1 = expected risk premium for variable 1
γ_n = loading factor for last variable
λ_n = expected risk premium for last variable

As in the CAPM, investors are rewarded only for taking systematic risk. Unlike the CAPM, systematic risk is measured by more than one variable.[12]

In the mid-1980s, Nai-Fu Chen, Richard Roll, and Stephen Ross identified five risk factors for the APT:[13]

- Changes in industrial production
- Changes in anticipated inflation
- Unanticipated changes in inflation
- The default premium on corporate bonds
- The return differential between long- and short-term bonds

APT tends to be a richer explanatory model than the CAPM because of its use of multiple factors.[14] The factors are intuitively appealing and tend to match the ways that people think about security returns. Nonetheless, like the CAPM, it is merely an approximation of reality. Both theories are widely used to predict the relationship between risk and expected return.

---

[12] Note that the form of the CAPM equation is indistinguishable from the form of the one-factor APT.

[13] Nai-fu Chen, Richard Roll, and Stephen A. Ross, "Economic Forces and the Stock Market," *Journal of Business,* July 1986.

[14] A careful distinction should be drawn between explanatory and predictive power. An APT formulation that includes the market portfolio as a factor, and adds other factors, has greater explanatory power than the CAPM *by construction*. This does not mean it will predict returns out-of-sample better than the CAPM, and preliminary investigation has shown that it does not.

A Call for a
New Equilibrium Theory

Some of the basic issues in asset pricing are not addressed by asset pricing models that look only at risks. An example is the difference in expected return between a municipal bond and a corporate bond of comparable default risk. The difference is due entirely to the bonds' differing tax status. Likewise, a CAPM or APT estimate of the expected return on real estate is likely to be unsatisfactory, because real estate is priced on the basis of marketability, tax status, and other nonrisk factors as well as on the basis of its risks.

In a 1984 article, Roger G. Ibbotson, Jeffrey J. Diermeier, and Laurence B. Siegel called for a *new equilibrium theory* (NET) that includes nonrisk factors in asset pricing because asset prices are determined *net* of investor-specific costs.[15] If such a theory were developed, the result would be an integrated framework that includes costs arising from all sources—including various risks, as well as taxability, marketability, and other costs—that affect the expected return on an asset.

A brief sketch of the proposed NET framework is as follows: the cost of capital for an asset is the aggregation (after translation to percent per annum terms) of all investors' capital costs to acquire, hold, and dispose of an asset. Investors look at each asset as a bundle of characteristics for which they have various preferences and aversions. These characteristics are translated into costs for which investors require compensation, in the form of expected returns. Thus, while all investors perceive the same expected return for an asset, each investor has individually determined costs for holding that asset. The decision to hold an asset is made on the basis of expected returns net of the individually determined costs. Table 3-1 summarizes the effect that these characteristics would have on expected return.

We now enumerate some of the investor costs which have a significant impact on asset pricing.

Risks

The risk characteristics captured by the CAPM and APT are in this category. In addition, residual risk (the risk resulting from a lack of portfolio diversification), regarded as diversifiable and uncompensated in the frictionless CAPM and APT worlds, is rewarded when it is impossible or costly to diversify. Assets like real estate and human capital are difficult to diversify and

---

[15] Roger G. Ibbotson, Jeffrey J. Diermeier, and Laurence B. Siegel, "The Demand for Capital Market Returns," *Financial Analysts Journal,* January/February 1984.

Table 3-1. Effects of Characteristics on Expected Returns on Assets

| Asset | Characteristics | | | | | | | | |
| | Risks | | | | | Information costs* | Marketability | | Miscellaneous factors |
	Stock market beta	Inflation	Real interest rate	Residual risk cost*	Taxability*		Search and transactions costs	Divisibility costs	
Large company stocks	Near one	Low positive	Positive?	Near zero	Low	Low	Low	Very low	Probably efficiently priced
Small company stocks	Varies	Low positive	Positive?	Low	Low	High	Medium*	Very low	
Treasury bonds	Near zero	Positive	Low	Near zero	High	Low	Low	Medium*	Efficiently priced
Corporate bonds	Low	Positive	Low	Near zero	High	Low	Low	Medium*	
Municipal bonds	Near zero	Positive	Low	Low	Zero	Low	Low	Medium*	
Treasury bills	Zero	Zero	High	Near zero	High	Low	Low	High*	
Houses, condos	Low	?	?	High	Negative	High	High*	Very high*	High management costs
Gold	Zero or negative	Negative?	?	Low	Low	Low	Low	Very low	No income; portable
Art	Low	Negative?	?	High	Low	Very high	Very high	Very high	Nonpecuniary benefits; no income
Foreign securities	Varies	Varies	?	Varies	Low	High	Varies	Low	
Human capital	High	?	?	Very high	Very high	High	High*	Very high*	Cannot sell, only rent or borrow against

NOTE: Low, medium, high, etc. refer to positive coefficients unless indicated to be negative.

Effects of Characteristics on Expected Returns on Assets:

High or Positive = raises expected return, lowering price

Low or Negative = decreases expected return, raising price

*Financial intermediaries are likely to be important in reducing these costs.

SOURCE: Reprinted from the article by Roger G. Ibbotson, Jeffrey J. Diermeier, and Laurence B. Siegel. "The Demand for Capital Market Returns," *Financial Analysts Journal*, January/February 1984.

must offer a higher expected return than other risk-comparable assets as compensation for this undesirable trait.

Taxes

All other things being equal, an asset is worth less, the greater the taxability of the cash flows (income and capital gain) from the asset. This effect is unequal across investors, who (in most countries) have differing tax brackets according to their income. Likewise, in most countries, some classes of investors are tax-exempt, such as pension funds, endowments, and foundations in the United States. Thus taxes are a heterogeneous cost affecting each investor's expectation of net return.

Marketability Costs

Marketability costs are all those costs involved with buying and selling an asset, such as information, divisibility, search, and transaction costs. Human capital cannot be sold, only rented. Such severe impairment of marketability causes human capital to be worth much less than liquid, risk-comparable assets. Real estate can be sold, but has high information and transaction costs as well as long waits to consummate a transaction. In contrast, government bonds and the stocks of large companies are among the most liquid investments imaginable. Differences in marketability costs should be expected to have a substantial impact on asset pricing.

Miscellaneous Pricing Factors

Included in this category are asset management, maintenance, and storage costs. Because these costs may differ across investors, they are sometimes treated as costs of capital (specific to the investor in the NET framework) rather than cash flow reductions (inherent in the asset). Also in this category are negative costs, such as the aesthetic benefits of holding works of art. Negative costs lower an asset's expected financial return, because part of the return is realized in nonpecuniary form.

Asset Pricing and the Supply of Capital Market Returns

Capital market prices are set by the interaction of supply and demand. Typically, this relation is expressed as the "supply of and demand for capital." By turning this relation around and viewing it as the "supply of and demand for *returns*," attention is focused on returns as the good being priced in the market. Capital market returns are the equilibrium compensation investors receive for holding assets with various characteristics. This compensation is set both by what investors demand and what the market is able to supply. Modern portfolio theory has traditionally focused on the demand side, but the supply side is important too.

From a macroeconomic perspective, Diermeier, Ibbotson, and Siegel observe that the supply of total investment returns equals income returns for all assets, plus growth in aggregate market value of investable assets, less new issues.[16] This observation makes possible a forecast of the total returns on aggregate financial assets, if we assume that the aggregate value of investable assets is a constant proportion of total social wealth. The GNP is considered the "return" on social wealth, and the return on investor wealth is consequently related to GNP growth. Based on a historical real GNP growth rate of 2.6 percent, a forecast of expected capital market returns can be made using the supply model. The GNP growth rate of 2.6 percent may be projected and combined with current yield and new-issue data to produce a forecast of a 5.4 percent per year *real* return on the aggregate of investable assets.

The supply model places in perspective the various demand-driven models, such as the CAPM and APT, which dominate thinking about investors' expected returns. Investors cannot expect a much greater or fear a much lesser return than that provided by businesses in the real economy, so that investors' expectations should be guided at least in part by the supply of market returns.

[16] Jeffrey J. Diermeier, Roger G. Ibbotson, and Laurence B. Siegel, "The Supply of Capital Market Returns," *Financial Analysts Journal*, March/April 1984.

PART 2

Institutional Investing

4
Asset Allocation

The global investment process involves three distinct but integrated sets of decisions. The first and foremost aspect of the process is setting normal *asset allocation policy*: identifying the asset classes appropriate for a specific investment portfolio and the proportions of these assets that would normally comprise the portfolio. The second aspect is conducting *active asset allocation* over time: determining the periodic deviations of actual asset class allocations from the normal policy allocations. The third aspect involves the structure of the securities held within each asset class and is referred to as *security selection.*

This chapter focuses on the first two aspects of the investment process—determining asset allocation policy and active asset allocation. (Security selection is covered in Chapter 5.) The first section of the chapter develops a framework for the investment process, distinguishing between the two kinds of allocation decisions. The second section discusses the policy aspect of this framework within the context of the increasingly borderless nature of a global investable capital market.[1] The third section discusses active global asset allocation. Active asset allocation can refer to a number of specific techniques, and this discussion draws clear distinctions between such approaches as market timing, fundamental analysis, and "black box" models.

---

[1]*Investable capital market* refers to those primary wealth generating capital assets that are available to the institutional investor for inclusion in the portfolio.

Conceptual Framework
for the Global
Investment Process

Figure 4-1 illustrates a conceptual framework for the investment decision
process and for evaluating the performance that results from these decisions.[2] Actual investment performance within this framework is determined
by the combined effects of asset allocation policy, active asset allocation, and
security selection. The figure also indicates the computational requirements
for return accountability, thereby providing a means of determining both
the importance and effectiveness of each component.

Quadrant I is the foundation of the decision-making process—asset allocation policy. Policy decisions are dictated by the investor's objectives and
constraints, along with expected long-term capital market conditions. Long-
term capital market conditions, including asset class returns, risks, and correlations, are referred to as *equilibrium* conditions. *Current* capital market
conditions are those that reflect the returns, risks, and correlations that
would be expected to arise periodically from discrepancies between current
capital market conditions and long-run equilibrium.

Current capital market conditions may provide opportunities for active
management to enhance returns or reduce risk by deviating from the policy
allocation. Quadrant II is the active asset allocation facet of the investment
process and Quadrant III depicts active security selection. Finally, Quadrant
IV is the total portfolio performance resulting from policy, active asset allocation, and active rather than passive security selection decisions.

This conceptual matrix can serve as both a performance attribution system
and as a means for understanding the investment decision-making process.
The performance of a portfolio constructed to represent the asset allocation
policy decision, depicted by Quadrant I, is determined by applying the normal, or policy, weight to the passive return of each asset class.[3] The sum of
these weighted returns across asset classes provides the contribution of policy
to the total performance of the portfolio over a given period.

---

[2]A discussion of this framework from a performance attribution perspective is provided by
Gary P. Brinson, Brian D. Singer, and Gilbert L. Beebower, "Determinants of Portfolio
Performance II: An Update," *Financial Analysts Journal*, May/June 1991. This article is an
update of Gary P. Brinson, L. Randolph Hood, and Gilbert L. Beebower, "Determinants of
Portfolio Performance," *Financial Analysts Journal*, July/August 1986.

[3]The term *passive*, applying to both weights and returns, refers to those which would have
been provided in the absence of any management decisions that attempt to distinguish market price from fundamental value or otherwise discern exploitable disequilibria. The term
active refers to the weights and returns determined by portfolio management techniques that
make such distinctions.

Security Selection	
Active	Passive
IV Actual portfolio return 13.41% (Wai*Rai) R-sqr: 100.0%	II Policy and allocation return 13.23% (Wai*Rpi) R-sqr: 93.3%
III Policy and security selection return 13.75% (Wpi*Rai) R-sqr: 96.1%	I Policy return (Passive portfolio benchmark) 13.49% (Wpi*Rpi) R-sqr: 91.5%

(Left axis: **Asset Allocation** — Active / Passive)

Wpi = policy (passive) weight for asset class i
Wai = active weight for asset class i
Rpi = passive return for asset class i
Rai = active return for asset class i

Active return contribution due to:

Asset allocation	II−I	−0.26%
Security selection	III−I	0.26
Other	IV−III−II+I	−0.07
Total	IV−I	−0.08

Figure 4-1. Framework for return accountability. *(Source: Gary P. Brinson, Brian D. Singer, and Gilbert L. Beebower, "Determinants of Portfolio Performance II: An Update,"* Financial Analysts Journal, *May/June 1991.)*

This performance is expanded in Quadrant II to reflect the combined impact of policy and active allocation decisions. The combined performance is obtained by multiplying active asset class weights by the passive returns of each asset class and summing across asset classes. The impact of active allocation decisions in the investment process can be obtained by subtracting the policy returns provided in Quadrant I from the combined policy and active management returns provided in Quadrant II.

The performance of a portfolio constructed to reflect the combined effect of asset allocation policy and security selection is provided by Quadrant III. This performance is calculated by summing across asset classes the product of the active returns achieved by security selection within each asset class and the normal (policy) asset class weights. The value added by security selection is obtained by subtracting the policy returns of Quadrant I from the combined policy and selection returns of Quadrant III.

Finally, Quadrant IV provides the total performance of the investment portfolio for a given period. Such performance is determined by multiplying the actual asset class weights by the actual asset class returns. Note that Quadrant IV contains an element of active performance, called *other,* that is not attributable to either active asset allocation policy or security selection in isolation. This element effectively represents the interaction of active asset allocation and security selection.[4] Within this framework, the global investment process is divided into policy and active portfolio decisions. Portfolio performance, therefore, is determined by the policy allocation and the active endeavors of asset allocation and security selection.

Figure 4-1 also contains the results of a study by Gary P. Brinson, Brian D. Singer, and Gilbert L. Beebower that used this framework to study the performance of 82 large, multi-asset U.S. pension portfolios from 1977 to 1987. At the bottom of each quadrant, *coefficients of determination* are reported.[5] This statistic indicates the percentage of variability in actual returns that can be explained by policy, by the joint effect of policy and active asset allocation, and by the joint effect of policy and security selection. Brinson, Singer, and Beebower found that differences in policy allocations accounted for 91.5 percent of the variations of returns across the sample of portfolios. Thus, relative skill in active management of the asset allocation weights and in selecting specific securities accounted for less than 10 percent of the portfolio return variation. This analysis made no effort to judge the relative merits of the various policies, but rather focused on the importance of policy versus active management decisions irrespective of the specific policies.

The average annual return generated by these 82 portfolios was 13.41 percent, slightly less than the average annual policy return of 13.49 percent. On average, active security selection contributed an extra 0.26 percent, but was offset by an equal average rate of loss from active asset allocation decisions.

The main contributor to both absolute total returns and to the variance of total returns was the asset allocation *policy* decision. Of course, the deci-

---

[4]The cross-product referred to as "other" performance effectively quantifies the ability to deviate from asset allocation policy in order to take advantage of active performance above or below passive performance.

[5]A coefficient of determination is the square of the correlation coefficient between two jointly distributed random variables. It is also referred to as R^2 or R-squared.

sion to adopt an asset allocation policy can be divided into two parts. First, the decision to hold any diversified asset mix (say, the market portfolio), rather than a riskless portfolio, accounts for a large share of the Quadrant I performance. Second, the deviation of the policy mix from the typical or market mix accounts for the rest of the Quadrant I performance. The results suggest that applying resources to the asset allocation policy process is imperative and that the procedure for determining appropriate variations in the asset mix could be improved.

Asset Allocation Policy

Asset allocation policy is concerned with the basic structure of a multi-asset portfolio. The policy indicates the long-term, equilibrium composition of the portfolio by specifying the asset classes that are permissible investment vehicles and the normal proportions of these assets within the portfolio. The structure of the portfolio and the resulting asset allocation policy are determined by the objectives of the investor, particularly with respect to risk tolerance and the equilibrium return and risk characteristics of the asset classes.

Investor Objectives

The first step in determining appropriate asset allocation policy is to identify and specify investor objectives and constraints. The general question being answered is, For what purpose are the funds to be invested? More specifically, does the investor require a minimum rate of return? Is there a maximum amount of risk which would be tolerable? When will the funds be required to extinguish future liabilities? In which currencies are the associated liabilities denominated? What degree of uncertainty is associated with these specifications?

As the global economy becomes more integrated, investors will be forced to take a broader view of these questions. The effects of international variables are not isolated within the international component of the portfolio. Rather, they extend beyond asset related factors to the structure of liabilities and future spending plans.

A multinational corporation, for example, might have liabilities in its pension plan that are denominated in both domestic and foreign currencies and have ultimate values which depend on foreign economic and political developments. Some institutional investors purchase foreign assets to hedge the impact of unexpected foreign inflation on future import prices. Others consider currency exposure to be a hedge against domestic inflation. In all of these cases, the appropriate investment policy requires evaluation of the currency risks discussed in Chapter 2.

Policy Specification of Asset Classes

Optimally, a global investor would simultaneously evaluate every asset in the world to determine policy allocations to each asset. This approach would yield efficient results if all relevant information were freely and readily available. Especially in a global environment, the reality is that information on individual assets is costly to obtain and difficult to analyze. In practice, the bundling of assets into asset classes makes it possible to analyze the world market, given limited resources.

Global portfolios provide a diversification benefit over domestic portfolios to such a degree that expansion beyond domestic frontiers has become practically a necessity. This potential for diversification can be illustrated with an example drawn from recent historical experience. Figure 4-2 presents a simple example of U.S. dollar returns for several hypothetical domestic and global balanced portfolios for the period from 1969 to 1990. The domestic portfolios consist of fixed allocations of U.S. equity and bond index funds. The global portfolios additionally include fixed allocations to a non-U.S. equity index fund and a nondollar bond index. All portfolios were rebalanced monthly. As mentioned in Chapter 2, this period contained both fixed and floating exchange rates, and was characterized by prolonged bouts of dollar strength and dollar weakness. This time period also saw dramatic changes in average global inflation rates and substantial changes in inflation differentials among countries. In short, this was a risky period for picking individual country markets in which to invest.

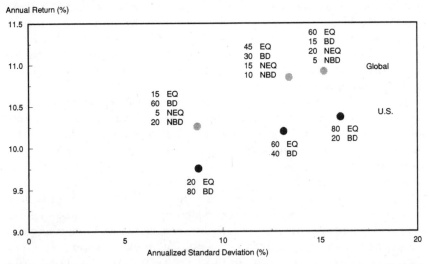

Figure 4-2. U.S. and global asset mixes: historical performance characteristics in U.S. dollars, year-end 1969–1990. (EQ = U.S. equities; BD = U.S. bonds; NEQ = non-U.S. equities; NBD = non-U.S. bonds.) *(Source: Brinson Partners, Inc.)*

In all cases the global portfolio generated higher returns than a domestic counterpart that had similar volatility. A "midrisk" domestic portfolio of 60 percent equity and 40 percent bonds, for example, generated an annual return of 10.2 percent, with a standard deviation of 13.2 percent. A global portfolio that also had a 60 to 40 allocation of equity to bonds, but included non-U.S. securities in each component, generated a 10.7 percent annual return with a standard deviation of 12.6 percent. While the dollar returns from non-U.S. equity and bond indexes were more volatile than returns from the respective U.S. markets over this period, the relatively low correlation of U.S. and non-U.S. assets suggests that both should have a significant role in the policy asset mix.

Policy Specification of
Asset Class Weights

The second asset allocation policy issue is the proportionate share of the various asset classes normally held in the portfolio. These are the weights that would be maintained in the absence of any information about the short-term performance of the various asset classes.

Market Value Policy Weights.   The performance of many global investment managers is measured relative to market-capitalization-based benchmarks. Although the Capital Asset Pricing Model discussed in Chapter 3 suggests that such an approach warrants consideration, market value weights are not always appropriate for a number of reasons. While it is helpful to have a benchmark against which an investor's performance can be evaluated, a market-capitalization-based benchmark might cause the information about the performance of the portfolio to be distorted relative to the objectives of the investor.

For example, when asset allocation policy reflects the relative capitalization of each market within an index, the policy shifts as market capitalizations change. This can be inappropriate when the investor's objectives are static or unrelated to market capitalizations. Second, strict application of the CAPM implies that all investors in the global market hold (or should hold) assets in proportion to their market weights. However, investors do not share common currencies. Because the local risks (say, inflation risk) facing Japanese investors differ from those facing U.S. or German investors, one might expect policy weights to be different across countries. Third, even the most broadly based current global indexes do not cover the full opportunity set available to global investors. In contrast to more narrowly defined markets, such as U.S. equities, a true index of the global market is neither identifiable nor capable of being held.

Customized Policy Weights. Establishing an allocation policy that takes account of investor's objectives and constraints, rather than simply adopting a market capitalization benchmark, requires information about the performance characteristics of the asset classes and how they interact. This information allows the investor to adopt a policy mix that, over time, would be expected to achieve the specified objectives. Determining a customized set of policy weights involves the simultaneous consideration of investor objectives, investor risk preferences, and long-term capital market expectations.

The most common approach to establishing customized policy weights is the mean-variance portfolio optimization procedure that was developed by the Nobel prize-winning economist, Harry Markowitz. The inputs necessary for this procedure are the expected returns and standard deviations for each asset class and the matrix of expected correlations of the returns for each asset class with every other. The output is a set of alternative portfolios, each having the minimum possible risk for a given expected return. The set of such portfolios, called optimal portfolios, describes a curve called the efficient frontier (see Figure 3-1). No one portfolio on the efficient frontier dominates any other, and the asset allocation policy decision involves selection of the efficient portfolio that best fits the investor's situation.

This quantitative approach to determining the policy weights generates precise asset mix recommendations. However, the results can be very sensitive to small changes in the inputs, requiring care in specification of the structure of expected long-run returns, risks, and correlations.[6] In that regard, two aspects of applying optimization techniques to the problem of policy weights are worthy of special consideration:

- The nature of constraints on the policy weights for U.S. versus non-U.S. assets

- The use of sound long-run equilibrium estimates to assure a consistent set of expected returns, risks, and correlations

Treatment of Non-U.S. Assets. On the first issue, recent analysis has called into question the standard practice of treating the assets of countries other than the United States as aggregate international indexes, with country weights that reflect relative market capitalizations, while U.S. asset policy weights are set at levels unrelated to their relative size in the global market.[7]

[6]Because the outputs of Markowitz optimization are too often used uncritically, it should be emphasized that the outputs are at best as accurate as the inputs, which are unavoidably subject to statistical estimation error. See Richard O. Michaud, "The Markowitz Optimization Enigma: Is 'Optimized' Optimal?" *Financial Analysts Journal*, January/February 1989.

[7]Gary P. Brinson and Denis S. Karnosky, "Global Asset Allocation Policy," in Robert Z. Aliber and Brian Bruce, eds., *Global Portfolios: Quantitative Strategies for Maximum Performance*, Business One Irwin, Homewood, Ill., 1991.

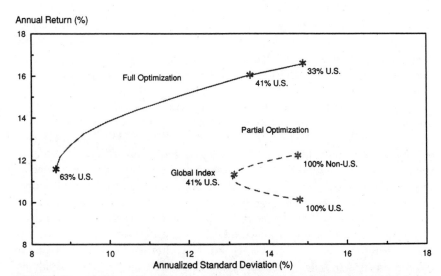

Figure 4-3. Global equities and bonds: full and partial historical optimizations in U.S. dollars, year-end 1974–1990. (100% U.S.-Cap. weighted 40 percent stock/60 percent bond. 100% Non-U.S.-Cap. weighted 47 percent stock/53 percent bond.) *(Source: Brinson Partners, Inc.)*

Often the normal allocation to U.S. assets, especially equities, is much larger than their relative market capitalization, while capitalization weights are assigned to assets within the non-U.S. component. Two alternative conclusions emerged from this study:

- Either the weights of U.S. assets in global portfolios are too large, given the market capitalization weights within the non-U.S. component

- Or the index weights within the non-U.S. component of global portfolios are suboptimal, given the normal weights that are assigned to the U.S. assets

Figure 4-3 illustrates these points, using actual dollar returns, standard deviations, and correlations for global equity and bond markets over the period from 1974 to 1990.[8] The lower curve is the frontier that is derived from a constrained optimization with four asset class indexes: U.S. equities, U.S. bonds, non-U.S. equities, and nondollar bonds. The endpoints represent pure domestic and international portfolios, with the mix of equities

---

[8] The use of historical (realized) returns in this analysis overstates the extent to which investors can expect to benefit in the future from relaxing the capitalization-weight restriction.

and bonds set to the relative market capitalizations at year-end 1990 in both cases. In this time period, the balanced portfolio of non-U.S. equities and bonds clearly dominated the U.S. balanced portfolio. Note that, based on this experience, the efficient set of global portfolios of these four indexes contained a maximum of 41 percent exposure to the U.S. markets. Since U.S. investors typically have normal exposures of at least 80 percent U.S. assets, this curve suggests that the normal U.S. weight is too large.

The upper frontier relaxes the restriction that non-U.S. assets are pre-aggregated into a unitary capitalization-weighted index called *international*. Instead, each individual country's equity and bond markets are treated as distinct asset classes. This approach gives portfolios that historically dominated portfolios based on aggregated non-U.S. indexes. Throughout the curve, the allocation among the individual non-U.S. markets is significantly different from their capitalization weights, suggesting that there are beneficial intermarket relationships which are lost when the non-U.S. assets are combined into indexes prior to optimization or other kinds of analyses. That is, use of aggregated non-U.S. equity and bond indexes might well lead to inefficient policy weights in global portfolios.

The Equilibrium Inputs. The asset allocation policy of an institutional investor should be guided by the basic philosophy that capital market behavior is ultimately a function of underlying economic fundamentals. This philosophy suggests that a normal asset allocation should be set in terms of normal asset class characteristics, rather than short-term historical observations. These normal characteristics are the return, risk, and covariance conditions that provide a long-term secular description of each asset class and of the relationships among asset classes.

Equilibrium asset class returns are those required by investors to forgo present consumption opportunities in favor of future consumption, to compensate for investment risk, and to protect the purchasing power of the investment capital. These considerations define three components of the equilibrium required return of an asset class—the real riskless rate, the risk premium, and the inflation premium, respectively.

In equilibrium, the real riskless rate is the marginal rate at which people are willing to forgo present consumption in favor of uncertain future consumption. This rate depends on both the time preference for consumption and the marginal efficiency of investment. This real riskless rate would be required by all investors from all assets.

Almost all assets offer a stream of future payoffs that, in real terms, is subject to uncertainty, or risk. Investors require a return premium to compensate for the uncertainty of these real payoffs. This premium is referred to as a risk premium and should be proportional to the compensable risk taken by an investor in the asset class. (A risk that cannot be avoided, such as market risk, is compensable in the framework of equilibrium asset pricing models; investors are not rewarded for the portion of total risk they can cheaply avoid; see Chapter 3.) The simplifying assumption that all investors require the same return per unit of risk incurred (i.e., that the price of risk is uniform across investors) would imply that all investors would require the same risk premium to be provided by a specific asset. In a fully integrated world the free flow of resources across borders would justify this type of assumption. Not only would all investors require the same real risk-free rate, but they would also require the same risk premium from a given asset.

However, it is likely that the marginal rate at which investors exchange risk for return is different across countries. This describes a world in which local markets are fully integrated but the global market is best viewed as segmented by national borders. The result is a partially segmented world in which resource flows are restricted because of transportation and transaction costs and political or cultural reasons. This suggests that local investors set the equilibrium risk premium for a globally held asset. Investors from another country, however, may require a different risk premium based on their price of risk. Thus, all investors would require the same real riskless rate, but different investors would require a different risk premium from the same asset. In this setting, opportunities for abnormal risk-adjusted returns in international investing may present themselves.

The equilibrium inflation premium is common to all asset classes but is potentially different for investors of different countries. To protect the required real return, consisting of the riskless rate plus the risk premium, a U.S. investor with dollar liabilities (or spending plans) would require an inflation premium to compensate for the expected long-term rate of U.S. price inflation. This premium would be required of all assets, domestic or foreign. A German investor with deutschemark liabilities, on the other hand, would require an inflation premium from both domestic and foreign assets that compensates for the expected rate of German inflation. Thus, U.S. and German investors would require different inflation premiums and hence different nominal rates of return to be provided by the same assets.

Combining these components gives equilibrium asset class returns. For a U.S. investor the equilibrium return for any global asset is equal to the common real riskless rate, a premium to compensate for expected U.S. inflation, and a risk premium that is unique to each asset. The risk premium is the only component that varies across assets and thus is the basic return variable that is relevant for global optimization. In a fully integrated world market in equilibrium, the risk premium is free of all currency considerations and would be the same for all investors, irrespective of their home currency. Currency con-

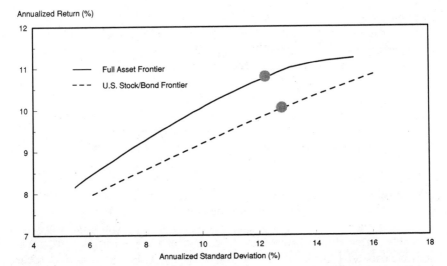

Figure 4-4.   Global versus domestic optimizations (in U.S. dollars). *(Source: Brinson Partners, Inc.)*

siderations would have no effect on the determination of policy weights for the various asset classes in a global portfolio.

One application of the optimization process to global markets is the Multiple Markets Index (MMI),[9] developed by Brinson Partners, Inc, which is discussed in Chapter 1. This global portfolio is designed to have a level of long term risk that is in line with the standard U.S. domestic balanced portfolio of 60 percent U.S. equities and 40 percent U.S. bonds. The equilibrium returns, risks, and correlations that were developed by Brinson Partners and used in the development of this normal portfolio are presented in Table 4-1.

Figure 4-4 presents two arrays of portfolios that are derived from these equilibrium inputs. The lower curve, labeled "U.S. Stock/Bond Frontier," gives the efficient combinations of U.S. equities and bonds. The upper curve, labeled "Full Asset Frontier," is derived from the global set of investable asset classes. The risk to return pattern of the MMI is marked on the upper frontier and compared to the risk to return profile of the 60-40 domestic portfolio on the lower curve. The global portfolios clearly dominated the U.S. balanced portfolios, offering higher equilibrium returns at each level of risk.

[9]The MMI policy weights are 40 percent U.S. equities, 15 percent non-U.S. equities, 20 percent U.S. dollar bonds, 5 percent non-U.S. dollar bonds, 3 percent high yield bonds, 5 percent venture capital, and 12 percent real estate.

Table 4-1. Equilibrium Asset Class Expectations for a U.S. Dollar-Based Investor

	Return (%)	Risk (%)	Correlations								
			1	2	3	4	5	6	7	8	9
1. U.S. large capitalization equities	10.71	16.50	1.00								
2. U.S. small capitalization equities	14.10	30.00	0.90	1.00							
3. International equities	10.75	17.00	0.60	0.60	1.00						
4. High-yield bonds	10.80	15.00	0.60	0.60	0.50	1.00					
5. Venture capital	18.10	45.00	0.30	0.40	0.15	0.35	1.00				
6. Dollar-denominated bonds	7.90	8.00	0.45	0.45	0.25	0.55	0.15	1.00			
7. Non-dollar-denominated bonds	7.45	12.20	0.25	0.20	0.60	0.25	0.10	0.30	1.00		
8. Real estate	9.80	14.00	0.35	0.40	0.30	0.25	0.25	0.20	0.15	1.00	
9. Cash	6.08	1.50	-0.10	-0.10	-0.15	-0.05	-0.10	-0.05	-0.10	0.25	1.00

SOURCE: Brinson Partners, Inc.

Active Asset Allocation

Asset allocation policy is established in accordance with normal capital market conditions and the institutional investor's risk tolerance. While the investor's risk tolerance is presumed to be constant over time and across risk levels, capital market conditions will vary, affording profitable opportunities to deviate from the policy asset mix. Such active asset allocations would reflect the constant risk tolerance of the investor but capital market conditions that are different from those used to identify the policy mix.

Active management techniques can be segregated into the broad categories of fundamental and market-timing models.[10] The distinction between these approaches is their orientation toward the present versus the future. Fundamental models generate opportunistic active allocations that are determined by estimates of discrepancies between current and equilibrium capital market conditions. Such models do not explicitly require forecasts of future market prices as such, but focus on actual current prices relative to equilibrium values. Market-timing models lead to active asset-mix decisions that are motivated by explicit forecasts of future price changes (returns).

An example of the difference in these approaches is the reaction to a significant increase in interest rates, such as in the early 1980s. The market-timing approach evaluates the prospect that interest rates will fall in the near future, generating a capital gain on a bond position. The fundamental approach, on the other hand, evaluates whether the higher current bond yields are attractive relative to equilibrium returns and risks. In that framework, bonds would be attractive because they offer superior rates of return, with no necessary forecast of lower interest rates. In fact, the total returns from long-term Treasury bonds from 1981 to the present would have been as high or higher had interest rates not declined. Reinvestment income at the higher interest rates would have equalled or exceeded the actual rate of price appreciation.

Fundamental Valuation

The fundamental determination of equilibrium returns, risks, and correlations presumes that the returns of and relationships between all asset classes are stable over time. Although observed risks and correlations may demonstrate short-run deviations from equilibrium, and the long-run equilibrium may also change over time (as with the unification of Germany), they can be treated as stationary at any point. As time passes and events reshape both investors' thinking and economic fundamentals, these equilibrium relationships would be subject to modification.

[10]Gary P. Brinson, "Asset Allocation vs. Market Timing," *Investment Management Review*, September/October 1988.

The expected returns that the asset classes provide over the investment horizon, on the other hand, reflect the *current* prices in the capital markets. As such, a state of disequilibrium reflects the deviation of expected asset class returns from equilibrium returns and/or variations in asset class risks or correlations. Thus, active asset allocations are motivated by deviations of expected returns, risks, and correlations from equilibrium capital market conditions. The discussion of portfolio construction in Chapter 5 expands the concept of fundamental valuation and the computation of expected asset class and security returns.

The long-term results of a fundamental approach to active investment management should reflect the objectives of the institutional investor. Although active asset class weights would often diverge from policy weights in response to these price-value discrepancies, the central tendency of the portfolio should be the policy mix. Thus, fundamental valuation dictates a long-term risk orientation for the portfolio that gives appropriate consideration of the investor's preferences toward risk. Simply stated, a fundamental valuation approach to active portfolio management seeks to manage portfolio risk to the investor's objectives.

Alternative Valuation Techniques

Alternative valuation models range from "black box" models to technical analysis of price chart patterns. Many of these approaches are motivated by investor forecasts of future prices, and they too lead to active asset allocations. A forecast, or timing, approach to active asset allocation does not specifically compare current prices with fundamental values, or current expected returns with long-run equilibrium-expected returns. Consequently, timing-based approaches involve an entirely different philosophical approach to the asset allocation question.

Black-box models provide for consistent application of historical macroeconomic relationships across asset classes. However, they are completely dependent on the repeatability of history. In their extreme quantitative form these models have become a pseudoscience. Technical analysis, in contrast, relies on the repeatability of history in a very different sense. Rather than evaluating relationships among asset classes, technical analysis attempts to divine future price trends from historical price patterns. Such an approach implies that even the weak efficient-market hypothesis is invalid since it presumes that investors are expected to repeat past mistakes.

The Optimal Active Allocation

Irrespective of the valuation model employed, the expected returns, risks, and correlations generated for each asset class form the foundation for actively managed asset allocation. Rather than determining the asset mix according to equilibrium returns, risks, and correlations, the active allocation is based upon comparison of the equilibrium values of these variables with the conditions that exist in the market at a specific point in time. This approach reflects a belief that the long-term relationships between asset classes are stable and deviations from the policy mix are appropriate only when the expected returns differ from those used to generate the policy allocation. Therefore, an active asset allocation that is different from the policy allocation implies a situation where expected asset class returns are in a temporary state of disequilibrium.

5
Portfolio Management

John Maynard Keynes, in what is perhaps the most famous passage in financial writing, vividly captured the problem of investment decision making. He compared it to

> newspaper competitions in which the competitors have to pick out the six prettiest faces from a hundred photographs, the prize being awarded to the competitor whose choice most nearly corresponds to the average preferences of the competitors as a whole; so that each competitor has to pick, not those which he himself finds prettiest, but those which he thinks likeliest to catch the fancy of the other competitors, all of whom are looking at the problem from the same point of view.[1]

In this chapter we tackle this problem and discuss how to identify and exploit investment opportunities that exist across and within global capital market asset classes. While Keynes actually managed a portfolio using the techniques of technical analysis that address the pricing of securities independent of their fundamental values, his beauty contest analogy applies to all of active portfolio management, which is the focus of this chapter. We begin with a discussion of passive management, because it forms a baseline against which active management techniques must be judged. We discuss passive management in some detail because of its recent greatly increased popularity. We then set forth a fundamental value-oriented approach to active management. Finally, we address the controversy regarding the advisability of certain aspects of currency hedging, and describe how derivative securities can be used to reconfigure portfolio risk and return.

[1] John Maynard Keynes, *The General Theory of Employment, Interest and Money*, Harcourt, Brace, Jovanovich, Inc., New York, 1936.

Passive Management

The goal of passive management is not to *beat*, but rather to *track* the performance of a benchmark or index of assets. Passive managers do not try to identify bargain prices or determine if a particular market is over- or underpriced. Instead, they employ indexing methods that will allow the portfolio (called an index fund) to replicate the benchmark returns as closely as possible.

Drawing on the insight provided by the efficient market hypothesis, a few fund managers introduced index funds in the 1970s, but they were largely ignored until the early 1980s. Today, indexing is a popular choice for both stock and bond funds. The reason for this remarkable growth is a belief that index funds can provide returns equal or superior to those of actively managed funds at lower cost.

Many studies have shown that unmanaged indexes outperform the median active manager on average. In fact, active management in the aggregate is a negative-sum game. Since, by construction, the aggregation of all active investors generates returns equal to the market, then after transaction costs, the average return of all active managers must be lower than that of the market.[2]

A passively managed fund may have both fixed and variable costs that are lower than those of an actively managed fund.[3] Lower fixed costs are primarily due to lower personnel costs—security analysts who can beat the market do not come cheap. The variable cost advantage stems from lower commissions, tighter bid-offer spreads, and less market impact than are found in the transactions of many, but not all, active managers.[4] All of these cost differentials are magnified when one considers that active equity managers typically turn over their portfolios at a rate of nearly 100 percent per year, while the S&P 500 index may have a turnover of 5 percent per year. Finally, management fees are about one-tenth as large for a passive fund as for an active fund.

Popular Index Fund Benchmarks

The first step when indexing is to decide what index to follow. In the United States the most popular equity benchmark is the Standard & Poor's 500 index.

---

[2]For a further elaboration of this point see William F. Sharpe, "The Arithmetic of Active Management," *Financial Analysts Journal,* January/February 1991.

[3]For an excellent comparison of costs between active and passive management see Brian R. Bruce, Heydon D. Traub, and Larry L. Martin, "Global Passive Management," in Robert Z. Aliber and Brian R. Bruce, eds., *Global Portfolios,* Richard D. Irwin, Inc., Homewood, Ill. 1991.

[4]These transaction costs are lower because passive managers typically trade patiently; they wait for favorable trading conditions to occur.

For U.S. investors in the international equity market, the most popular is the EAFE (Europe, Australia, Far East) index constructed by Morgan Stanley Capital International.[5] Global investors in Europe tend to follow either the EAFE or the Goldman Sachs/FT-Actuaries World Indices. For U.S. bonds the Salomon Broad Investment Grade ("BIG") Index or Lehman Brothers Government/Corporate Bond Index is typically used. For world bonds, popular indexes are the Salomon Brothers World Government Bond Index and the J.P. Morgan Government Bond Index.

Methods of Indexing

Once an index has been chosen, a method must be selected for achieving performance that tracks the index as efficiently as possible. A near perfect match between portfolio and index returns can be achieved by adjusting portfolio holdings to mirror index composition changes. Unfortunately, this method of "full replication" is expensive because an index can itself have substantial turnover and many securities in an index may be relatively illiquid or small and subject the portfolio to rebalancing costs. This problem is particularly severe for broad-based bond indexes. In order to reduce these costs while introducing as little tracking risk as possible, techniques such as sampling and optimization have been introduced.

Sampling involves selecting a subset of the index to hold instead of the whole index. The reasoning is that one can construct a subset that will mimic the entire index with only minimal tracking error. For equities, two popular methods of sampling include size-stratified sampling and industry sampling. In size-stratified sampling, the companies in the index are divided into size categories and stocks are selected to represent each category in its proper capitalization weight. Industry sampling involves dividing the index into industry groups and replicating the same industry distribution in the portfolio, but with fewer stocks representing each industry. For bonds, sampling is performed on characteristics such as duration and credit quality, while diversification across issuers is maintained.

Probably the most complex technique for tracking an index is optimization. For a given number of securities (selected from the universe of securities, not just those in the index) the optimizer selects those that will minimize tracking error. As the constraint on the number of securities is loosened, tracking error continues to drop.

---

[5]A more comprehensive discussion of equity index construction and the qualities of specific indexes is contained in Chapter 7.

Weighting Issues

The most frequently used portfolio weighting methods employed in passive management are market capitalization and Gross National Product (GNP) or Gross Domestic Product (GDP) weights.

Market capitalization, the most popular method, requires the least rebalancing because a security's value and its weight in a capitalization-weighted index move in lockstep. Rebalancing is only required for composition changes and dividend reinvestment. Market-capitalization weighting has caused some consternation when applied to both domestic and international investing (See Chapter 4). With respect to international investing, many indexes are capitalization-weighted according to the size of a country's equity market. But as will be seen in Chapter 6, this may not be an ideal way to hold global equities; for example, capitalization weights are not necessarily reflective of a country's economic strength as measured by GDP or GNP. This was particularly a concern in the late 1980s as the remarkable run-up in Japanese stocks made it an extremely large percentage of the EAFE and other indexes. Many fund managers felt that continued tracking of a capitalization-weighted international equity index would reduce, not increase diversification in their portfolios.

For these reasons, some investors prefer to hold a GDP-weighted portfolio of international securities.

Active Management

Active asset allocation and security selection attempt to provide the investor with added value through periodic adjustment of the structure of the portfolio relative to its fundamental policy norms. The magnitude and frequency of the changes will reflect the particular style of the investment manager, as some approaches produce frequent and large changes, while others show long periods of constancy or a series of small changes. The key consideration is a conviction that market conditions periodically offer the opportunity to enhance the performance of the portfolio.

The choice between active and passive management of a portfolio involves two basic issues:

1. The investor's opinion on the efficiency of markets, e.g., whether opportunities to earn excess returns from active management exist

2. The perceived ability of a given investor to recognize and exploit such opportunities, if they exist

Relative to evaluating domestic opportunities, the active management task is complicated for the global investor by differences in basic factors such as tax laws, accounting conventions, trade settlement systems, and economic reporting across nations. In addition, there is the matter of managing currency exposures.

Nonetheless, we believe that while the efficient market hypothesis has originated many useful analytical tools, its underlying homogeneity assumptions are not viable in a global environment. As a practical matter, there are opportunities for investors to add value through active management of global asset classes. In fact, the very complexities of the global market that concern passive investors are among the factors that provide a basis for active management.

Figure 5-1 indicates each year's best and worst performing asset classes among several that were available to global investors since December 31, 1969. The graph clearly depicts broad variation in asset class returns over this period. An asset class may have been the worst performing one year and the best in the subsequent year. Active management of the asset allocation decision provides the opportunity to add value by potentially capturing or avoiding these wide return variations. To describe a way that value can be added through long-term, fundamental analysis, we set forth a consistent, objective valuation process that is based on the sustainable earning power of assets.

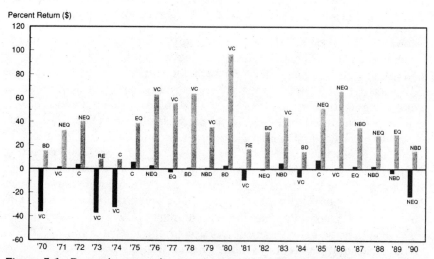

Figure 5-1. Best and worst performing global assets: 1970–1990—Annual returns. (EQ: U.S. equities; C: cash; BD: v.s. bonds; VC: venture capital; NEQ: non-U.S. equities; NBD: non-dollar bonds; RE: U.S. real estate.) *(Source: Brinson Partners, Inc.)*

Asset Valuation

Since assets and asset classes represent claims on future income, their values can be determined in a consistent fashion by summing the present value of all future cash flows. In an uncertain world, the investor's projection of future cash flows must be discounted by a discount rate that is higher than the nominal riskless rate. Thus, the discount rate is a risk-adjusted rate and reflects a premium for the uncertainty of future cash flows.

It is important to consider all cash payments that accrue to the benefit of the asset owner. In the case of equities, for example, the economic income to the stockholder includes cash that is retained as earnings within the corporation and cash that is disbursed to repurchase stock, in addition to the direct flow of dividends.

Cash Flow Forecasting.   The task of evaluating the cash flow potential of assets has become increasingly complicated by change and innovation in capital markets. Hybrid securities, such as convertible bonds and equity index-linked certificates of deposit, are being introduced at a rapid pace. High-yield, or "junk," bonds have payment streams with risk characteristics resembling those of equities. The explosion of debt financing in the 1980s, on the other hand, resulted in some corporations having balance sheets that were heavily exposed to monetary assets. Equity in these firms represented claims on financial, rather than real assets. Analysis of the associated income streams requires special attention to these shifts in the asset composition of firms.

Global Equity Assets.   To determine future cash flows, an equity analyst needs to estimate the expected future earnings of the company. Both domestic and international earnings analyses involve the evaluation of global and local economic developments, industry growth, currency exposures and individual company growth. This may require analyses of both domestic and foreign sources of income and the influence of foreign as well as domestic competition.

While foreign equity asset valuations reflect the same considerations as domestic equity assets, the information required for cash flow forecasting is often much more difficult to obtain and interpret. Furthermore, the variety of accounting standards evident among even the major investment market countries complicates the interpretation of that information. The International Accounting Standards Committee (IASC) was established in 1973 to achieve some reconciliation of accounting interpretations. The goal of the IASC, however, is not to standardize accounting practices. IASC statements are not enforceable and local accounting procedures need not conform to IASC standards. Consequently, progress toward standardization remains slow and the efficiency of global capital markets continues to be reduced by the limited availability of information and by the difficulty of interpreting that which is available.

In general, the IASC accommodates a broader range of accounting standards than the generally accepted accounting principles (GAAP) of the United States. The IASC recognizes that accounting procedures are not necessarily right or wrong but simply reflect differing approaches and objectives. Table 5-1 provides a summary of the major accounting differences that exist among six major international trading nations. The following examples provide a flavor of some of the more important differences between U.S. GAAP and IASC standards.

- *Acquisitions.* IASC standards permit both the purchase and pooling-of-interests methods of accounting for acquisitions. However, the requirements for using these methods are much less strict outside the United States.

- *Goodwill.* The IASC allows goodwill to be treated either as an asset, as does GAAP, or as a contra-equity adjustment. Moreover, the IASC allows a wider range of amortization periods than GAAP and upward revaluations of goodwill not allowed in the United States.

- *Market Value Revaluation.* GAAP requires the recording of assets at historical cost, whereas the IASC allows periodic upward revaluation to market value. If revaluations are properly implemented, IASC statements may provide more information than GAAP statements.

- *Foreign Currency Translation.* Foreign countries, as well as the United States, tend to use an all-current method of accounting for currency translation gains and losses. However, many foreign countries flow currency translation gains or losses through the income statement while U.S. companies account for them as an adjustment to shareholders' equity.

- *Earnings per Share.* In the United States, earnings per share is an often-quoted accounting ratio and is reported according to strict specifications.[6] The IASC does not provide a set of specifications for calculating earnings per share, and foreign companies are able to report various and incomparable measures.

While obviously troublesome for the analyst, these differences also provide exploitable opportunities for those investors willing to incur the costs of obtaining the necessary information. Evaluation of foreign equities should involve, where possible, the adjustment of foreign financial statements to GAAP, allowing for consistent analysis of cash flows across countries. The IASC recommends that companies provide a statement of changes in financial position that should provide enough information to

---

[6]These specifications were set forth in 1969 by Opinion 15 of the Accounting Principles Board (APB). The APB has since been replaced by the Financial Accounting Standards Board (FASB).

Table 5-1. Summary of Generally Accepted Accounting Principles for Major Industrialized Countries

	United States	Canada	France[a]	Japan	Great Britain[b]	West Germany
Marketable securities (current asset)	Lower of cost or market	Lower of cost or market	Lower of cost or market	Cost (unless price declines considered permanent)	Lower of cost or market	Lower of cost or market
Bad debts	Allowance method	Allowance method	Allowance method for identifiable uncollectible accounts	Allowance method	Allowance method	Allowance method for identifiable uncollectible accounts
Inventories—Valuation	Lower of cost or market	Lower of cost or market	Lower of cost or market	Lower of cost or market	Lower of cost or market	Lower of cost or market
Inventories—Cost Flow Assumption	FIFO, LIFO, average	FIFO, average	FIFO, average	FIFO, LIFO, average	FIFO, average	Average (unless physical flow is FIFO or LIFO)
Fixed assets—Valuation	Acquisition cost less depreciation	Acquisition cost less depreciation	Acquisition cost less depreciation	Acquisition cost less depreciation	Acquisition cost less depreciation	Acquisition cost less depreciation
Fixed assets—Depreciation	Straight-line declining balance, sum-of-the-years-digits	Straight-line accelerated	Straight-line accelerated	Straight-line, declining balance, sum-of-the-years-digits	Straight-line, declining balance, sum-of-the-years-digits	Straight-line accelerated

Research and development	Expensed when incurred	Expense when incurred	Generally expensed when incurred, but may be capitalized and amortized	Expensed when incurred or capitalized or amortized	Expensed when incurred	Expensed when incurred
Leases	Operating and capital lease methods	Operating and capital lease methods	Operating lease method	Operating lease method	Operating lease method	Operating lease method
Deferred taxes	Deferred tax accounting required	Deferred tax accounting required	Book-tax conformity generally required so deferred tax accounting not an issue	Book-tax conformity generally required so deferred tax accounting not an issue	Deferred tax accounting required based on probability that liability or asset will crystallize	Book-tax conformity generally required so deferred tax accounting not an issue
Investments in Securities 0–20%	Lower of cost or market	Cost (unless price declines considered permanent)	Lower of cost or market	Cost (unless price declines considered permanent)	Lower of cost or market	Cost (unless price declines considered permanent)

(Continued)

79

Table 5-1. Summary of Generally Accepted Accounting Principles for Major Industrialized Countries (Continued)

	United States	Canada	France[a]	Japan	Great Britain[b]	West Germany
Investment in Securities: 20%–50%	Equity method	Equity method	Equity method	Cost (unless price declines considered permanent)	Equity method	Cost (unless price declines considered permanent)
Investment in Securities: greater than 50%	Consolidation required	Consolidation generally required	Consolidation required	Consolidation not required (except in certain listings with the Ministry of Finance)	Both parent company and group (consolidated) financial statement presented	Consolidation required
Corporate acquisitions: accounting method	Purchase and pooling of interest methods	Purchase method (pooling permitted only when acquired cannot be identified)	Purchase method	Purchase method	Purchase and pooling of interest methods	Purchase method

Amortization of goodwill	Amortized over maximum of 40 years	Amortized over maximum of 40 years	Amortization required	Amortized over maximum of 5 years	Goodwill either written off immediately against a retained earnings reserve or capitalized and amortized over its expected useful life	Amortized over a period of 4 to 14 years

[a] Generally accepted accounting principles in France permit periodic revaluation of tangible fixed assets and investment to current market values. However, the book/tax conformity requirement in France results in immediate taxation of unrealized gains. As a consequence, revaluations are unusual.

[b] Generally accepted accounting principles in Great Britian permit periodic revaluations of land, buildings, and certain intangibles to current market values. The firm credits a revaluation reserve account, a component of shareholders' equity.

SOURCE: Clyde P. Stickney, Roman L. Weil, and Sidney Davidson, from *Financial Accounting: An Introduction to Concepts, Methods, and Uses*, 6th Ed., Exhibit 14.4, "Summary of Generally Accepted Accounting Principles for Major Industrialized Countries," copyright © 1991 by Harcourt Brace Jovanovich, Inc., Reprinted by permission of the publisher.

generate a cash flow statement similar to that required in the United States.[7]

Special tax considerations can have a significant impact on the expected cash flows provided by equity assets. Table 5-2 indicates effective withholding tax rates facing U.S. investors in foreign assets. These rates are approximate and vary across investors; also, investors domiciled outside the United States would experience different withholding tax rates. Note that the effective tax rates are reported as net of reclaimed taxes, that is, taxes that are withheld but later refunded to the investor. Thus, statutory or stated rates are often higher than the effective rates shown.

Global Fixed-Income Assets.   Global fixed-income securities require analysis of the risk of expected coupon and principal payments. Risk subsumes both the probability of receiving cash flows and the timing of their receipt. Although fixed-income cash flows are less dependent on the economic environment than those of equity assets, default or quality risk must be taken into consideration in establishing each security's discount rate. As with equity assets, the uncertainty should be accounted for by incorporating a risk premium, reflective of quality risk, into the rate at which expected cash flows are discounted.

With respect to the timing of cash flows, explicit option provisions, such as the call features of corporate bonds, and implicit option provisions, such as the prepayment option embedded in mortgage-backed securities, must be appropriately accounted for in bond analysis. These considerations would be reflected in the timing of the return of principal, typically shifting this expected cash flow to an earlier date.

Table 5-2 also indicates the various withholding taxes that apply to coupon income from the bonds of various countries. Some withholding taxes are avoidable, however. The tax on some foreign bonds, for example, currently applies only to securities held at the end of the tax period. This tax could be avoided through transactions, eliminating ownership (from the tax authority's viewpoint) by using the bonds as collateral against borrowed funds until after the tax date, when the repurchase agreement, or "repo," would be unwound. Taxes are also reclaimable for many foreign bonds, impacting the timing but not the magnitude of the future cash flows.

Global Real Estate Assets.   A global real estate investor is required to perform similar cash flow analyses. Real estate cash flow analysis, in many respects, combines fixed-income and equity asset considerations. Debt-type

---

[7]These and other accounting distinctions are discussed in David F. Hawkins, "Dealing with International Accounting Diversity: International Accounting Standards," *Accounting Bulletin #1*, Merrill Lynch & Co., Inc., May 1990.

Table 5-2. Effective Withholding Tax for U.S. Investors

Country	Dividends (%)	Interest (%)	Capital Gains (%)	Comment
Australia	15.0	10.0	As income	Interest tax reclaimable by tax-exempt funds.
Austria	12.5	10.0	0.0	
Belgium	15.0	0.0	0.0	
Canada	15.0	0.0	0.0	
Denmark	15.0	0.0	0.0	
Finland	15.0	N/A	0.0	
France	15.0	15.0	0.0	No interest tax for bonds issued after 1987. Dividends include government paid *avoir fiscal.*
Germany	15.0	0.0	0.0	
Hong Kong	0.0	0.0	0.0	
Italy	15.0	12.5	0.0	
Japan	15.0	10.0	0.0	
Luxembourg	7.5	N/A	0.0	
Mexico	0.0	0.0	0.0	A 35 percent tax for dividends not paid out of distributable profits.
Netherlands	15.0	0.0	0.0	
New Zealand	15.0	0.0	0.0	
Norway	15.0	N/A	0.0	Capital gains tax of 40 percent if held less than 3 years.
Singapore	0.0	N/A	N/A	
Spain	0.0	15.0	N/A	
Sweden	15.0	N/A	0.0	
Switzerland	15.0	5.0	0.0	
United Kingdom	15.0	27.0	0.0	Interest tax reclaimable by tax-exempt funds. Certain government bonds are free of interest tax.
United States	0.0	0.0	0.0	

SOURCE: This material reproduced Courtesy of Euromoney Books, extracted from *The G. T. Guide to World Equity Markets 1989,* 1988; Morgan Stanley Capital International *Perspective* (various issues); and Brinson Partners, Inc.

exposure arises from the rental income generated by the property. The equity aspect reflects both direct claims on capital resources and, in some instances, participations in tenant revenue or income. As we note in Chapter 13, the real estate investor can think of each property as a portfolio of debt and equity assets. The combination of these analyses generates an expected stream of revenues to be provided by each property.

Discount Rate Determination. The discounting of expected cash flows by the equilibrium expected rate of return of the asset identifies the asset's current equilibrium value. As explained in Chapter 4, the equilibrium expected return, or the discount rate, for an asset that generates uncertain future cash flows is comprised of three components:

1. The real riskless rate (uniform for every asset)

2. An expected inflation premium (uniform for every asset)

3. A risk premium (specific to each asset)

The real riskless rate is that which is required by the investor to forgo present consumption for future consumption. The expected inflation premium is the return premium that is required to protect the purchasing power of the invested funds. Finally, the asset-specific risk premium is the compensation for the uncertainty of the future real income stream expected to be generated by each asset.

The real riskless rate and the inflation premium are constant across all assets for a given investor. For a U.S. investor, the inflation premium for all assets, including non-U.S. assets, covers the investor's expectations for U.S. inflation. Therefore, the risk premium is the only distinguishing feature between the equilibrium discount rate of one asset and that of another. However, the definition and therefore the measurement of equilibrium risk is ambiguous.

Even in this environment of increasingly integrated capital markets, the dominant participants of almost every local market are local investors. A survey of the literature suggests that local institutional investors in major countries currently maintain domestic equity and bond holdings of about 60 to 80 percent. The investible capital market available to but not necessarily held by U.S. investors was comprised of 49 percent domestic assets as of December 31, 1990, down from 55 percent as of December 31, 1969, according to estimates by Brinson Partners, Inc. The integration of global markets will work over time to further reduce this fundamental segmentation, and risk premiums will tend to equilibrate.

However, the process has just begun. The generally lower volatility in domestic markets relative to unhedged foreign markets, the greater availability of information on domestic assets, and the persistence of official barriers to capital flows provides a perceived degree of comfort that would suggest a long adjustment period.

Based on the assumption that local investors remain the dominant force in establishing local asset risk premiums a global investor can evaluate the expected returns on assets according to the equilibrium price of risk as set by local investors in each national market. Although many approaches could be used, a good top-down working model would establish equilibrium risk premia for local asset classes and then derive the individual asset risk premium from those of the local market asset classes. The global investor would tend to hold assets in countries where the expected reward for taking risk is high relative to other countries.

Global Portfolio Construction

Exploitable opportunities may exist when the expected return implied by the current market price of an asset is different from its equilibrium discount rate. The expected rate of return is implied by the combination of the asset's current market price and the investor's cash flow expectations for the asset. In fact, the discount rate is the only link between expected cash flows and the current price of an asset. For example, an asset that is expected to generate cash flows of $5 at the end of year 1, $10 after year 2, and $15 after years 3, 4, and 5 and is priced at $43.64 would have an expected return of 10 percent:

$$\$43.64 = \frac{\$5}{(1+0.10)^1} + \frac{\$10}{(1+0.10)^2} + \frac{\$15}{(1+0.10)^3} + \frac{\$15}{(1+0.10)^4} + \frac{\$15}{(1+0.10)^5}$$

If this implied expected rate of return of 10 percent exceeds the equilibrium discount rate required to compensate for the perceived risk of the asset, then an opportunity exists to buy this asset at a price below fundamental value. If the equilibrium discount rate were 7 percent, then the fundamental value computed by discounting the cash flows at that rate would be $47.79. Thus, a market price of $43.64 would be attractive.

Whether or not an investment opportunity exists outside the local market (for an investor whose currency of denomination is different from that of the asset) depends on exchange rate considerations. Investors domiciled outside the local market require an inflation premium that compensates for their own expected inflation, not the premium that is offered in the local market. Thus, the required return to a U.S. investor from a foreign asset consists of the real riskless rate, the expected U.S. inflation rate, and the risk premium on the asset.

Exchange rates provide the means by which the inflation premiums provided in the local markets are translated into an inflation premium for the U.S. investor. Under certain conditions (see Chapter 2), the expected rate of change in the dollar price of a foreign currency is equal to the expected inflation differential between the U.S. and the other country. Assuming the required conditions hold, a 4 percent expected rate of inflation in the United States and a 3 percent expected rate in Germany would translate to an expected (sometimes called required) 1 percent rate of appreciation of the deutschemark against the U.S. dollar.

Managing Currency Exposure

The long-term returns of U.S. dollar and non-dollar bonds indicate that these two asset classes would be expected to generate similar long-term returns to a U.S. investor, but the risks are different. Volatility of exchange rates is the primary source of this risk differential. The implication is that hedging the currency exposure of non-dollar bonds, for example, would decrease volatility over the long term, with no reduction in return. This observation has prompted some investors to adopt a policy of fully hedging the currency exposure in global portfolios. That policy decision, in turn, has a significant effect on the nature of any active management decision. However, the decision to incorporate hedged or unhedged assets into the investment policy requires consideration of additional factors, some specific to individual investors.

The case for hedging typically rests on the idea that currency fluctuations introduce a risk that has no payoff. As with other nonsystematic or uncompensated risk, the investor should be willing to pay some appropriate price to dispose of that risk. Some analysts have argued that the price of currency hedging is zero, offering the elusive "free lunch." In this case, volatility is reduced by hedging, with no material loss in return.[8] Ironically, others have argued that there is an expected positive gain to both parties in a currency

---

[8]Andre F. Perold and Evan C. Schulman, "The Free Lunch in Currency Hedging: Implications for Investment Policy and Performance Standards," *Financial Analysts Journal*, May/June, 1988.

transaction, implying that there is an optimal, partially hedged position for all global investors.[9]

The ability of currency hedging to reduce volatility of assets within a portfolio, however, does not address the full range of investor objectives. Figure 5-2 shows two efficient frontiers for global assets, based on historical data. One frontier includes fully hedged non-U.S. assets, while the other is based on the performance of unhedged non-U.S. assets. The hedged portfolios are clearly dominant over the range of low- to middle-risk levels, offering higher returns for equivalent risk. These results are consistent with the conventional arguments that are made in favor of currency hedging.

Figure 5-3, however, considers this historical record from another perspective and shows a very different result. When the volatility of liabilities of the investor (e.g., a pension fund) are also a consideration, unhedged currency exposure can have a significant benefit. Unhedged foreign currency exposure provides a buffer against the effects of unexpected changes in U.S. inflation relative to that of other countries. To the extent that U.S. liabilities are affected by unexpected changes in the rate of U.S. inflation, exchange rate changes would tend to offset these effects.

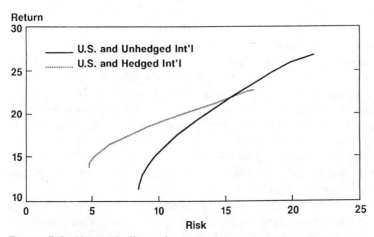

Figure 5-2. Historical efficient frontiers, assets only: 1974–1988 *(Source: Brinson Partners, Inc.)*

[9] Fischer Black, "Equilibrium Exchange Rate Hedging," *Journal of Finance,* July 1990.

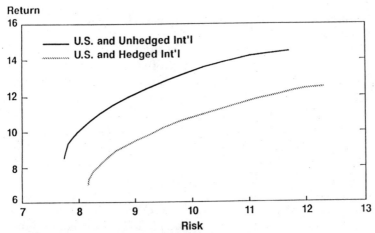

Figure 5-3. Historical efficient frontiers, assets less active liabilities: 1974–1988 *(Source: Brinson Partners, Inc.)*

Futures, Options, and Other Derivatives

Active management can be implemented without actually altering the asset class structure of the investment portfolio. A nonintrusive method of active management is implemented through the use of derivative securities. This section discusses the use of derivative securities in implementing many active asset allocation and security selection decisions.

The fundamental benefits of derivative securities are transaction facilitation and flexibility. Derivative securities enable the immediate implementation of investment decisions, often greatly reducing transaction costs. The decision to move assets from U.S. equities to U.S. fixed-income securities, for example, can be effected immediately by selling equity futures and purchasing fixed-income futures. Rather than incur transaction costs that might arise from the negative market impact of selling large blocks of equity securities and buying fixed-income assets, the initial futures implementation enables a more orderly and less costly transition.

Derivative securities enable the specification of almost any expected return distribution likely to be realized by an asset. As such, derivatives offer the potential to create synthetic securities with desired return and risk characteristics. Perhaps the most common example of this application is *hedging*, where synthetic cash securities are created by selling futures against an asset position. However, derivatives offer more flexibility than this simple application would suggest. As shall be seen later in this chapter, options, for example, can be combined with other derivatives and/or underlying assets to create almost any return distribution.

Implementation within the Investment Process

Asset Allocation Policy. Chapter 4 outlined a conceptual framework for the investment process that identified three major stages of decision making—asset allocation policy, active asset allocation, and security selection. Asset allocation policy identifies the asset classes and the proportions of these asset classes that are normally held by a portfolio. The decisions associated with establishing policy require little consideration of derivative securities. Derivatives possess no fundamental return and risk characteristics beyond those of the underlying assets. Instead, a derivative security merely provides a means of altering, typically for a short time horizon, the return and risk characteristics of an asset. Since asset allocation policy is based on long-term investor objectives, the potential policy application of derivative securities is limited to techniques, such as portfolio insurance, that can use short-term instruments to achieve long-run goals. Currency hedging and, recently, the use of managed commodity futures as a risk-reducing asset class have become more common applications of derivative securities at the policy level; however, the major uses of derivatives are in the active phase of the investment process.

Active Asset Allocation. The active asset allocation process can make extensive use of derivative securities. As noted, derivatives enable the immediate implementation of investment decisions without incurring the potentially high transaction costs that would be associated with shifting portfolio assets. At the asset class level, derivatives can be used to change the systematic (market) risk of the portfolio. In effect, the portfolio manager can target an equity beta or a bond duration within a portfolio without altering the asset composition of the portfolio. The systematic risk can be controlled by transacting in derivative securities that replicate the performance of the portfolio benchmark. Such securities include futures contracts on equity indexes and government bonds and notes. Options provide the ability to alter systematic risk contingent upon the price performance of asset classes.

To implement an active asset allocation decision with derivative securities, the investment manager increases (reduces) the effective exposure to an asset class, by buying (selling) futures against that asset class. Reducing the equity beta or fixed-income duration to zero would be equivalent to a zero allocation to stocks or bonds, respectively. Thus the availability of futures contracts on the major asset classes makes it easy and inexpensive to implement active asset allocation decisions.

Security Selection. The nonsystematic (nonmarket) risk of an investment portfolio can also be modified by transacting in securities that are derivatives of the individual assets. Such securities include options on underlying equity or fixed-income securities, collateralized mortgage obligations, Primes, Scores, and other derivative securities. While the analysis of options on individual assets is almost identical to that of index options, the impact of implementation is largely on the nonsystematic portion of portfolio risk. The effect on systematic portfolio risk is often negligible.

Futures

A futures contract is an instrument that conveys the *obligation* either to buy or sell an asset at a predetermined price and delivery date. As such, the futures market is little more than a standardized market for forward delivery contracts in which counterparty risk has been transferred to the clearing corporation of the exchange. The major difference between futures contracts and forward contracts is that all of the terms of each forward contract are negotiated between buyer and seller, while the terms (except price) of a futures contract are standardized or prespecified. Thus, futures contracts avoid problems of "coincidence of wants" and are, in general, a more efficient means of trade. In addition, futures positions are marked-to-market according to their daily price fluctuations and require a payment of "earnest money" or margin based on these fluctuations. If the contract is not transferred in the secondary market prior to the specified delivery date (contract expiration), the asset is delivered in exchange for the predetermined price. Since futures contracts exist for financial assets, commodities, market indexes, and currencies, they can be used to transfer risk at the asset class level.

Futures are often used to create synthetic cash at the asset class level. The sale of index futures against an asset class portfolio modifies the income stream in a manner that replicates the income of a cash-equivalent asset. In order to understand the concept of synthetic cash, consider the purchase of an equity portfolio that is equivalent to the S&P 500 and the sale of an equivalent dollar amount of S&P 500 futures contracts for delivery in three months. This combination of transactions provides the income stream of the S&P 500 for the 3 months prior to contract expiration. All price risk is eliminated by the futures contract. As such, the combination provides an income stream that is similar to a cash equivalent. To fixed-income investors this set of transactions applied to bonds and the bond futures contract creates a synthetic 3-month spot interest rate.

If the asset portfolio is actively managed and, therefore, not compositionally equivalent to the futures index, then the sale of futures creates synthetic cash by eliminating the systematic (market) risk of the portfolio, retaining the portfolio alpha and the nonsystematic risk. By preserving desired portfolio characteristics (the alpha) and eliminating market risk, selling futures

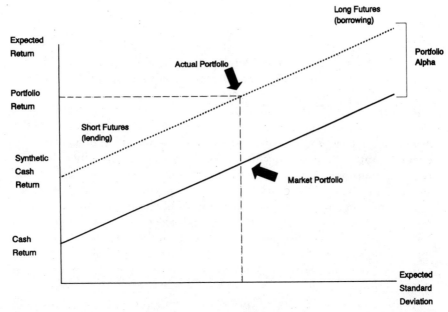

Figure 5-4. Capital market line with synthetic cash. *(Source: Brinson Partners, Inc.)*

against a portfolio can thus produce a risk configuration not achievable by allocating away from the equity portfolio and into cash.

A positive cash position created by selling futures against an asset class portfolio is the equivalent of lending. Synthetic cash does not necessarily need to be positive in quantity, however. If equity futures are *bought* instead of being *sold* against the equity portfolio, the equity position is effectively leveraged (cash is borrowed) and the synthetic cash position becomes negative. Figure 5-4 plots the expected return and risk of the market portfolio, the investment portfolio (the beta of the portfolio is assumed to equal 1), and the effect of selling or buying futures in conjunction with the portfolio.

Similar results are achieved in fixed-income portfolios by the purchase or sale of government bond and note futures contracts. A fixed-income portfolio hedge would be based on the interest rate sensitivity of the fixed-income portfolio and the futures contract and on the yield beta of the portfolio with respect to the futures contract.[10]

---

[10]The interest rate sensitivity of a portfolio is given by its modified duration. The yield beta is the beta of the portfolio yield with respect to the yield of the futures contract.

Options

Options are also effective vehicles for managing the risk of asset classes or asset exposures, providing considerably more flexibility than that afforded by futures contracts. An option provides its owner with the *right*, but not the obligation, to participate in the price appreciation or depreciation of the underlying asset. That is, options constitute nonsymmetric, contingent claims on the cash flows of an asset. A put option, for example, provides the owner with the right to benefit from the price depreciation of an asset. For example, rather than selling futures contracts to create synthetic cash, a portfolio manager may wish to allocate portfolio assets to cash only in the event of a decline of the market value of the portfolio. This can be implemented by purchasing puts on the asset portfolio. Such a strategy is sometimes called *portfolio insurance* because it provides a nonzero lower bound on the market value of the portfolio, which does not exist for equity portfolios in isolation. The lower bound is determined by the strike price of the put option, and the safety of the "insurance" provided is dependent upon the liquidity of the put.

Figure 5-5 depicts the payoff pattern of a put option and the return distribution created by purchasing a put in conjunction with an underlying asset position. Combining the put option with the asset position creates a synthetic security with a truncated return distribution; insurance against a loss has been purchased at the cost of a lower return for each asset price above the strike price of the put option.

Options can be sold as well as purchased. Selling an option is often referred to as *writing* an option. One versatile application of options is the creation of synthetic securities through the simultaneous purchase and sale of put and call options. In the absence of transaction costs, options can theoretically be used to create any return distribution with respect to the underlying asset price.

Global Asset Derivatives

In a global investment environment, the number of derivative securities that can be used to allocate actively between national markets and to alter the return distribution of individual assets is increasing rapidly. Although the list changes rapidly, Table 5-3 identifies as of late 1991 some of the derivative securities that can be employed by global investors to implement both active asset allocation and security selection decisions.

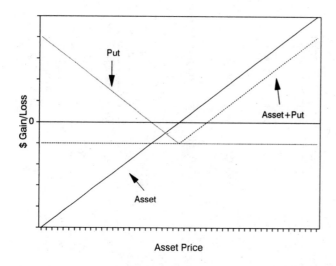

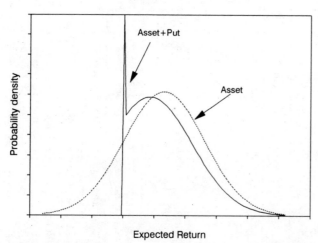

Figure 5-5. Asset and put option. (Top) Payoff pattern. (Bottom) Return distribution. *(Source: Brinson Partners, Inc.)*

Table 5-3. International Derivative Securities: Fixed-Income, Equity, and Exchange Rate

Currency of denomination	Contract (* = options)	Trading venue	Trading hours (local time)	Contract size	Contract months
(a) International Fixed-Income Futures and Options Contracts					
Australian dollar	90-day bank accepted bills*	Sydney Futures Exchange	8:30 a.m.–12:30 p.m. 2:00 p.m.–4:30 p.m. 4:40 p.m.–2:00 a.m.	A$500,000	Mar., Jun., Sep., Dec.
	3-year Treasury bond*	Sydney Futures Exchange	8:30 a.m.–12:30 p.m. 2:00 p.m.–4:30 p.m. 4:40 p.m.–2:00 a.m.	A$100,000	Mar., Jun., Sep., Dec.
	10-year Treasury bond*	Sydney Futures Exchange	8:30 a.m.–12:30 p.m. 2:00 p.m.–4:30 p.m. 4:40 p.m.–2:00 a.m.	A$100,000	Mar., Jun., Sep., Dec.
Canadian dollar	Bankers' acceptances	Montreal Exchange	8:20 a.m.–3:00 p.m.	C$1,000,000	Mar., Jun., Sep., Dec.
	10-year Treasury bond	Montreal Exchange	8:20 a.m.–3:00 p.m.	C$100,000	Mar., Jun., Sep., Dec.
European currency unit	3-month ECU interest rate	London Int'l. Financial Futures Exch.	8:05 a.m.–4:05 p.m.	ECU1,000,000	Mar., Jun., Sep., Dec.
	6 to 10-year ECU bond	Paris Financial Futures Exch.	9:00 a.m.–4:00 p.m.	ECU100,000	Mar., Jun., Sep., Dec.
French franc	3-month PIBOR*	Paris Financial Futures Exch.	8:30 a.m.–4:00 p.m.	FF5,000,000	Mar., Jun., Sep., Dec.
	7 to 10-year government bond*	Paris Financial Futures Exch.	9:00 a.m.–4:30 p.m.	FF500,000	Mar., Jun., Sep., Dec.

Currency	Instrument	Exchange	Hours	Contract Size	Months
German mark	3-month Euromark interest rate*	London Int'l. Financial Futures Exch.	8:00 a.m.–4:10 p.m.	DM1,000,000	Mar., Jun., Sep., Dec.
	Euromark deposit	Singapore Int'l. Monetary Exch.	8:15 a.m.–6:00 p.m.	DM1,000,000	Mar., Jun., Sep., Dec.
	German gov't bond*	London Int'l. Financial Futures Exch.	7:30 a.m.–4:00 p.m.	DM250,000	Mar., Jun., Sep., Dec.
	8.5 to 10-year gov't bond	Deutsche Terminboerse	8:00 a.m.–5:00 p.m.	DM250,000	Mar., Jun., Sep., Dec.
	3.5 to 5-year gov't bond	Deutsche Terminboerse	8:00 a.m.–5:00 p.m.	DM250,000	Mar., Jun., Sep., Dec.
Hong Kong dollar	3-month HIBOR	Hong Kong Futures Exchange	9:00 a.m.–3:30 p.m.	HK$1,000,000	Mar., Jun., Sep., Dec.
Japanese yen	3-month Euroyen deposit*	Tokyo Int'l. Financial Futures Exch.	9:00 a.m.–12:00 p.m. 1:30 p.m.–3:30 p.m.	¥100,000,000	Mar., Jun., Sep., Dec.
	3-month Euroyen deposit*	Singapore Int'l. Monetary Exch.	8:00 a.m.–6:10 p.m.	¥100,000,000	Mar., Jun., Sep., Dec.
	10-year gov't bond*	Tokyo Stock Exchange	9:00 a.m.–11:00 a.m. 12:30 p.m.–3:00 p.m.	¥100,000,000	Mar., Jun., Sep., Dec.
	Japanese gov't bond*	London Int'l. Financial Futures Exch.	7:00 a.m.–3:00 p.m.	¥100,000,000	Mar., Jun., Sep., Dec.
	20-year gov't bond	Tokyo Stock Exchange	9:00 a.m.–11:00 a.m. 12:30 p.m.–3:00 p.m.	¥100,000,000	Mar., Jun., Sep., Dec.
Netherlands guilder	Guilder bonds	Financiele Termijnmarkt Amsterdam	9:00 a.m.–5:00 p.m.	DG250,000	Mar., Jun., Sep., Dec.

(Continued)

Table 5-3. International Derivative Securities: Fixed-Income, Equity, and Exchange Rate (Continued)

Currency of denomination	Contract (* = options)	Trading venue	Trading hours (local time)	Contract size	Contract months
		(a) International Fixed-Income Futures and Options Contracts			
U.K. pound sterling	3-month sterling deposit	London Int'l. Financial Futures Exch.	8:20 a.m.–4:02 p.m.	£500,000	Mar., Jun., Sep., Dec.
	Long gilt*	London Int'l. Financial Futures Exch.	8:30 a.m.–4:15 p.m.	£50,000	Mar., Jun., Sep., Dec.
U.S. dollar	30-day interest rate	Chicago Board of Trade	7:20 a.m.–2:00 p.m.	$5,000,000	All months
	1-month LIBOR	Chicago Mercantile Exchange	7:20 a.m.–2:00 p.m.	$3,000,000	All months
	90-day Treasury bill*	Chicago Mercantile Exchange	7:20 a.m.–2:00 p.m.	$1,000,000	Mar., Jun., Sep., Dec.
	3-month Eurodollar deposit*	Chicago Mercantile Exchange	7:20 a.m.–2:00 p.m.	$1,000,000	Mar., Jun., Sep., Dec.
	Eurodollar deposit*	Singapore Int'l. Monetary Exch.	7:45 a.m.–6:20 p.m.	$1,000,000	Mar., Jun., Sep., Dec.
	3-month Eurodollar deposit*	London Int'l. Financial Futures Exch.	8:30 a.m.–4:00 p.m.	$1,000,000	Mar., Jun., Sep., Dec.
	3-month Eurodollar deposit	Tokyo Int'l. Financial Futures Exch.	9:00 a.m.–12:00 p.m. 1:30 p.m.–3:30 p.m.	$1,000,000	Mar., Jun., Sep., Dec.

2-year Treasury note	Chicago Board of Trade	7:20 a.m.–2:00 p.m. 5:00 p.m.–8:30 p.m.	$200,000	Mar., Jun., Sep., Dec.
5-year Treasury note	Chicago Board of Trade	7:20 a.m.–2:00 p.m. 5:00 p.m.–8:30 p.m.	$100,000	Mar., Jun., Sep., Dec.
6.5 to 10-year Treasury note*	Chicago Board of Trade	7:20 a.m.–2:00 p.m. 5:00 p.m.–8:30 p.m.	$100,000	Mar., Jun., Sep., Dec.
U.S. Treasury bond*	Chicago Board of Trade	7:20 a.m.–2:00 p.m. 5:00 p.m.–8:30 p.m.	$100,000	Mar., Jun., Sep., Dec.
Treasury bond	Tokyo Stock Exchange	9:00 a.m.–11:00 a.m. 12:30 p.m.–3:00 p.m.	$100,000	Mar., Jun., Sep., Dec.
U.S. Treasury bond*	London Int'l. Financial Futures Exch.	8:15 a.m.–4:10 p.m.	$100,000	Mar., Jun., Sep., Dec.
Municipal bond index	Chicago Board of Trade	7:20 a.m.–2:00 p.m.	$1,000 x-index	Mar., Jun., Sep., Dec.

(Continued)

97

Table 5-3. International Derivative Securities: Fixed-Income, Equity, and Exchange Rate (Continued)

Currency of denomination	Contract (* = options)	Trading venue	Trading hours (local time)	Contract size	Contract months
		(b) International Equity Futures and Options Contracts			
Australian dollar	All Ordinaries Share Price Index*	Sydney Futures Exchange	9:30 a.m.–12:30 p.m. 2:00 p.m.–4:10 p.m. 4:40 p.m.–2:00 a.m.	A$100 x index	Mar., Jun., Sep., Dec.
Canadian dollar	Toronto 35 Index	Toronto Futures Exchange	9:30 a.m.–4:15 p.m.	C$500 x index	All months
French franc	CAC 40 Stock Index	Paris Financial Futures Exch.	10:00 a.m.–5:00 p.m.	FF200 x index	All months
German mark	DAX Stock Index	Deutsche Terminboerse	9:30 a.m.–4:00 p.m.	DM100 x index	Mar., Jun., Sep., Dec.
Hong Kong dollar	Hang Seng Index	Hong Kong Futures Exchange	10:00 a.m.–12:30 p.m. 2:30 p.m.–3:30 p.m.	HK$50 x index	All months
Japanese yen	Tokyo Stock Price Index (TOPIX)	Tokyo Stock Exchange	9:00 a.m.–11:00 a.m. 12:30 p.m.–3:10 p.m.	¥10,000 x index	Mar., Jun., Sep., Dec.
	Nikkei Stock Average	Osaka Securities Exchange	9:00 a.m.–11:15 a.m. 12:30 p.m.–3:10 p.m.	¥1,000 x index	Mar., Jun., Sep., Dec.
	Nikkei 225 Stock Index*	Chicago Mercantile Exchange	8:00 a.m.–3:15 p.m.	$5 x index	Mar., Jun., Sep., Dec.
	Nikkei Stock Index	Singapore Int'l. Monetary Exch.	8:00 a.m.–2:15 p.m.	¥500 x index	Mar., Jun., Sep., Dec.
	Osaka Stock Futures 50	Osaka Securities Exchange	9:00 a.m.–11:00 a.m. 12:30 p.m.–3:10 p.m.	Sum of shares representing one trading unit.	Mar., Jun., Sep., Dec.

Netherlands guilder	EOE Dutch Stock Index	Financiele Termijnmarkt Amsterdam	9:15 a.m.–4:30 p.m.	DG200 x index	Jan., Apr., Jul., Oct.
	Dutch Top 5 Stock Index	Financiele Termijnmarkt Amsterdam	9:45 a.m.–4:30 p.m.	DG200 x index	Jan., Apr., Jul., Oct.
U.K. pound sterling	Financial Times Stock Exchange	London Int'l. Financial Futures Exch.	8:35 a.m.–4:10 p.m.	£25 x index	Mar., Jun., Sep., Dec.
U.S. dollar	Standard & Poor's 500*	Chicago Mercantile Exchange	8:00 a.m.–3:15 p.m.	$500 x index	Mar., Jun., Sep., Dec.
	Major Market Index	Chicago Board of Trade	8:15 a.m.–3:15 p.m.	$500 x index	All months
	NYSE Composite Stock Index*	New York Futures Exchange	9:30 a.m.–4:15 p.m.	$500 x index	Mar., Jun., Sep., Dec.
	Value Line Stock Index	Kansas City Board of Trade	8:30 a.m.–3:15 p.m.	$500 x index	Mar., Jun., Sep., Dec.

(Continued)

Table 5-3. International Derivative Securities: Fixed-Income, Equitys and Exchange Rate (Continued)

Currency of denomination	Contract (* = options)	Trading venue	Trading hours (local time)	Contract size	Contract months
(c) International Exchange Rate Futures and Options Contracts					
Australian dollar	U.S. dollar/ Australian dollar*	Chicago Mercantile Exchange	7:20 a.m.–2:00 p.m.	A$100,000	Spot, Mar., Apr., Jun., Jul., Sep., Oct., Dec.
	U.S. dollar/ Australian dollar*	Sydney Futures Exchange	8:30 a.m.–4:30 p.m. 4:40 p.m.–2:00 a.m.	A$100,000	Mar., Jun., Sep., Dec.
Canadian dollar	U.S. dollar/ Canadian dollar*	Chicago Mercantile Exchange	7:20 a.m.–2:00 p.m.	C$100,000	Spot, Jan., Mar., Apr., Jul., Sept., Oct., Dec.
German mark	U.S. dollar/ deutschemark*	Chicago Mercantile Exchange	7:20 a.m.–2:00 p.m.	DM125,000	Spot, Jan., Mar., Apr., Jul., Sep., Oct., Dec.
	U.S. dollar/ deutschemark*	Singapore Int'l. Monetary Exch.	8:20 a.m.–5:10 p.m.	DM125,000	Mar., Jun., Sep., Dec.
Japanese yen	U.S. dollar/ Japanese yen*	Chicago Mercantile Exchange	7:20 a.m.–2:00 p.m.	¥12,500,000	Spot, Jan., Mar., Apr., Jul., Sep., Oct., Dec.
	U.S. dollar/ Japanese yen*	Singapore Int'l. Monetary Exch.	8:15 a.m.–5:05 p.m.	¥12,500,000	Mar., Jun., Sep., Dec.
	U.S. dollar/ Japanese yen	Tokyo Int'l Financial Futures Exch.	9:00 a.m.–12:00 p.m. 1:30 p.m.–3:30 p.m.	$50,000	Mar., Jun., Sep., Dec.

Swiss franc	U.S. dollar/Swiss franc*	Chicago Mercantile Exchange	7:20 a.m.–2:00 p.m.	SF125,000	Spot, Jan., Mar., Apr., Jul., Sep., Oct., Dec.
British pound	U.S. dollar/British pound*	Chicago Mercantile Exchange	7:20 a.m.–2:00 p.m.	£62,500	Spot, Jan., Mar., Apr., Jul., Sep., Oct., Dec.
	U.S. dollar/British pound	Singapore Int'l. Monetary Exch.	8:25 a.m.–5:15 p.m.	£62,500	Mar., Jun., Sep., Dec.
U.S. dollar	U.S. dollar index*	New York Cotton Exchange	8:20 a.m.–3:00 p.m.	$500 x index	Mar., Jun., Sep., Dec.

SOURCE: *Futures: 1992 Reference Guide to Futures/Options Markets.*

Conclusion

This discussion of portfolio management has touched on a broad range of issues. The active management issues addressed can be approached from many perspectives. The global perspective that is the theme of this book imposes greater demands on the active manager than ever before, but it can provide substantial benefits to investors willing to do the required analysis. The remaining segmentation in global markets creates opportunities for the investor with superior analytical ability.

The proliferation of derivative securities has expanded dramatically the means by which a portfolio manager can implement active management decisions. Thus, portfolio management now extends beyond the analysis of assets to include the evaluation of complex implementation decisions made possible by derivative securities. Like security selection, these implementation decisions can be an important contributor to portfolio performance.

PART 3
The Equity Market

6
Stock Markets
Around the World

The world is full of stock markets. The European Community alone has 40 organized exchanges. Looking farther afield, it is hard to imagine a more unlikely locale for an equity marketplace than the almost unpopulated African desert country of Botswana. Botswana has only two major towns, Gaborone (near the South African border) and Francistown (near Zimbabwe). Nevertheless, Botswana has a stock market. It is not an exchange but a corporation (Stockbroker's Botswana Ltd.) that makes a market in six stocks. The market capitalization is $205 million, of which foreign investors own 10 percent, and the percentage is rising.

Botswana's market is interesting not so much for its investment opportunities (though they may be attractive) but for what it indicates about the natural human drive to exchange. Wherever one looks for institutions that facilitate exchange, one usually finds them. This chapter discusses the world's institutions of exchange as they relate to corporate equities. We characterize the world's equity markets in terms of their size, as measured by market capitalization (market price times number of shares outstanding), and review the historical and current institutional facts pertaining to the developed world's leading equity marketplaces. Finally, we address emerging equity markets and summarize their diverse characteristics.

The Equity Market
Capitalization of the World

The world equity market has grown phenomenally in the past generation and as of year-end 1990 its market capitalization was approximately $8.3 trillion. The greatest contribution to this growth came in Japan, where equity capitalization grew from $15 billion in 1960 to $2755 billion in 1990. The

U.S. equity market grew from $347 billion to $2754 billion over the same period. European and other markets have also grown greatly in size and importance. Figure 6-1 shows the growth of world equity market capitalization from 1960 to 1990.

The 1980s were unusually favorable to world equities, the 1987 crash notwithstanding. During this decade market capitalization roughly quintupled. The chief source of this increase was capital appreciation, since new issues were not particularly prevalent. In fact, the supply of U.S. equities actually shrank in several of the years as retirement of issues (by repurchase and takeovers) exceeded new issuances.

At the beginning of 1991, U.S. and Japanese equity market capitalizations were approaching $3 trillion, and the various European markets totaled $2 trillion. Britain has the lion's share of European equity although Germany, France, and perhaps Italy have larger economies as measured by GNP.

Figure 6-2 shows current equity market capitalizations for the world's more developed markets. These measures of capitalization attempt to cap-

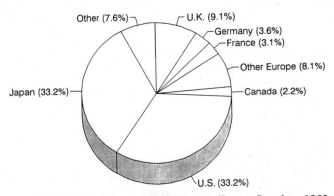

Figure 6-1. World equity market capitalization. *(Source: Data from 1960 was collected by the authors. Data from 1990 is from the Salomon-Russell Global Equity Indices.)*

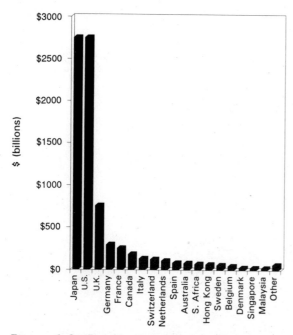

Figure 6-2. Developed equity market capitalization
(December 1990). *(Source: Data from the Salomon-Russell
Global Equity Indices.)*

ture the total equity capitalizations of the countries, not just that which is
available to global investors. The size of the Japanese market is overstated
because of the large amount of crossholdings (one company holding the
stock of another). Even after correcting for crossholding, the market is still
remarkably large relative to Japan's population and GNP. The German market's value is understated because much corporate equity does not trade and
is in private hands; consequently, it is unreported in Figure 6-2. Figure 6-3
shows an alternative measure of capitalization, which removes crossholdings,
restricted and government-held shares, and other shares not available to institutional investors outside the home country. The relative sizes of the countries
are dramatically changed, since some countries have a large restricted equity
sector. The United States and the United Kingdom are by far the most accessible markets, relative to their total capitalizations.

Equity Markets in the Developed Countries

Stock exchanges are a prominent feature of the financial landscape of
developed countries. However, the institutions of these exchanges are by no

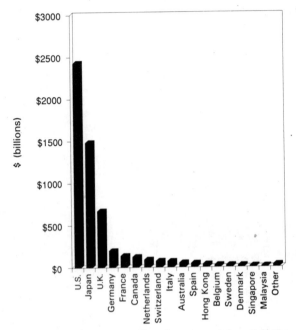

Figure 6-3. Available developed equity market capitalization (December 1990). *(Source: Data from the Salomon-Russell Global Equity Indices.)*

means homogenous. Informed global portfolio selection depends as much on knowledge of these country-specific or exchange-specific traits as it does on the study of the companies' fundamental merits. Such market characteristics include:

- Monetary policy and currency behavior
- Political institutions
- Prospects for economic growth
- Security market organization and legal structure
- Industrial organization of the national economy and characteristics of key companies
- Price limits, transaction and withholding taxes, brokerage commissions, settlement structure and other factors affecting returns

In the following pages we examine equity market institutions for the world's developed countries. We focus on aspects of the country markets that tend to be stable over time. Table 6-1 summarizes key information about the stock markets in 24 developed countries. Except where noted, trading volume and number of issues are for the principal stock exchange

Table 6-1. Developed Markets Around the World

Country	Principal exchange	Other exchanges	Total market capitalization ($billions)	Available market capitalization ($billions)	Trading volume ($billions)	Domestic issues listed	Total issues listed	Auction mechanism	Official specialists	Options/ futures trading	Price limits	Principal market indexes
Australia	Sydney	5	82.3	53.5	39.3	n/a	1496	Continuous	No	Yes	None	All Ordinaries—324 issues
Austria	Vienna	–	18.7	8.3	37.2	125	176	Single	Yes	No	5%	GZ Aktienindex—25 issues
Belgium	Brussels	3	48.5	26.2	6.8	186	337	Mixed	No	Few	10%	Brussels Stock Exchange Index—186 issues
Canada	Toronto	4	186.8	124.5	71.3	n/a	1208	Continuous	Yes	Yes	None	TSE 300 Composite Index
Denmark	Copenhagen	–	29.7	22.2	11.1	n/a	284	Mixed	No	No	None	Copenhagen Stock Exchange Index—38 issues
Finland	Helsinki	–	9.9	1.7	5.2	n/a	125	Mixed	n/a	n/a	n/a	KOP (Kansallis–Osake–Pannki) Price Index
France	Paris	6	256.5	137.2	129.0	463	663	Mixed	Yes	Yes	4%	CAC General Index—240 issues
Germany	Frankfurt	7	297.7	197.9	1003.7	n/a	355	Continuous	Yes	Options	None	DAX; FAZ (Frankfurter Allgemeine Zeitung)
Hong Kong	Hong Kong	–	67.7	37.1	34.6	n/a	479	Continuous	No	Futures	None	Hang Seng Index—33 issues
Ireland	Dublin	–	8.4	6.4	5.5	n/a	n/a	Continuous	No	No	None	J&E Davy Total Market Index

(Continued)

Table 6-1. Developed Markets Around the World (Continued)

Country	Principal exchange	Other exchanges	Total market capitalization ($billions)	Available market capitalization ($billions)	Trading volume ($billions)	Domestic issues listed	Total issues listed	Auction mechanism	Official specialists	Options/futures trading	Price limits	Principal market indexes
Italy	Milan	9	137.0	73.2	42.6	n/a	317	Mixed	No	No	10–20%	Banca Commerziale—209 issues
Japan	Tokyo	7	2754.6	1483.5	1602.4	n/a	1576	Continuous	Yes	No	10% down	TOPIX—1097 issues; TSE II—423 issues; Nikkei 225
Luxembourg	Luxembourg	—	1.5	0.9	0.1	61	247	Continuous	n/a	n/a	n/a	Domestic Share Price Index—9 issues
Malaysia	Kuala Lumpur	—	37.0	14.2	10.6	240	282	Continuous	No	No	None	Kuala Lumpur Composite Index—83 issues
Netherlands	Amsterdam	—	112.1	92.4	80.4	279	569	Continuous	Yes	Options	Variable	ANP—CBS General Index—51 issues
New Zealand	Wellington	—	6.7	5.3	2.0	295	451	Continuous	No	Futures	None	Barclay's Industrial Price Index—40 issues
Norway	Oslo	9	18.4	7.9	14.1	n/a	128	Single	No	No	None	Oslo Bors Stock Index—50 issues
Singapore	Singapore	—	28.6	15.6	8.2	n/a	324	Continuous	No	No	None	Straits Times Index—30 issues; SES—32 issues
South Africa	Johannesburg	—	72.7	n/a	8.2	n/a	n/a	Continuous	No	Options	None	JSE Actuaries Index—141 issues

Spain	Madrid	3	86.6	46.8	41.0	n/a	368	Mixed	No	No	10%	Madrid Stock Exchange Index—72 issues
Sweden	Stockholm	—	59.0	24.6	15.8	n/a	151	Mixed	No	Yes	None	Jacobson & Ponsbach—30 issues
Switzerland	Zurich	6	128.5	75.4	376.6	161	380	Mixed	No	Yes	5%	Societe de Banque Suisse—90 issues
United Kingdom	London	5	756.2	671.1	280.7	1911	2577	Continuous	No	Yes	None	Financial Times (FT) Ordinaries—750 issues; FTSE 100; FT 30
United States	New York	6	2754.3	2429.2	1787.1	n/a	2234	Continuous	Yes	Yes	None	S&P 500; Dow Jones Industrial Average; Wilshire 5000; Russell 3000

NOTES: Market capitalizations (both total and available) are as of December 31, 1990, except for South African market capitalization, which is from 1988. Available differs from total market capitalization by subtracting out crossholdings, closely held and government-owned shares, and takes into account restrictions on foreign ownership. Number of issues listed are from 1988 except for Malaysia which is from 1990. Trading volume data is 1990 except for Switzerland, which is from 1988. Trading institutions data is from 1987.

SOURCE: Market capitalizations (both total and available) for all countries except the United States and South Africa are from the Salomon-Russell Global Equity Indices. U.S. market capitalization (both total and available) is from the Frank Russell Company. All trading volume information (except for Switzerland) and Malaysian total issues listed is from the *Emerging Stock Markets Factbook: 1991*, International Finance Corp., 1991. Trading institutions information is from Richard Roll, "The International Crash of 1987," *Financial Analysts Journal*, September/October 1988. South African market capitalization, number of issues listed for all countries (except Malaysia), and Swiss trading volume are reproduced courtesy of Euromoney Books extracted from *The G. T. Guide to World Equity Markets: 1989*, 1988. All other information was collected by the authors.

of each country. Seven of the most prominent markets are treated first. We then briefly review the smaller developed markets of Europe. Finally, we review the rest of the world's developed markets.

The United States

In the 1990s it is proper to regard the United States as just another country—as it may well always have been. The distinguishing feature of the United States is its size. The United States ranks fourth in both land area and population and is far and away the world's largest national economy. The European Community (EC) has more people and may be more diversified than the United States, but it is in no sense a single country; Japan's economy is half the size of the United States. For sheer bulk the United States simply has no peers.

The population, production, and wealth of the United States are remarkably evenly distributed across the vast land. The Northeast, Midwest, South, and West are roughly equal in population and each has about the population of a major European country.

The human and economic diversity of the United States is unequalled: it is a melting pot for European, African, Asian, and New World peoples. Likewise, it is economically diverse, with a foothold in literally every area of economic activity. Yet the United States, with its fairly well-educated work force and high capital investment per person, has specialized in the broad general field known as *high tech*. High technology refers not only to the familiar computer and aerospace fields, but to agriculture, education, finance, law, and medicine. If it is surprising to find agriculture in this list, consider that it has the greatest capital intensity and least labor intensity of any of these fields. Agriculture occupies much of the U.S. land area but an astonishingly tiny 2 percent of its population—resources with which the United States is the world's largest food *exporter*.

Stock market capitalization in the United States is heavily concentrated in the traditional marketplace, the New York Stock Exchange (NYSE). Execution is less heavily concentrated than listing. The National Association of Securities Dealers Automated Quotation (NASDAQ) market has the second largest capitalization among U.S. equity markets. The NASDAQ market comprises over-the-counter (OTC) stocks that meet the listing qualifications of the National Association of Securities Dealers (NASD). Rather than trading through specialists, the NASDAQ and other OTC stocks trade through one or more *market makers*. Market makers are brokers who have committed to buying and selling shares in particular companies at their stated prices and quantities. The OTC market (inclusive of the NASDAQ) commands an increasing share of trading in NYSE-listed companies, as well as all of the trading in the thousands of unlisted firms. Chicago's Midwest Stock

Exchange is the third largest U.S. equity marketplace, after the NYSE and NASDAQ markets, but its listings tend to overlap the NYSE and American Stock Exchange (ASE). The ASE, which was once dominant in non-NYSE stocks, specializes in smaller and less financially secure firms, both seasoned and emerging. Finally, a "third market" consists of over-the-counter trading in exchange-listed securities by nonexchange member firms, and a "fourth market" which refers to the increasing amount of institutional trading that is done directly between buyer and seller to avoid the fees associated with the use of exchanges, brokers, and dealers.[1]

Because of its size and diversity, the United States has been able to afford a relatively isolated economic position. Trade with outside partners, while highly visible, is a far smaller portion of economic activity than is the case for smaller developed countries. This isolation has led U.S. investors to hold home-country equities far out of proportion to their importance in the world, even to this day. Only 30 years ago, while European investors facing limited opportunities in their home countries were busy diversifying across borders, international investing was practically unknown in the United States. Today, while many investors do not hold a single share of a non-U.S. company, most recognize that non-U.S. markets offer various opportunities.[2] The change from 1960 to the 1990s in attitudes toward global investing will continue to be of great benefit to investors in the long run.

Japan

Only 45 years ago a devastated land, Japan has risen like a phoenix. Despite the recent sharp downturn in Japanese stock prices, the country remains the premier growth market of recent history. Japan is remarkable in many aspects, not just for its capital markets. A 1927 writer noted that Japan "bears a strong likeness to the British Isles, similarly separated from [a great and densely populated] continent," with similar land area and

---

[1]The "first market" consists of the exchanges and the "second market" is the tradition-al OTC market including the NASDAQ.

[2]Some U.S. investors try to diversify internationally by buying shares of U.S. companies with multinational exposure. This strategy has produced mixed reviews: see Bertrand Jacquillat and Bruno Solnik, "Multinationals are Poor Tools for International Diversification," and Dennis Logue, "Multinationals are Good Tools for International Diversification," both in Peter L. Bernstein, ed., *International Investing*, Institutional Investor Books, New York, 1983. Another way for U.S. investors to diversify internationally without trading directly in a foreign market is through the use of American Depositary Receipts (ADRs). These are usually issued by a foreign branch of an American bank, most frequently by Morgan Guaranty Trust. About 60 ADRs are listed on the NYSE. ADRs can be bought and sold like any other shares, and have the advantage of paying dividends in U.S. dollars, not the local currency. ADRs can also be converted into ordinary (non-U.S.) shares for a small fee.

population.[3] In six decades, the semideveloped Japan of 1927 came to be, by some measures, the richest country in the world, with an economy more than twice the size of its likewise extraordinary counterpart off Europe's mainland.

The Japanese economy has some of the attributes of a public-private partnership, with MITI (Ministry for Trade and Information) helping businesses overcome international competition.[4] But product quality, not collusion, has been the key to Japan's success in international business.

Recent history has been less favorable. The Japanese stock market fell 39.5 percent in 1990 (the largest annual decline in that market's modern history), was flat in 1991, and had fallen 27.5 percent through June 1992. In land-poor Japan, one indicator of real trouble in the Tokyo markets is the price of golf course memberships. These trade in a secondary market in accordance with golf course land values. In 1990, as the once boundless optimism of the Kabutocho (the Tokyo stock market district) crumbled, leveraged investors sold memberships to meet margin calls. Because of the link between golf memberships and real estate values, the falling membership prices may point to trouble in the real estate market as well.

Although Japan's population and GNP are half that of the United States, its equity capitalization is only marginally smaller. The Tokyo Stock Exchange (TSE), Japan's principal trading venue, lists about 1600 stocks, on par with London and New York. The exchange has two "sections" or categories of listings. The first section of the TSE (1200 stocks) contains large and important companies, and the second section (400 stocks) has more lenient listing requirements. Several hundred more stocks are traded on an over-the-counter market. Margin buying is widespread, which is perhaps due to the onetime perception that the market would continue upward forever. To prevent a wave of forced selling to meet margin requirements as the market declined in 1990, the Ministry of Finance reduced the margin requirement.

The "Big Four" of Japanese brokerage houses are Nomura, Daiwa, Nikko, and Yamaichi. These firms sometimes try to support or stabilize stock prices using the *eigyo tokkin*, a fund used to move stocks or the market in a desired direction.[5] However, competition during the 1980s caused the Big Four's

---

[3] *The World Almanac 1927*, New York, World, p. 635. Population and land area comparisons are between Japan (*excluding* its extraterritorial possessions in 1927) and the British Isles (Britain and Ireland combined).

[4] Despite its reputation for remarkable business vision, MITI is not infallible. In the 1970s, MITI objected to Toyota's decision to pursue U.S. automobile exports.

[5] In September 1990, Daiwa, along with three smaller firms, was fined by the Tokyo Stock Exchange and the Ministry of Finance for artificially inflating the price of Fujita Tourist Enterprises. This was the first regulatory action of its kind taken since 1980.

share of total trades to decline from 60 to 34 percent. Meanwhile, foreign brokerage firms, which handled only 4 percent of all trades in 1988, had captured 10 percent of the market by 1990.

Unlike the United States and the United Kingdom, which eliminated fixed-rate commissions in 1975 and 1986 respectively, Japan still has them. In September 1990 they were reduced to be more in line with international standards.

Many of Japan's leading companies are parts of *zaibatsu,* or corporation groups originally controlled by a family. As share ownership has become widespread, the influence of the leading families has declined, but the similarity of many corporate names reflects their heritage. For example, there is Sumitomo Bank, Sumitomo Trust, and Sumitomo Metal Industries. Other *zaibatsu* include Mitsubishi and Mitsui. Today, the bulk of Japan's most important companies are independent; Sony and Toyota are well-known examples.

The United Kingdom

The Thatcher era (1979–1990) saw the long-suffering British economy dramatically revived by massive tax cuts, improved labor productivity, and the entrepreneurial zeal associated with privatization of government-owned corporations. As of this writing, however, the dynamic phase of British business growth seems to have lost momentum. The near future depends in large part on the unpredictable effects of Britain's increasing willingness to coordinate economic policies with the other members of the EC.

The International Stock Exchange (ISE), provocatively named to attract both foreign issues and foreign investment, was formed in 1973 by consolidating all British regional exchanges and the Dublin exchange in Ireland with the London Stock Exchange. By number of issues (stocks and bonds) listed, the ISE is by far the largest financial marketplace in the world.[6] The prevalence of foreign issues (some 700 foreign firms are listed) and fixed-income issues (bonds outnumber equities) overstates its size, but counting British domestic equities alone, it is the largest stock market in Europe and trails only the U.S. and Japan in capitalization.

In October 1986 another major reorganization occurred. The "big bang" was an attempt to create a competitive brokerage market similar to that of the modern (post-1975) United States and enhance London's historical position as a financial center. Specific aspects of the reorganization included:

---

[6]India's Bombay Stock Exchange lists more stocks than any exchange in a developed country, but the stocks listed are small and few are liquid.

- Allowing foreign and domestic banks (both investment and commercial) to purchase exchange memberships
- Elimination of the colorful but antiquated trading floor and replacing it with a computer-oriented system
- Dissemination of price quotes to nonexchange members
- Abolition of fixed-rate commissions
- Replacing jobbers (roughly equivalent to specialists in the United States) with market makers

The planned internationalization of the London exchange has been quite successful. For example, 50 percent of the trades of some French blue-chip stocks are executed at the ISE. A smaller but significant proportion of U.S. business is executed in London, as is the preponderance of trading in Irish companies.

The British stock market is notable for the consistency of its composition over time. Of the 30 issues that were in the BZW Equity Index in 1919, 24 were still there (with a few name changes) in 1962. Because of Britain's tremendous global reach in trade and merchandising, many firms in the index are household names outside Britain. Principal industries include manufacturing, consumer goods, international trade, banking, and utilities—the anchors of a mature and diversified economy.

Germany

The German economic miracle after World War II paralleled that of Japan, with Germany having the advantage of better-developed prewar economic, technological, and educational institutions. Germany became the most prosperous large country in Europe, surpassing Britain by the 1960s.

In the 1970s Germany widened its lead with a conservative, hard-money policy that had been abandoned by practically every other country in the world, including Japan for a period. Germany was thus well-prepared for the revolutionary events of 1989, in that the cost of assimilating the eastern lands, while astronomical, could be paid. Market euphoria in response to the 1990 German reunification dissipated, however, as the true costs began to be felt.

The German stock market system (eight exchanges plus an institutionally complex OTC market) is oddly out of rhythm with the booming economy. A Deutsche Bank board member described the market as "primitive, old-fashioned, and customer-averse."[7] German investors are unusually averse to

---

[7] *The Economist*, December 16, 1989, survey page 20.

taking equity positions: as of 1986 only one of every 13 Germans owned shares or invested in a mutual fund. The amount deposited in savings accounts exceeded equity market capitalization. Equity capitalization amounts to 20 percent of GNP, compared to 51 percent in the United States, 85 percent in the United Kingdom, and 132 percent in Japan.

Germany's publicly traded stock market is small not because the economy is small but because its bond market, private equity market, and merchant banking (integrated commercial and investment banking) sector are so large. The German publicly traded stock market is the second largest in Europe. The current trend is toward greater public ownership and trading of corporate equities.

Principal industries include a powerful automotive sector, chemicals and other heavy industries, pharmaceuticals, and banking. The largest non-financial corporation is Daimler-Benz, manufacturer of the Mercedes-Benz and a claimant to the invention of the automobile.

France

The French equity market is Europe's third largest and, along with the Dutch market, one of the world's oldest. The Paris Bourse originated in the 1500s, but equity trading was not its *raison d'être* until the 1700s; the exchange mainly traded bonds. While France has seven exchanges, Paris is responsible for 95 percent of the trading volume.

The French economy is one of the most prosperous in the world. Yet the French stock market has been turbulent over almost the entire postwar period, and it was unrewarding to investors until quite recently. A comparative study of French investments, conducted in the 1970s, found that stocks, bonds, bills, and inflation had successively *higher* returns—the exact opposite of the relation that might be expected, and of what is observed in most countries.[8] A dramatic upsurge in stock prices in the 1980s erased earlier losses.

The stock market in France is unusually diverse in the variety of investment structures. Equity investments include common shares in limited companies and joint-stock companies; two classes of preferred stock; investment certificates representing equity in public-private partnerships; and participation bonds. Several classes of investment funds and unit trusts exist, and a great many specialized funds have become popular in the last decade.

[8] Bertrand Jacquillat and Richard Roll, "French Index-Linked Bonds for U.S. Investors?" in Peter L. Bernstein, ed., *International Investing*, Institutional Investor Books, New York, 1983. Of course, the result is period-specific. When the study is updated, the normal relationship (that riskier assets beat safer ones) reappears. The risk-reward relationship across countries is summarized in Laurence B. Siegel and Paul D. Kaplan, "Stocks, Bonds, Bills, and Inflation Around the World," in Frank J. Fabozzi, ed., *Managing Institutional Assets*, Harper & Row, New York, 1990.

Unlike most other countries that have over-the-counter trading in listed securities, French law requires that all listed securities be traded at the exchange, through a stockbroker who is an exchange member. Fixed-rate commissions were in place until July 1989, when they were eliminated so as to be competitive with other countries.

Chief industries include automobiles, travel and leisure, and consumer goods. Several of the world's largest banks are French.

Canada

Canada and the United States have the world's longest undefended border with 75 percent of the Canadian population living within 100 miles of the United States.[9] This entente has yielded a fruitful trading relationship for both countries. Seventy to 80 percent of Canada's trade is with the United States; Canada, not Japan, is the largest trading partner for the United States. Along with the United States, Canada leads the world on a per capita GNP basis, after adjusting for consumer price differences. The importance of trade between the two countries may even increase as provisions of the United States–Canada free trade agreement are gradually enacted over the next decade. While peaceful and prosperous, Canada has an unsettling lack of cohesiveness. British Columbia is a keystone of the North American arch of the Pacific Rim, a demographic and economic continuity that runs from Alaska to Mexico. Alberta is part of the resource-rich empty quarter that takes up much of the North American West. Canada's prairie provinces are much like those of the United States. Ontario mirrors the characteristics of the U.S. states that face it across the Great Lakes, while the maritime provinces resemble New England. Quebec, the largest province as measured by gross domestic product, sometimes sees itself more as a separate country than part of Canada.

The on-again, off-again secessionist movement in Quebec casts a pall on the investment climate. Quebec can survive on its own; while the rest of Canada will be poorer if Quebec leaves, it too will survive. The question is why the separation should be considered at all. At a time when the fractious nations of the EC find it profitable to band together and do away with costly economic borders, it is troublesome that the Canadians consider erecting internal borders and imposing costs that did not previously exist. Yet the fragmentation of the country, as described above, may result in such a dismemberment for cultural and social reasons, in defiance of economic logic.

[9]Judy Jones and William Wilson, *An Incomplete Education*, Ballantine Books, New York, 1987.

The Canadian equity market is dominated by the Toronto Stock Exchange, which lists a diverse group of industrial, financial, and natural resource stocks. The Vancouver exchange is a haven for penny mining and energy stocks. The fast-growing Montreal exchange has increased its share of trading from 10 to 17 percent over the past decade.

The market capitalization of listed equities on Canadian exchanges is huge ($606 billion on the Toronto exchange), primarily due to the listing of large U.S. and British companies. Canadian companies, which account for most of the trading on the exchanges, total about $200 billion. The historical Canadian concentration in extractive industries, agriculture, and energy has changed substantially in recent decades, and the structure of corporate Canada resembles that of the other highly developed countries.

Australia

Like Canada, Australia offers the happy combination of industrial prosperity and a wealth of natural resources. Australia is often compared to Canada in other ways: both countries are large, sparsely populated, and predominantly English-speaking. But differences between the two countries run quite deep. Australia is culturally and politically cohesive. Almost every Australian lives near the sea, and its people are rarely exposed to a harsh climate.

The Australian stock market developed historically at Melbourne, but Sydney, the largest city, now has the leading exchange. In all, Australia has six stock exchanges, one in the capital of each state. Each exchange is a wholly owned subsidiary of the Australian Stock Exchange Limited, which was formed in 1987 to unify the country's equity marketplaces. In 1984, the brokerage industry was deregulated and fixed commissions were abolished in favor of fully negotiable rates.

The Australian market has been somewhat more volatile than that of comparable countries such as the United States, Canada, and the United Kingdom. For example, stocks more than doubled in the extravagant boom of 1986 to 1987, then gave up almost all of those gains in the October 1987 crash.

The principal stocks are industrial, banking, and natural resource companies. Broken Hill Proprietary (BHP), Australia's largest company, is a conglomerate offering a cross section of the Australian economy.

Other Developed European Markets

Here we survey 11 countries in descending order of their 1991 equity capitalization. The relatively new Euroequity market is discussed last.

Italy has matched Great Britain in GNP, but its stock market is notably less well developed. Milan, the heart of the rich industrial north, is the site of the principal stock exchange. Stock prices rallied dramatically in the 1980s, bringing Italy's equity capitalization up to about $150 billion; as recently as 1979, the bottom of a 2-decade bear market, it had been $8 billion. Unlike most modern markets, Milan still uses the "open outcry" method. A few stocks are highly liquid, notably Fiat, which has been a perennial leader in European car sales. But most stocks are fairly closely held: it is said that two-thirds of the country's market capitalization is controlled by a few families.

Switzerland's reputation for banking safety and privacy has been a magnet to foreign capital. The equity market plays a secondary role to the credit market, but it is still Europe's fourth largest with an aggregate market value far out of proportion to the country's size. The three principal exchanges, Zurich, Geneva, and Basel, function essentially as one because orders are executed at whichever exchange has the best price. These exchanges list a large number of foreign issues. Of the few hundred Swiss equities, only several dozen are large enough for institutional trading. Swiss money managers, including the money management activities of the banks, are among the largest and most influential in the world, controlling over $1 trillion.

The Netherlands has a long history of international trade and capital market activity going back to the United East India Company[10] for which shares were listed in 1602. The Dutch focus on trading has remained intact as the country exports about 60 percent of its GNP, with Germany as the largest trading partner. The stock exchange is in Amsterdam and the market has a global flavor. Half of the listed issues are foreign, and foreigners own 40 percent of the market capitalization. Royal Dutch, the multinational petroleum company, has a commanding share of equity market capitalization. Of special note are the global investment trusts, such as Robeco, a model international equity portfolio formed in the 1930s. It is listed on 19 exchanges, more than any other firm in the world.

Spain's astonishing growth in the recent past has been closely associated with the emergence of democratic institutions. No longer poor by any measure, northeastern Spain (Catalonia) is part of developed Europe, while the rest of the country is moderately well developed. The principal stock exchange is at Madrid, and lists about 400 companies. Banks comprise about two-fifths of market capitalization. A securities commission, formed in 1988 to regulate the markets and oversee the electronic linking of the four Spanish exchanges, has encouraged foreign investment. Non-Spanish

---

[10] Outside the Netherlands, the United East India Company is usually called the Dutch East India Company.

investors have responded by generating about 40 percent of total trading volume.

Sweden is the industrial powerhouse of the Nordic group of countries. In the past, Sweden's neutrality in foreign affairs has precluded membership in the EC, but an October 1990 announcement suggested that the country may apply for EC membership in the near future. The only stock exchange is at Stockholm. Stock ownership, paradoxically, is both dispersed and concentrated. Sweden has the world's broadest individual participation in the market: 50 percent of adults hold some shares. But a few families control large blocks of stock. The Wallenberg family alone, directly or indirectly, controls more than 20 percent of the Stockholm exchange's value. Volvo, the automotive giant, is the largest company.

Belgium has an export-oriented economy linked closely to that of Germany. The principal stock exchange, the Brussels Bourse, lists mainly industrial companies and banks. An approximately value-weighted portfolio of Belgian equities can be held by purchasing the shares of one company, Société Générale de Belgique, which is said to own 30 percent of the value of all publicly traded Belgian stocks. An interesting twist in Belgian economic history occurred in 1988 when Carlo de Benedetti, an Italian businessman, tried and failed to obtain a controlling share in this remarkable company.

Denmark's economy is dominated by industrial and banking companies. The only stock exchange, at Copenhagen, lists about 300 companies, and is completely open to foreigners. Historically, the exchange took a back seat to the busy over-the-counter market, but recent reforms have encouraged more exchange activity. The construction of bridges linking Denmark to both Germany and Sweden is likely to increase Denmark's economic prominence in the near future. The bridge project has been described as even more dramatic in its expected impact than the tunnel across the English Channel.

Austria's tiny market, centered on the Vienna Stock Exchange, prospered greatly in the 1980s along with other central European markets. Banking, chemicals, and insurance are the principal industries. Austria's historical ties to Hungary may cause the Austrian economy to become more prominent if Hungary can manage successful entry into the central European economy.

Norway, a resource-rich country, first became financially prominent in the 1970s when rising energy prices pushed Norwegian stock prices up. The market moved further upward in the 1980s, and crashed in 1987, in tandem with the rest of the world. Norway then experienced one of its most spirited rallies after the crash, but the 1990 oil shock caused a decline. As of June 1992 the market was 36 percent below its July 1990 peak. The Oslo exchange is the only one of any importance, although there are 10 in all. Much of the market value of Norwegian stocks is represented by Norsk Hydro, the national electric company.

Finland is a relative newcomer to the world capital market, with equity financing overtaking traditional debt financing in the 1980s. The Helsinki Stock Exchange lists about 70 domestic issues, many of which are available to foreigners. While the market is dominated by industrial shares, the largest single company is the Union Bank of Finland.

Ireland's market has a grand past: in the nineteeth century the three Dublin exchanges made up a major national capital market, listing 60 railroad issues as well as shares in other industries. Today's Irish stock market is small, but the 1973 unification of the Dublin exchange (there is now only one) with the numerous British exchanges to form the International Stock Exchange of the United Kingdom and Republic of Ireland is boosting liquidity and market capitalization.

The *Euroequity market* refers to the stocks of companies issuing equity in countries other than their own. Companies using this approach are as diverse as Repsol, Spain's government oil company, and the Euro Disney Resort, a Parisian venture. The market has flourished because domestic markets cannot supply enough financing for these companies, while investors in other countries are looking for means to diversify beyond their borders. The 1990 adoption by the U.S. Securities and Exchange Commission (SEC) of Rule 144A, allowing institutions to trade unregistered securities, has also buoyed this market. Non-U.S. companies may now make whatever offerings they wish without having to undergo the burdensome SEC registration and disclosure process. The U.K.'s Warburg Securities is the principal handler of Euroequity issues.

Other Developed Markets

Hong Kong, along with Singapore, is the financial capital of southeast Asia. It gained its prominence after 1949, when the former leader, Shanghai, suffered a Communist takeover. Despite the impending repossession of the British colony by mainland China in 1997, Hong Kong remains a vibrant business center as well as a city-state that is world-renowned for its sophistication and excitement.

Despite its glittering prosperity, Hong Kong's future is clouded. The mainland Chinese have vowed to leave Hong Kong's capitalist system alone for at least 50 years beyond 1997, and there are reasons to believe that China cannot afford to do otherwise: Hong Kong is the conduit through which Japan and other countries have been moving low-tech, labor-intensive operations to China. Nonetheless, there is an exodus of corporate headquarters and a rapid brain drain. The massacre of June 4, 1989 in Beijing's Tiananmen Square only served to increase tensions.

Despite recent setbacks, it is only a matter of time before mainland China reemerges as a rapidly developing country. Investors desiring exposure to this opportunity should consider Hong Kong's market. The economy of Hong Kong is so closely interwoven with the mainland economy that investors in Hong Kong stocks would almost certainly benefit from positive changes in China.

Singapore emerged as the richest Asian country outside Japan following its separation from the Malay Federation in 1965. Singapore benefits from the uncertainty in Hong Kong: numerous corporations are moving their headquarters to Singapore. In fact, the Hongkong Land Company is the largest company listed on the Singapore Stock Exchange.

While Singapore stocks have fluctuated wildly in the past, like those of Hong Kong, Singapore's market has become more stable in recent years as the country has become more developed. An exception was the crash of 1987, when Singapore's market fell about as much as that of any other market in the world.

New Zealand's economy is dominated by agriculture and forest products. Since most farms are small businesses, forest product companies form the largest component of the stock market—about one-third of total market capitalization. The New Zealand Stock Exchange has trading floors in three locations, with Wellington dominant.

South Africa is a resource-rich country with by far the most developed capital market in Africa. Companies extracting gold, platinum, diamonds, and other natural resources form a highly visible component of the market. In fact, the Johannesburg Stock Exchange is informally divided into two sections, one for mining and the other for industrial, financial, and other firms. The sections have separate price indexes.

Prior to the U.S. legalization of gold ownership by individuals in 1975, South African gold shares were a favorite vehicle for American investors desiring gold exposure. Since that date U.S. investment in South African equities has declined drastically. The principal cause of falling levels of investment in South Africa, however, has been distaste for South Africa's apartheid policies. While many investors have simply gotten out of the South African market, others have sought "constructive engagement," concentrating their investments in companies believed to treat nonwhites fairly, and otherwise trying to influence outcomes in the region.

Emerging Markets

Some of the most interesting and high-returning markets are located in the emerging countries, those attempting the transition from third world to first world status. South Korea and Taiwan are the largest and most successful members of this group, with credible claims to first world membership. Each has a market capitalization about equal to that of Sweden. Unusual barriers exist in some of these markets. For example, it is difficult for non-Koreans to purchase Korean stocks. Investors often capture returns in these markets by holding shares of single-country mutual funds ("country funds"), or mutual funds that diversify across emerging markets.

Which markets qualify as "emerging" is subjective. We classify Taiwan and South Korea in this category, despite their large size, because of volatility and barriers to entry. Since almost every non-Communist country has some kind of market, the category of emerging markets includes some that barely function. Table 6-2 summarizes key points of information about 20 emerging markets. Figure 6-4 shows recent market capitalizations of 15 of these markets. The following section reviews the institutional settings of the most notable emerging markets.

Asian and Pacific Rim Countries

South Korea's remarkable growth over the past decades has hit some stumbling blocks recently: its labor cost advantage over Japan is shrinking, there is political instability in the wake of democratic reforms, and it even has a trade deficit.

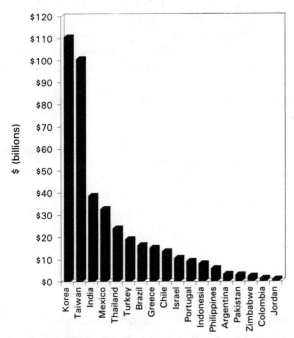

Figure 6-4. Emerging equity market capitalization (December 1990). (*Source:* Emerging Stock Markets Factbook: 1991, *International Finance Corporation.*)

Table 6-2. Emerging Markets Around the World

Country	Principal exchange	Other exchanges	Market capitalization ($billions)	Trading volume ($billions)	Total issues listed	Auction mechanism	Principal market indexes
Argentina	Buenos Aires	4	3.3	0.9	179	n/a	Buenos Aires Stock Exchange Index
Brazil	São Paulo	9	16.4	6.2	581	Continuous	BOVESPA Share Price Index—83 issues
Chile	Santiago	–	13.6	0.8	215	Mixed	IGPA Index—180 issues
Colombia	Medellin	1	1.4	0.1	80	n/a	Bogota General Composite Index
Greece	Athens	–	15.2	3.8	145	Continuous	Athens Stock Exchange Industrial Price Index
India	Bombay	14	38.6	27.3	2435	Continuous	Economic Times Index—72 issues
Indonesia	Jakarta	–	8.1	3.9	125	Mixed	Jakarta Stock Exchange Index
Israel	Tel Aviv	–	10.6	5.5	267	Single	General Share Index—all listed issues
Jordan	Amman	–	1.0	0.4	105	n/a	Amman Financial Market Index
Mexico	Mexico City	–	32.7	11.8	199	Continuous	Bolsa de Valores Index—49 issues
Nigeria	Lagos	–	1.4	n/a	131	Single	Nigerian Stock Exchange General Index
Pakistan	Karachi	–	3.0	0.2	487	Continuous	State Bank of Pakistan Index

(Continued)

Table 6-2. Developing Markets Around the World (Continued)

Country	Principal exchange	Other exchanges	Market capitalization ($billions)	Trading volume ($billions)	Total issues listed	Auction mechanism	Principal market indexes
Philippines	Makati	1	5.9	1.2	153	n/a	Manila Commerical & Industrial Index—25 issues
Portugal	Lisbon	1	9.2	1.6	181	Single	Banco Totta e Acores Share Index—50 issues
South Korea	Seoul	–	110.6	76.0	669	Continuous	Korea Composite Stock Price Index
Taiwan	Taipei	–	100.7	718.0	199	Continuous	Taiwan Stock Exchange Index
Thailand	Bangkok	–	23.9	22.2	214	Continuous	Securities Exchange of Thailand Price Index
Turkey	Istanbul	–	19.1	5.7	110	Continuous	Istanbul Stock Exchange Index—50 issues
Venezuela	Caracas	1	8.4	2.2	66	Continuous	Caracas Stock Exchange Price Index
Zimbabwe	n/a	–	2.4	0.1	57	n/a	Reserve Bank of Zimbabwe Industrial Index

NOTES: Market capitalizations, trading volume, and total issues listed are as of 1990. Market capitalization, trading volume, and total issues listed for Brazil are São Paulo only. Trading volume for the Philippines is for both Manila and Makati. Total issues listed for India is Bombay only. Trading institutions information is from 1987 and 1988.

SOURCE: Market capitalizations, trading volume, and total issues listed are from the *Emerging Stock Markets Factbook: 1991*, International Finance Corp., 1991. Trading institutions information is from Richard Roll, "The International Crash of 1987," *Financial Analysts Journal*, September/October 1988. Additional trading institutions information is reproduced courtesy of Euromoney Books extracted from *The G. T. Guide to World Equity Markets: 1989*, 1988. All other information was collected by the authors.

The Korea Stock Exchange is marked by low liquidity and limited foreign participation. Foreign ownership is restricted and crossholdings and government ownership mean that only 10 to 15 percent of listed shares are actively traded. In an effort to prop up prices, the Korean government in May 1990 established a stabilization fund to buy stocks during bear markets. Beginning January 1, 1992, non-Koreans were allowed to invest directly in Korean equities. However, non-Korean ownership is restricted to 10 percent of total market capitalization and trading is allowed in only about 30 percent of listed companies.

In one of the more curious episodes in recent memory, the Korean government announced in 1990 that security transactions would have to be executed under the real names of the transacting parties. This announcement prompted such a massive sell-off, in an already jittery market, that the government withdrew the proposal.

Taiwan's market is not for the faint of heart: the Weighted Price index on the Taiwan exchange rose from a low of 880 in the mid-1980s, peaked at 12,682 in February 1990, and crashed to 3600 by September. Unlike developed markets, only 10 percent of trading volume is institutional; individual Taiwanese are the major players.

There are many instances of manipulation in the Taiwan market. One technique, called *ramping*, involves company officials openly buying up large blocs of stock. After buying the stock they disseminate falsehoods designed to push the stock higher. During this period they sell out their holdings to uninformed investors. While such activity is observed in every market, the Taiwanese authorities openly admit to its existence and are cracking down. In a policy reform designed to attract foreign participation, non-Taiwanese institutional and individual investors were permitted to invest in equities directly, and local fund managers were allowed to invest foreigners' funds.

Malaysia has been closely linked with Singapore since they separated in 1965. For many years the Singapore stock exchange was the principal venue of trading for Malaysian stocks, and Malaysia's Kuala Lumpur Stock Exchange (KLSE) had little importance. In October 1989, the two exchanges were decoupled. To give the KLSE a boost, all Malaysian companies (as of January 1, 1990) were required to delist from Singapore and list on the KLSE. (Singapore retaliated by requiring Singapore companies to delist from the KLSE.) Trading volume has exceeded all expectations, but the exchange has not been able to keep up with volume and settlement remains troublesome. For investors unwilling to transact in Kuala Lumpur, a thriving over-the-counter market in Malaysian stocks has arisen in Singapore.

Thailand has gotten recognition in recent years as a particularly dynamic emerging economy. Thailand's recent GNP growth rate compares with those of Japan and the United States in their best years. The Securities

Exchange of Thailand, in Bangkok, is the principal trading venue. Siam Cement is by far the largest listed company, and 5 of the top 10 companies are banks.

After decades of political turmoil, *Indonesia* (Asia's second largest oil producer behind China) has started to develop along the lines of its Pacific Rim neighbors. While equities have been traded there since 1912, its first real boom started in 1988, after foreigners were allowed to participate.

Thanks to high oil prices and political instability, *the Philippines* equity market fell 39 percent in local currency terms in 1990. In 1991, the market was up 54 percent and through May 1992 was up another 25 percent. The nation has two stock exchanges (Manila and Makati), with the latter dominant. The two exchanges are expected to merge in the near future.

India has a complex and richly textured stock market, with 15 exchanges. The largest, at Bombay, lists more companies (mostly small) than any other in the world. While most Indians remain poor, stock market returns have been on par with those of other successful developing countries. Non-Indians are currently barred from participation, except indirectly by purchasing shares in the India or India Growth Funds. Neighboring *Pakistan* has a small equity market, which has provided good returns and moderate volatility to investors in recent years. In 1991, foreigners were allowed to purchase stocks directly.

The Americas

In the late 1970s, *Mexico* looked like a sure bet. As a major oil exporter, with soaring revenues from tourism, Mexico seemed to be headed for lasting prosperity. Mexicans looked to the United States as an economic role model and became fascinated with all things American. But the Mexican crash of 1981 to 1982, paralleling the worldwide decline of that period but much worse, changed growth expectations. Ever since, *la crise* (the crisis) has been a fixture of Mexican economic life. Despite the economic difficulties, the stock market boomed in the mid-1980s, and after crashing once more in late 1987, has risen dramatically. Now, once again, Mexico seems poised for rapid growth if the North American free trade agreement (NAFTA) is concluded.

The central exchange for Mexican securities is in Mexico City. Over 200 companies are listed. Foreigners can purchase individual securities, but a large proportion of foreign investment is in country funds.

Brazil's large size and success in developing some sectors of the economy tends to mask its economic failures. Consequently, Brazil's market has failed to provide a positive real return over the 1980s and was the worst performing equity market in 1990 (down 68 percent in U.S. dollar terms). Volatility is high, with occasional spectacular booms and devastating slumps. Like many other South Americans, some Brazilians refer to the 1980s as the "lost decade": their economy stagnated during a world boom.

Bovespa (Bolsa de Valores de São Paulo, the São Paulo stock exchange) is Brazil's largest, listing about 600 companies, most of modest size. The Rio de Janeiro exchange, with many of the same listings, has less activity. Astonishingly, Bovespa subsumes the second most active stock-index futures market in the world, exceeded only by Chicago's Mercantile Exchange. In an attempt to provide more liquidity, the Rio and São Paulo exchanges are considering a merger. In March 1991 foreigners were allowed to directly purchase the shares of individual companies.

Other South American countries have relatively undeveloped stock markets. For example, *Chile*'s telephone company (Companía de Teléfonos de Chile) bypassed the country's stock exchange (which has substantial capitalization but limited liquidity) and floated its issue in the U.S. American Depositary Receipt market. *Argentina*, sometimes referred to as a formerly developed country, has seen its once-proud stock exchange decline from 669 listings in 1962 to fewer than 200 recently. *Venezuela* was the world's best performing market in 1990 (up 571 percent in U.S. dollar terms). *Colombia* has two principal exchanges (Bogotá and Medellín). They have about equal capitalization and trading volume.

Europe and the Middle East

Several small European countries have markets that are best characterized as emerging. The most important of these are *Greece* and *Portugal*. Prior to the mid-1980s, the Athens and Lisbon stock exchanges had insignificant capitalization and little liquidity. Both exchanges have recently experienced a boom, with trading in Athens growing from $0.55 billion in 1989 to $3.8 billion in 1990. Capitalization of the Lisbon exchange grew almost thirtyfold between 1985 and 1990, but remains small. Returns in both markets have been respectable in recent years.

Bridging Europe and the Middle East, *Turkey* has over 500 stocks listed on the Istanbul Stock Exchange. This once-active market reopened in 1986 after being closed for decades. It has been one of the best-performing markets in recent years. *Israel* has the second largest Middle Eastern stock market, with nearly 300 listed companies. Market capitalization exceeds $5 billion. The Israeli market was traditionally dominated by commercial banking stocks, which accounted for about three-fifths of total capitalization until the October 1988 government acquisition of several of the largest banks.

This action pared the supply of equities and reduced the banks' share of capitalization to about 30 percent. Of the several stock exchanges scattered around the Arab world, *Jordan* is the only active one, albeit barely. Because of the Gulf war, daily volume was $500,000 in late 1990, down from $2.6 million in 1989. While the Middle East is a great repository of wealth, most of it is closely held and does not trade.

African Markets

As noted, South Africa has by far the largest capital market in Africa. Other capital markets are scattered around sub-Saharan Africa, notably in *Nigeria* and *Zimbabwe*. An oil-exporting country, Nigeria prospered in the 1970s and early 1980s, but lagged afterwards. Foreigners are currently banned from direct investment and there are no country funds. Returns in the Zimbabwe market were poor over the 1976 to 1984 period and excellent thereafter.

A New Kind of Emerging Market

The revolutionary events of 1989 have raised the possibility that capital markets will emerge in the formerly Communist countries of central and eastern Europe. In central Europe, eastern Germany has merged with its western counterpart and is essentially capitalist; Poland, Hungary, and the Czech lands are all experimenting with equity markets and have a very good chance of success. In these cases the countries have long since emerged as local powers and functioning economies; what is emerging—or reemerging—is the capital market sector.[11] This factor differentiates the liberated countries of central Europe from the other emerging markets, in which basic economic development and capital markets are emerging in tandem.

Farther east, the republics of the former Soviet Union have suffered 70 years of Communism rather than 40. The difference affects the expected outcome. It will be more difficult for these countries to develop democratic and economically free institutions and patterns of thought, but high education levels and the rapid pace of change in Russia proper gives encouragement over the long-run. Romania and Bulgaria, with their historically close ties to Russia, face some of the same difficulties.

As Communism crumbles around the world, more capital markets will emerge. Before China's Tiananmen Square massacre in 1989, that country, not those of central Europe, appeared to be the next market to sprout from

---

[11]Before Communism, all of these countries had some form of capital market. In fact, Budapest was home to the world's fourth largest stock exchange in 1900.

the Communist bloc. The old stock exchange at Shanghai was even reopened, although the bulk of equity trading in China takes place over the counter in Shenzhen (near Hong Kong), not on the Shanghai exchange floor. This new class of emerging markets may provide as much opportunity to investors as the markets traditionally regarded as emerging.

7
Historical Returns on World Equities

A U.S.-based investor would have seen his or her investment of a dollar in the Japanese stock market at the beginning of 1970 grow to $39.28 in 21 years.[1] A dollar investment in Australian stocks, made at the same time, would have grown only to $4.75. This illustrates that global investing can provide a very wide range of results. Although aggregating the results across countries may give the illusion of a single return from global investing, the differences between returns in countries' equity markets are very significant. This chapter highlights some of these differences.

Market Indexes

There is no shortage of indexes purporting to track various markets. In this section we discuss the general characteristics of a good index; focus on the details of a particular form of index (market-value-weighted total return index); and then evaluate some of the popular indexes in use around the world.

Characteristics of a Good Index

Like all measurement tools, the quality of an index depends in large part on how the index is intended to be used. The Dow Jones Industrial Average (Dow) is calculated in a very different fashion than the Wilshire 5000 total

---

[1]This result assumes no transaction costs or taxes are paid. The return quoted is a total return. A total return assumes that all periodic payments of a security are immediately reinvested in that same security. Returns are in U.S. dollars (that is, unhedged).

return index. The broad purpose of both indexes is to measure U.S. stock market performance; because each index serves different clienteles with different requirements, both are useful. Regardless of its eventual purpose, a quality index should:

- Reflect what an investor, or a hypothetical investor facing no transaction costs or taxes, could achieve in the market that the index purports to measure
- Be reflective of a broad class of securities, either by containing all the securities in the class or by careful selection of a subset
- Have a reasonably long back history
- Be updated in a timely fashion

The most common function of an index is to provide a benchmark for portfolio performance. An index that can be traded by an investor in live action is a fair benchmark. Some indexes form the basis for an index fund, or portfolio designed specifically to match (not beat) the underlying index. An index for which an index fund cannot be constructed is generally a poor index.[2]

Indexes may be broad or narrow, but narrow indexes such as the Dow are useful primarily because their returns are related to the broad market. The Dow is recalculated every 30 seconds. This recalculation has meaning because, in any given 30-second period, most of the 30 stocks in the Dow will have traded. A recalculation of the Wilshire 5000 every 30 seconds would have little meaning because few of the more than 5000 stocks in the index would have traded. Over the long run, however, the broad-based Wilshire 5000 index provides a better indication of changes in most investors' wealth than does the narrowly defined Dow.

A reasonably long history is a useful property of an index because investors use indexes to compare prices, returns, and other variables at different points in time. Without a history that spans diverse economic scenarios, this comparability function is compromised. For exactly this reason, when launching an index modern index constructors often reconstruct a historical record to make the index more useful; and scholars have back-dated other indexes far beyond their original launch dates. Finally, because investors are primarily concerned with history as it influences current and future outcomes, the index should be updated so that the insights it provides can be put to use as soon as possible.

---

[2]Geometric indexes are a case in point. A geometric index is constructed by multiplying the percentage changes of the components together and cannot be replicated by any actual strategy.

Market-Value-Weighted
Total Return Indexes

Market-value-weighted total return indexes are a relatively recent vintage because of the intense computational requirements needed to calculate and update the index. Researchers and practitioners are drawn to this type of index because it purports to track the market more precisely than any other kind of index and takes into account all sources of return.

There are five important characteristics to a well-constructed market-value-weighted index:

1. It is broad, reflecting all securities in a particular market.

2. Each security's return is weighted according to its market value at the beginning of the period over which the return is measured.[3]

3. Total returns, consisting of capital appreciation and dividend income, are measured.

4. Dividend income is recorded in the period received and is reinvested quickly in the market.

5. Stocks which are delisted, go bankrupt, or become worthless have their last return included in the index. This procedure eliminates the selection bias favoring companies that succeed. For example, in constructing an index of NYSE stocks, one should use the following rule: if a stock is delisted from the NYSE, the first stock quote off the NYSE (even if it is zero) should be used as if it were the last NYSE quote.

Market-value-weighted indexes (market indexes for short), in which each stock or country is weighted according to the market value of its outstanding shares, are used throughout this book, except where data constraints make them unavailable. Market value weighting captures what would happen to a sum of money invested at a particular time, presuming that the initial investment was divided between all of the market's securities in proportion to each security's total value.

As an example, let's construct an index for a market with two firms. Cheap Inc. has 10 shares outstanding and a $50 share price. Dear Ltd. has 10 shares outstanding and a $100 share price. The market capitalization is thus $500 for Cheap and $1000 for Dear; total market capitalization is $1500. Assume that after one year, Cheap's stock rises to $75 while Dear remains at $100. The total market value is now $1750. The capital appreciation for the market over this period is $250, representing a 16.7 percent

---

[3]The *market value* is defined as the price per share multiplied by the number of shares outstanding.

gain on the initial investment of $1500. A 16.7 percent annual capital gain return means that a market index initialized at 1.000 would grow in one year to 1.167. A proper index also takes into account dividend payments. Assume that Cheap did not pay a dividend, but that Dear paid an end-of-year dividend of $10 per share, or $100 total. In a market index, dividends are invested in all market segments in proportion to the segments' market value. After one year, market capitalizations are $750 for Cheap and $1000 for Dear; consequently, 43 percent of the dividend ($43) is invested in Cheap and 57 percent ($57) in Dear. The market values are now $793 for Cheap and $1057 for Dear, or $1850 for the market, a 23.3 percent increase (total return) over the $1500 initial investment. The market index, initialized at 1.000, is now 1.233. The 23.3 percent increase is composed of a 16.7 percent capital gain and a 6.6 percent dividend (income) return.

In the 1960s, James Lorie and Lawrence Fisher of the University of Chicago compiled data on security returns for the University's Center for Research on Security Prices (CRSP). The CRSP index was the first well-constructed index of the U.S. stock market's performance and satisfies all five criteria. Investors can study not only the aggregate index but all information that went into constructing it, including returns on individual stocks, industrial sectors, and other groupings of securities. Other indexes constructed along the same lines have proliferated since that time.

Popular Indexes Evaluated

The Standard & Poor's 500 (S&P 500) and the Dow Jones Industrial Average (Dow) are the most popular indexes of U.S. stock performance currently in use. The S&P 500 is broad enough to capture most of the value in the U.S. equity market, but it has two limitations. First, the index omits midcapitalization and small U.S. stocks. Broad indexes such as the Russell 3000 and Wilshire 5000 have been introduced to capture the totality of the U.S. market. Second, the S&P index measures only capital appreciation and not total returns. The exclusion of dividend returns can be overcome because a number of sources, including Ibbotson Associates' *Stocks, Bonds, Bills, and Inflation Yearbook*, make available S&P 500 dividend returns and total returns.

The Dow, calculated since 1885, is price-weighted, which means that the prices of 30 large stocks are summed and divided by a constant. Originally, the sum was divided by the number of stocks in the index, so that the level of the Dow was the average stock price of its components. But over more than 100 years, the divisor has been adjusted to reflect stock splits and other capital changes, so that the level of the Dow is much higher than the price of any of the component stocks. The Dow, like the S&P 500, measures only capital appreciation. Despite its shortcomings, even a narrow average of major stocks such as the Dow will track the market to a large extent; as such, the Dow has provided investors with an indication of short-term market trends for over a century. However, over the long term, the Dow has misrepresented the market as a whole because its scope is restricted to the largest companies and it ignores dividends.

The best-constructed index of Japanese equities is the TOPIX index, which is a market value index of all section I stocks on the Tokyo Stock Exchange. The index measures only capital appreciation and not total returns. The exclusion of dividend returns can be overcome because a number of sources make total returns available.[4] The widely quoted Nikkei average is a price-weighted average of 225 stocks and resembles the Dow Jones average.

In the British market, the *Financial Times* (FT) constructs a suite of indexes. The FT 30 is composed of 30 industrial stocks and is a geometric index which imparts a bias when viewed over the long term.[5] The FT-SE 100 or "Footsie" is a market-value-weighted index of the 100 largest companies (ranked by market value) listed on London's International Stock Exchange. This index is the most popular because it is calculated every minute during the trading day and forms the basis for trading on stock index options. The FT All-Ordinaries index is broad (about 750 stocks). All of these indexes ignore dividend payments. Barclays de Zoete Wedd (BZW) calculates a value-weighted total return index that dates back to 1919. Since 1962 this index has been based on the FT All-Ordinaries index.

The two primary indexes of the French stock market are the CAC-40 and CAC-240.[6] Both are value-weighted indexes that are composed of the larger stocks trading on the Paris Bourse.

Since 1958 the newspaper, *Frankfurter Allgemeine Zeitung* (FAZ), has published the most popular index on the Frankfurt exchange. It is a value-weighted index that is composed of 100 of the largest stocks traded at Frankfurt. The Deutscher Aktienindex (DAX) is a value-weighted index that was introduced in 1988 and tracks 30 of the most heavily traded stocks at Frankfurt. The FAZ is calculated only once a day, whereas the narrower DAX is calculated every minute.

Supranational Indexes

The lack of cohesion between local-country indexes has spawned a cottage industry of supranational index constructors. The leading supranational

---

[4]See, for example, Yasushi Hamao, "Japanese Stocks, Bonds, Inflation, 1973–1987," *The Journal of Portfolio Management*, Winter 1989.

[5]As noted earlier, the returns on a geometric index cannot be achieved by an actual investor.

[6]CAC stands for *Campagnie des Agents de Change*, which is the French brokers' association.

suites of indexes are constructed so as to be closely comparable across countries. They are the Morgan Stanley Capital International (MSCI); the FT-Actuaries World Indices constructed by Goldman Sachs, the Financial Times, and County NatWest Wood Mackenzie; and the Salomon-Russell Global Equity Indices.

Of these, MSCI has by far the longest back history. The FT-Actuaries World Indices are noted for the large number of securities covered and their consistent exclusion of issues restricted as to foreign ownership. The Salomon-Russell Indices are constructed in "available capital" form, representing a careful evaluation of crossholdings, closely held and government-owned shares, and restrictions on foreign ownership. Ibbotson Associates, among others, is a distributor of many of these series.

Historical Returns

The historical returns of the world's stock markets range from spectacular to mediocre. Table 7-1 contains the annualized returns and standard deviations for the world's developed stock markets for the period 1970–1990. The returns and standard deviations are reported in the U.S. dollar (US$), Japanese yen (¥), German deutschemark (DM), British pound (£), and in each market's local currency. All returns are total returns and are before transaction costs or taxes, including dividend taxes withheld at the source. In local currency terms, Hong Kong was the pacesetter at 20.7 percent, while Swiss stocks were the laggards at 5.3 percent. The United States finished with a below average 10.0 percent.

The highest standard deviation of annual returns was that of Singapore (54.8 percent), followed closely by Hong Kong and Norway. The U.S. and Canadian markets, with standard deviations of 16.6 percent and 17.7 percent, respectively, offered the least volatile returns to local investors.

In U.S. dollar terms, Hong Kong with a 19.2 percent return edged out Japan. Italy trailed the field at 6.4 percent. South Africa, with a shorter data history, had a negative return. Figures 7-1 and 7-2 show the growth of a U.S. dollar and a unit of local currency, respectively, in four of the leading equity markets over the 1970 to 1990 period.

More action is found in the world's emerging and less-developed stock markets. Table 7-2 contains U.S. dollar returns and standard deviations for some of these markets.

The Argentine market vividly demonstrates the importance of taking into account currency fluctuations. The compound annual return measured in the peso (formerly the austral) was 415.3 percent, but only 22.6 percent when

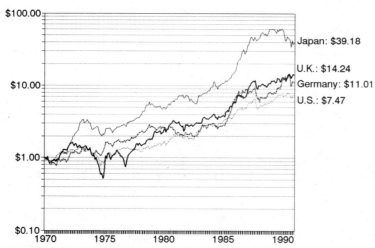

Figure 7-1. Growth of one U.S. dollar invested in leading equity markets (1969=$1.00). (*Source: Morgan Stanley Capital International.*)

measured in U.S. dollars. The difference between the dollar-denominated and peso-denominated return indicates the effect that the rapid depreciation of the peso had on returns to the international investor. The peso depreciation is attributable to persistent high inflation rates in Argentina.

The proposition introduced in Chapter 3, that riskier assets need to offer

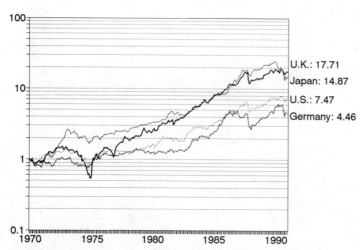

Figure 7-2. Growth of one local currency unit invested in leading equity markets (1969=1.00). (*Source: Morgan Stanley Capital International.*)

Table 7-1. Returns in Developed Stock Markets (1970–1990)

First Line: Compound Annual Return

(Second Line: Standard Deviation)

Country	US$(%)	¥(%)	DM(%)	£(%)	Local(%)
			Currency		
United States	10.0	5.1	5.4	14.7	10.0
	(16.6)	(21.9)	(23.7)	(24.8)	(16.6)
Japan	19.1	13.7	14.1	20.3	13.7
	(38.7)	(31.8)	(37.1)	(42.1)	(31.8)
United Kingdom	13.5	8.4	8.7	14.7	14.7
	(34.7)	(33.2)	(37.8)	(37.5)	(37.5)
Germany	12.1	7.0	7.4	13.3	7.4
	(33.8)	(29.5)	(27.6)	(30.6)	(27.6)
France	12.4	7.3	7.7	13.6	11.9
	(33.3)	(30.5)	(30.5)	(33.2)	(29.4)
Canada	10.1	5.1	5.4	11.2	10.5
	(17.9)	(25.5)	(23.1)	(21.9)	(17.7)
Netherlands	15.3	10.1	10.5	16.6	11.2
	(20.7)	(22.9)	(23.8)	(26.4)	(23.6)
Italy	6.4	1.6	1.9	7.5	9.4
	(44.8)	(34.8)	(38.9)	(38.7)	(39.3)
Australia	7.7	2.9	3.2	8.8	9.6
	(28.5)	(29.9)	(34.7)	(30.7)	(29.4)
Switzerland	11.6	6.6	6.9	12.8	5.3
	(27.4)	(23.7)	(22.8)	(25.7)	(24.2)
Spain	8.5	3.6	3.9	9.6	10.1
	(35.5)	(29.2)	(30.0)	(36.4)	(28.5)
Hong Kong	19.2	13.8	14.2	20.5	20.7
	(53.9)	(55.5)	(56.8)	(59.9)	(53.8)
Belgium	15.8	10.6	10.9	17.0	13.2
	(26.1)	(22.7)	(22.6)	(26.3)	(24.6)
Denmark	15.5	10.3	10.6	16.7	14.1
	(32.9)	(34.5)	(38.2)	(39.2)	(37.6)
Sweden	15.5	10.3	10.6	16.7	15.9
	(26.3)	(27.0)	(30.1)	(31.6)	(30.4)
Singapore	15.1	10.0	10.3	16.4	12.0
	(55.3)	(54.4)	(57.3)	(62.3)	(54.8)
Austria	15.3	10.1	10.4	16.5	10.4
	(44.1)	(41.4)	(32.6)	(38.7)	(32.6)
Norway	14.9	9.7	10.1	16.1	14.9
	(54.8)	(66.1)	(52.2)	(52.8)	(52.0)
South Africa	−6.5	−10.2	−9.0	−4.5	8.8
	(49.3)	(49.0)	(42.5)	(53.7)	(32.9)

SOURCE: Calculated from Morgan Stanley Capital International annual returns. South African data are from the FT-Actuaries World Indices and cover the period 1981–1990.

a higher return, is partially borne out by the data. Figure 7-3 is a plot of the compound annual return and standard deviation (in U.S. dollars) for some the world's largest stock markets over the period from 1970 to 1990. The relation between volatility and realized return is a loose one. For example, Singapore, Hong Kong, and Norway all had virtually the same standard deviation, but their U.S. dollar returns ranged from 15 percent in Norway to 19 percent in Hong Kong. Likewise, although the United States and Spain had about the same return, the U.S. investor faced a standard deviation of 17 percent in his home country's market, while the Spanish market generated a 36 percent standard deviation in U.S. dollars.

Figure 7-4 is a plot of returns and standard deviations for the same countries, but in the markets' local currency. Figures 7-3 and 7-4 are on the same scale revealing that the risk-reward relationship is tighter when portrayed in local currency terms.

These results illustrate that investors' expectations and what actually happens do not always coincide. For example, the data in Figures 7-3 and 7-4 do not invalidate the proposition that investors expect riskier investments to provide a higher return. Instead, it merely indicates the extent to which those expectations were realized over the period studied.

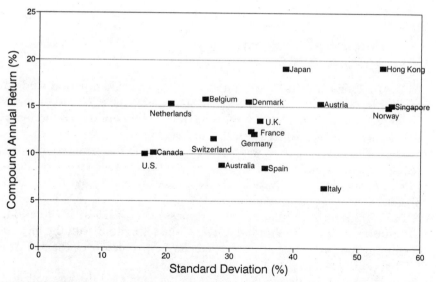

Figure 7-3. Risk versus reward of equities: returns in U.S. dollars (1970–1990). (*Source: Morgan Stanley Capital International.*)

Table 7-2. Emerging and Undeveloped Stock Market Returns

Country	Compound annual return (US$) (%)	Standard deviation (%)	Period covered
Argentina	22.6	121.2	1978–1988
Brazil	0.0	60.2	1976–1990
Chile	31.1	60.2	1976–1990
Colombia	33.5	64.7	1985–1990
Greece	5.4	56.9	1976–1990
India	17.7	29.1	1976–1990
Jordan	9.2	36.3	1979–1990
Malaysia	12.0	20.5	1985–1990
Mexico	17.4	58.4	1976–1990
Nigeria	–5.3	34.1	1985–1990
Pakistan	12.8	5.7	1985–1990
Philippines	50.5	149.9	1985–1990
Portugal	28.3	134.9	1987–1990
South Korea	30.6	46.2	1976–1990
Taiwan	44.5	79.0	1987–1990
Thailand	22.9	53.1	1976–1990
Turkey	157.7	522.9	1987–1990
Venezuela	35.3	235.2	1985–1990
Zimbabwe	14.3	64.7	1976–1990

SOURCE: The IFC Emerging Markets database provided by the International Financial Corporation, an affiliate of the World Bank.

Period-by-Period Returns from 1970 to 1990

While the long-run returns are important, subsets of the period studied reveal information hidden in the long-run statistics. Table 7-3 breaks down the 21-year period studied in Table 7-1 into four 5-year periods plus the 1-year 1990 return. The returns are calculated in U.S. dollars.

The 1970 to 1974 period was a notably poor one for world equity markets, but there was wide divergence in how the 1973 to 1974 recession affected equity markets. Japan weathered the storm quite well, but the United Kingdom had its worst crash in history.

During the recovery that dominated most of the 1975 to 1979 period, all countries except Italy fared well. The United Kingdom, with the biggest decline in the previous period, posted the best return over the 1975 to 1979 period.

The 1980 to 1984 period had mixed results. Japan led the way, with the United States, a below average performer in the two previous periods, finishing second. Most of the U.S. return occurred in the near doubling of

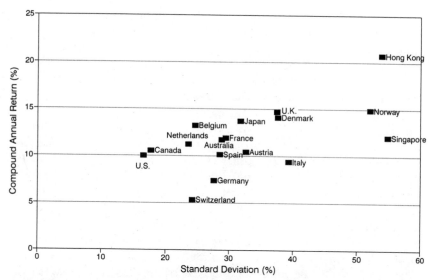

Figure 7-4. Risk versus reward of equities: return in local currency (1970–1990). (*Source: Morgan Stanley Capital International.*)

stock prices from mid-1982 to mid-1983. The French market was hammered in the 1981 to 1982 period when Mitterand's Socialist government was elected; for the 5-year period France roughly tied with Switzerland for last place.

The second half of the 1980s was the best period for the U.S. investor in world equity markets since good international stock records began to be

Table 7-3. Stock Market Compound Annual Returns Denominated in U.S. Dollars.

Five-Year Periods, 1970–1989, and One-Year Period, 1990.

Country	1970–1974	1975–1979	1980–1984	1985–1989	1990
Australia	−9.65	21.28	4.61	24.06	−15.99
Canada	4.41	18.02	6.57	16.89	−12.20
France	−0.59	22.35	−1.20	39.98	−13.23
Germany	4.90	15.87	0.90	34.17	−8.73
Italy	−9.37	−1.28	8.34	39.44	−18.26
Japan	15.78	18.78	17.07	41.44	−36.01
Netherlands	−0.25	24.25	12.09	31.61	−1.85
Switzerland	3.80	22.66	−1.79	28.09	−5.00
United Kingdom	−11.93	33.14	11.35	27.75	10.30
United States	−3.42	13.30	14.51	19.81	−2.08

SOURCE: Morgan Stanley Capital International.

kept. Every market posted double-digit compound annual returns in U.S. dollars over the 5 years.[7] Japan, a consistent gainer in the previous 15 years, won again, with a startling 41.4 percent compound annual return. The returns for the other markets were related to their ability to spring back from the nearly worldwide October 1987 crash. The slow recovery of the U.S. market showed as it and Canada brought up the rear.

October 1987 was a significant month in world capital market history. The October 19, 1987 equity price collapse was the first truly synchronous international stock price event, and it represents a degree of integration previously unobserved. The crashes of 1929 in the United States and 1974 in the United Kingdom were each mirrored in the other country's market, had ramifications for still other markets, but were hardly simultaneous across countries. In contrast, the 1987 crash represented a massive revaluation of world equities over a little more than one day.[8] Virtually every major stock market experienced double-digit declines (in both local and U.S. dollar terms) in the last 2 weeks of the month. Only Japan escaped the world crash; while its October return was terrible by any standard, it was less than half as severe as the typical decline in other countries. Nevertheless, the results for all of 1987 are quite divergent because of differential performance before and after October. For example, in local currency terms, Germany had a 38.4 percent decline, the United States had a 3.9 percent gain, and Japan had an 8.8 percent gain for the year.

The postcrash bull market came to an abrupt halt in 1990. The Japanese market had the worst year in its history with a 36 percent decline in dollar terms and a 40 percent decline in yen terms. The United States, a laggard for many of the last 20 years, turned in a relatively good performance with only a 2 percent decline. This performance contrasts sharply with the relation of the two markets in 1987.[9]

The breadth of the 1990 bear market is also interesting. In dollar terms, 9 of the 10 countries in Table 7-3 posted a total return loss for the year, with the markets falling for much of the year. In local currency terms, all ten posted a total return loss for the year. The international crash of 1987 lasted less than a month. While far less abrupt, the market decline of 1990 represents substantial correlation across countries over a reasonably long time period, suggesting that these correlations may be rising as the global market becomes more integrated.

---

[7]Substantial appreciation of most non-U.S. currencies against the dollar were responsible for a portion of these U.S.-dollar denominated returns.

[8]See Richard Roll, "The International Crash of October 1987," *Financial Analysts Journal*, September/October 1988.

[9]In 1987 virtually all of the downward action for the U.S. market occurred in October and November. The Japanese market of 1990 was in an almost unbroken decline for the entire year.

Correlations of Equity Returns

One of the foremost arguments for international investing is that it provides risk diversification. The amount of diversification provided by a portfolio of international stocks depends in part on the correlation of returns between the portfolio's component countries. Table 7-4 presents correlations between monthly total returns of some of the larger equity markets over the 1970 to 1990 period. To be relevant, it is necessary to convert the returns to a common currency and U.S. dollar returns are used.

At one time, countries tended to cluster into "equity blocs," within which stock markets were highly correlated but between which correlations were low. These blocs corresponded roughly to the better-known currency areas: there were yen and deutschemark blocs, and the U.K. and U.S. stock markets were correlated with countries around the world, showing the global reach of these countries. Today, as the world economy becomes more integrated, these clusters are disappearing, with correlations between countries becoming more evenly distributed.

Exceptions to this rule include the continental European countries and the United States and Canada. The United States and Canadian economies are closely linked. This closeness is reflected in the correlation between the country's respective stock markets. The correlation of .72 is the highest for any pair of countries represented in Table 7-4. The bloc formed by continental Europe is described by the data in Table 7-5.

Systematic Risk and the Stock Market: Country Returns in a World CAPM Setting

In Table 7-6, the monthly *alphas* and *betas* for several countries are measured over the 132 months from January 1980 to December 1990. Alphas are risk-adjusted excess returns relative to the world stock market and betas are a measure of market risk (see Chapter 3). The alpha is expressed in percent per *month* and is positive for countries that have beat the world market on a risk-adjusted basis. Countries that were beaten by the world market have negative alphas. Interestingly, none of the alphas is significant (the

Table 7-4. Correlations of Monthly Equity Total Returns Denominated in U.S. Dollars (1970–1990)

	Australia	Canada	France	Germany	Italy	Japan	Netherlands	Switzerland	United Kingdom	United States
Australia	1.00									
Canada	.59	1.00								
France	.35	.43	1.00							
Germany	.27	.31	.59	1.00						
Italy	.26	.29	.48	.39	1.00					
Japan	.26	.27	.41	.40	.40	1.00				
Netherlands	.39	.55	.59	.66	.39	.43	1.00			
Switzerland	.41	.48	.61	.71	.42	.45	.71	1.00		
United Kingdom	.46	.53	.52	.41	.37	.37	.63	.56	1.00	
United States	.47	.72	.42	.35	.24	.28	.57	.50	.50	1.00

SOURCE: Morgan Stanley Capital International.

Table 7-5. Correlations of Monthly Equity Total Returns
Denominated in U.S. Dollars (1970–1990)

	Belgium	France	Germany	Netherlands	Switzerland
Belgium	1.00				
France	.67	1.00			
Germany	.66	.59	1.00		
Netherlands	.66	.59	.66	1.00	
Switzerland	.67	.61	.71	.71	1.00

SOURCE: Morgan Stanley Capital International.

alpha t-statistics fall within the range of -2 to $+2$), suggesting substantial integration of world equity markets over the short run.[10]

The smaller European markets had the highest alphas with Sweden, Denmark, Austria, and Italy leading the way. Europe was not without its stragglers as Switzerland and Norway had among the lowest alphas measured.

The North American markets had widely divergent results. The alpha for the United States was virtually zero (0.07 percent) while Canada recorded a disappointing -0.40 percent.

Asian markets had the same diverse performance as the European markets. The 1990 collapse notwithstanding, Japan still had the highest excess return in Asia (0.38 percent), with Hong Kong close behind at 0.29 percent. The 1980s were less kind to Singapore and Australia as both countries underperformed the world index on a beta-adjusted basis.

---

[10]The following regression was run to determine the values reported in Table 7-6:

$$r_s - r_f = \alpha_s + \beta_s(r_w - r_f) + \epsilon$$

where

r_s = monthly return (in U.S. dollars) of the country

r_f = monthly riskless rate, proxied by the total return on U.S. Treasury bills

α_s = monthly excess return of the country

β_s = beta of the country

r_w = monthly return on the world index

ϵ = error term

For computational simplicity, this differs from the World CAPM equation presented in Chapter 3. Here, returns on U.S. Treasury bills, not a global portfolio of locally riskless assets, are used to construct the market risk premium.

Table 7-6. Monthly Total Returns: Regressions on World Index (1980–1990)

	Monthly alpha (%)	Monthly alpha t-statistic	Beta	Unadjusted R^2
Australia	−0.08	−0.12	0.96	0.27
Austria	0.49	0.74	0.52	0.09
Belgium	0.31	0.65	0.91	0.37
Canada	−0.40	−1.04	0.96	0.51
Denmark	0.52	1.12	0.67	0.25
France	0.04	0.08	1.02	0.40
Germany	0.06	0.11	0.87	0.33
Hong Kong	0.29	0.36	0.93	0.18
Italy	0.45	0.74	0.89	0.26
Japan	0.38	0.88	1.17	0.55
Netherlands	0.33	0.97	0.92	0.54
Norway	−0.09	−0.15	1.05	0.33
Singapore	−0.12	−0.19	0.94	0.27
Spain	0.36	0.67	0.84	0.28
Sweden	0.77	1.54	0.90	0.35
Switzerland	−0.28	−0.77	0.90	0.49
United Kingdom	0.23	0.59	1.09	0.56
United States	0.07	0.25	0.82	0.63

SOURCE: Morgan Stanley Capital International.

8

Equity Returns over the Very Long Run

The Earliest Equity Markets

The story of world equity markets begins in the Middle Ages in southern France. A water mill at Bazacle, near Toulouse, had been built in the 800s for the purpose of milling grains. By the 1100s, ownership of the Bazacle mill had been divided into shares, which were sometimes traded. The prices of these transactions are the world's oldest stock quotations. Bazacle water mill share prices were quoted on a more or less continuous basis beginning in the 1400s, with the stock trading on the Paris Bourse from the 1600s to the modern era. In 1946 the French government, apparently having little appreciation of capital market history, nationalized the mill (long since turned into an electrical generating station), making it a part of the national electric company, Électricité de France.

The next chapter in the story takes place in the age of discovery. As Europeans set out to colonize the globe in the 1600s, joint-stock companies were established to administer trade with the new colonies. Like public utilities today, which are granted local service monopolies, these companies were granted trading rights to particular parts of the globe. The British and Dutch East India companies owned trading rights in various parts of Asia and thrived for centuries, becoming the de facto rulers of the colonies where they traded. These companies were dissolved with the end of the colonial empires, but not before they had provided high returns to their investors.

The Hudson's Bay Company had perhaps the least promising endowment: the right to trade in Canada's arctic Hudson Bay region. Yet the firm evolved into a department store chain and today is one of Canada's leading companies, traded on the Toronto Stock Exchange.

The story of France's Mississippi Company is a classic illustration of the risks of international investing. The company had the enticing right to trade in the French-owned Mississippi Valley area of North America, which now makes up about one-third of the United States. Although the stock price crashed in 1720, the precrash share price was high enough to make the company's market capitalization exceed the wealth of France. Long after the company's investors lost their trading rights, the Mississippi Valley grew tremendously in value, perhaps now exceeding the wealth of France. Thus, Mississippi Company shareholders did not participate in the growth of the Mississippi Valley.

The Mississippi Company story indicates that nonmarket considerations, such as political events, can cause the value of *claims* on an asset to diverge from the value of the asset itself. This divergence creates an investment risk that is not inherent in the asset.

Looking at very long-run returns tells a great deal about the history of a country, not just in terms of its capital markets, but also with respect to its economic life, culture, and politics. This chapter focuses on long-run historical returns for the United States and United Kingdom, the countries with the longest continuous capital market return histories.

History of U.S. Stock Returns

When Benjamin Franklin died in 1791, he left a small fortune to be invested for a period of 200 years, to benefit medical students and fund scientific research. Remarkably, his instructions were carried out faithfully for two centuries and the fund was liquidated on June 30, 1991. How would one dollar from Franklin's legacy have fared over this period? If invested in U.S. stocks, and if transactions costs and taxes could have been avoided, the dollar would have grown to over $9 million.[1] This section takes a look at the U.S. equity market and how the remarkable returns experienced by the Franklin bequest were achieved.

When the United States was emerging as a nation, centralized markets for stocks and bonds already existed in Europe. London, Paris, Brussels, Amsterdam, and other cities had functioning stock exchanges. The United States, which was eventually to become the world's largest equity market,

---

[1]In fact, the original £1000 (about $5000) grew only 400-fold, to about $2 million, because of spending. Because the proceeds of the liquidation were used to fund another charitable trust, Franklin's investment will last well beyond 200 years.

did not have a central stock exchange, but brokers and traders often gathered to do business in specified locations, particularly outdoors in New York, Philadelphia, and Boston.

In May 1792, a group of security brokers met under a buttonwood tree at 68 Wall Street in New York and pledged "not to buy or sell from this day for any person whatsoever, and any kind of public stock at a less than one quarter percent commission on the specie value, and that we will give preference to each other in our negotiations." The New York Stock Exchange (NYSE) officially began with this Buttonwood Agreement providing the basis for a fixed-fee brokerage market that survived for 183 years.

Stocks have traded over the counter for years in the U.S., but the market became more formalized in 1971 when the NASDAQ quotation system began. Since its inception, the NASDAQ market has been the fastest-growing of U.S. equity markets and now is surpassed only by the NYSE in terms of trading volume and market capitalization.

On "May Day," May 1, 1975, competitive brokerage fees were instituted, bringing the NYSE in line with American antimonopolistic tradition. The year 1975 also saw the Securities and Exchange Commission (SEC) require that ticker tapes reporting the prices of stock trades be consolidated. Thus, all trades of NYSE-listed issues, including non-NYSE executed trades, were reported together and available nationwide. As a result, regional exchanges became more important second markets for NYSE- and AMEX-listed companies.

Today, we think of 100 million share days as being slow at the NYSE, but this is a recent phenomenon. The NYSE's slowest day was on March 16, 1830 when 31 shares were traded. The exchange's first 100 million share day did not occur until August 18, 1982. The busiest day to date is October 20, 1987, when volume was 608 million shares—just exceeding the previous record of 604 million shares on October 19, 1987.

Since its founding, the NYSE's dollar value of listed shares, size of trading volume, and number of listed companies have all steadily increased—current levels would have been scarcely conceivable to its founders. Today's U.S. stock market capitalization is heavily concentrated at the NYSE, which lists virtually every important U.S. firm.[2] The Exchange's greatest expansion has been in the dimension of return. Annual returns over the period are presented in Tables 8-1, 8-2, and 8-3; together they form a continuous series from 1790 to 1990.

---

[2]There are a number of exceptions. Well-known firms like MCI Communications and Apple Computer qualify to be listed on the NYSE but elect not to.

Returns up to 1871, shown in Table 8-1, are based on linking of various indexes with undocumented characteristics.[3] By these calculations, a dollar invested at the end of 1789 would have grown to $569.23 by 1871 representing an 8 percent compound annual return.

The Cowles Index provides more reliable data on NYSE returns. These returns are available for the period 1872 to 1925 and are presented in Table 8-2.[4] A dollar invested in this NYSE index at the end of 1871 would have grown to $36.58 in 54 years, representing a compound annual return of 6.9 percent. It is noteworthy that only about 25 percent of this return, or 1.8 percent per year, is due to capital appreciation. The balance comes from reinvestment of dividends.

Annual return data for a value-weighted portfolio of all NYSE stocks from 1926 to 1990 are shown in Table 8-3. A dollar invested in a market portfolio of NYSE stocks at the end of 1925 would have grown to $436.27 in 65 years, for a compound annual return of 9.8 percent, about half from dividend reinvestment and half from capital appreciation.

Linking these three return series together, a dollar invested in the U.S. stock market over this 201-year period would have grown to a little over $9 million by the end of 1990 for a compound annual return of 8.3 percent. After taking into account inflation, the $9 million shrinks to about $400,000. While these results assume no transaction costs or taxes, actual investors facing these costs would still have earned a very high long-run return. Tax rates were zero or low until the 1930s, and transaction costs can be minimized by a buy-and-hold strategy. Of course, it is necessary to transact somewhat in order to track the changing composition of the indexes and to reinvest dividends.

---

[3] These indexes are generally narrow, representing a limited number of prominent stocks. Despite this feature, these indexes, like the Dow, probably track market trends reasonably well and thus provide useful information for this analysis. While the stocks may have traded on the NYSE, the pre-1871 indexes do not represent the NYSE as a whole, and are reported only to capture early period returns. These indexes, except for the Cowles Index, may suffer from survivorship bias, which means that firms that fail are not considered, biasing returns upward, and from other indeterminate biases. William N. Goetzmann and Roger G. Ibbotson are currently constructing a new return series that seeks to fix the flaws present in the pre-1926 indexes used in this chapter.

[4] The Cowles index is generally considered to be the first high-quality, broad-based index of U.S. stock market returns. In the 1930s, Alfred Cowles collected both monthly value-weighted capital appreciation returns and monthly dividend yields on all NYSE-listed stocks. Using the assumption that dividend returns equaled promised yields, the authors combined these data to construct the total returns and cumulative wealth index (initialized to 1.0000 at December 31, 1871) shown here. Survivorship bias is corrected for by including the last return after delisting or failure of a stock. Unfortunately, Cowles' capital appreciation returns are based on each stock's average price over a month, not the month-end closing price so that yearly returns measure price changes from (on average) mid-December to mid-December.

Table 8-1. U.S. Stock Market Annual Returns (1790–1871)

Year	Year-end total return (%)	Year-end total return index	Year-end capital appreciation index	Year	Year-end total return (%)	Year-end total return index	Year end capital appreciation index
1789		1.00	1.00				
1790	27.82	1.28	1.22	1830	20.92	35.52	4.98
1791	12.96	1.44	1.32	1831	−7.79	32.75	4.34
1792	−7.56	1.33	1.15	1832	37.58	45.06	5.76
1793	15.62	1.54	1.28	1833	0.09	45.10	5.48
1794	27.88	1.97	1.57	1834	22.25	55.14	6.42
1795	−0.51	1.96	1.48	1835	10.86	61.13	6.80
1796	−8.62	1.79	1.28	1836	−17.20	50.61	5.29
1797	−3.45	1.73	1.17	1837	−7.52	46.81	4.63
1798	27.76	2.21	1.44	1838	−7.20	43.44	4.06
1799	21.04	2.68	1.67	1839	−13.62	37.52	3.30
1800	26.59	3.39	2.03	1840	13.54	42.60	3.59
1801	−33.36	2.26	1.25	1841	−13.36	36.91	2.93
1802	17.10	2.65	1.40	1842	−14.40	31.59	2.36
1803	13.48	3.00	1.52	1843	77.08	55.95	4.06
1804	53.34	4.60	2.26	1844	16.58	65.22	4.53
1805	6.91	4.92	2.31	1845	11.30	72.59	4.82
1806	10.17	5.42	2.43	1846	2.97	74.75	4.72
1807	−41.34	3.18	1.30	1847	5.00	78.49	4.72
1808	59.16	5.06	2.01	1848	5.00	82.41	4.72
1809	25.54	6.36	2.42	1849	9.06	89.88	4.91
1810	−11.14	5.65	2.03	1850	33.81	120.27	6.33
1811	−0.34	5.63	1.92	1851	0.53	120.90	6.05
1812	−8.55	5.15	1.66	1852	31.52	159.01	7.65
1813	15.23	5.93	1.83	1853	−9.81	143.41	6.52
1814	73.57	10.30	3.09	1854	−23.50	109.71	4.66
1815	8.51	11.17	3.19	1855	12.22	123.12	5.00
1816	3.30	11.54	3.14	1856	20.50	148.36	5.77
1817	21.70	14.05	3.67	1857	−20.21	118.37	4.31
1818	13.88	16.00	3.99	1858	−11.94	104.24	3.58
1819	−5.06	15.19	3.59	1859	−3.78	100.30	3.27
1820	19.41	18.13	4.11	1860	22.94	123.31	3.85
1821	10.90	20.11	4.35	1861	17.86	145.33	4.35
1822	1.50	20.41	4.20	1862	53.91	223.68	6.48
1823	10.60	22.58	4.43	1863	46.56	327.82	9.18
1824	11.44	25.16	4.72	1864	0.18	328.41	8.73
1825	−6.73	23.46	4.17	1865	13.08	371.37	9.44
1826	3.78	24.35	4.11	1866	4.46	387.93	9.39
1827	7.99	26.30	4.24	1867	9.01	422.89	9.77
1828	−0.46	26.18	4.01	1868	14.15	482.72	10.66
1829	12.22	29.38	4.30	1869	−8.89	439.81	9.18
				1870	8.90	478.95	9.54
				1871	18.85	569.23	10.86

SOURCE: "Historical Record: Stock Prices 1789–Present (Data Bulletin 1975–1)," pp. 8–12, Foundation for the Study of Cycles, Irvine, Calif. The Foundation uses its internal index for 1789 to June 1831; the Cleveland Trust Company railroad stock index from July 1831 to February 1854; the Clement-Burgess Index from March 1854 to July 1871; and the Cowles index for August to December 1871. We used these indexes to construct returns and a cumulative wealth index initialized to 1.000 at December 31, 1789. Dividend income in each year is assumed to be the average over the period 1872 to 1985.

Table 8-2. New York Stock Exchange Value-Weighted Annual Returns (1872–1925)

Year	Total return (%)	Income return (%)	Capital appreciation return (%)	Year-end total return index	Year-end capital appreciation index
1871				1.00	1.00
1872	12.07	5.26	6.81	1.12	1.07
1873	−7.05	5.70	−12.75	1.04	0.93
1874	9.35	6.54	2.81	1.14	0.96
1875	2.79	6.89	−4.10	1.17	0.92
1876	−11.44	6.51	−17.95	1.04	0.75
1877	−2.35	7.02	−9.38	1.01	0.68
1878	11.91	5.78	6.13	1.13	0.73
1879	48.08	5.12	42.96	1.68	1.04
1880	23.39	4.70	18.69	2.07	1.23
1881	7.76	4.78	2.98	2.23	1.27
1882	1.95	4.84	−2.89	2.27	1.23
1883	−3.33	5.18	−8.51	2.20	1.13
1884	−13.15	5.69	−18.84	1.91	0.91
1885	26.37	6.31	20.06	2.41	1.10
1886	13.44	5.09	8.35	2.74	1.19
1887	−2.76	3.85	−6.61	2.66	1.11
1888	1.88	4.24	−2.36	2.71	1.08
1889	7.56	4.18	3.38	2.92	1.12
1890	−9.67	3.88	−13.55	2.64	0.97
1891	21.85	4.01	17.84	3.21	1.14
1892	5.89	4.28	1.61	3.40	1.16
1893	−15.70	4.16	−19.86	2.87	0.93
1894	2.49	5.03	−2.54	2.94	0.91
1895	5.20	4.62	0.58	3.09	0.91
1896	1.67	3.97	−2.30	3.14	0.89
1897	16.80	4.15	12.65	3.67	1.00
1898	22.70	3.90	18.80	4.50	1.19
1899	10.31	3.72	6.59	4.97	1.27

(*Continued*)

Table 8-2. New York Stock Exchange Value-Weighted Annual Returns (1872–1925) (Continued)

Year	Total return (%)	Income return (%)	Capital appreciation return (%)	Year-end total return index	Year-end capital appreciation index
1900	17.23	3.21	14.02	5.82	1.45
1901	20.23	4.50	15.73	7.00	1.68
1902	5.10	3.85	1.25	7.36	1.70
1903	−14.81	3.71	−18.52	6.29	1.38
1904	30.41	4.65	25.76	8.17	1.74
1905	19.84	4.18	15.66	9.80	2.01
1906	6.66	3.53	3.13	10.45	2.07
1907	−29.37	3.96	−33.33	7.38	1.38
1908	42.88	5.38	37.50	10.54	1.90
1909	19.12	4.93	14.19	12.56	2.17
1910	−7.87	4.31	−12.18	11.57	1.91
1911	5.53	4.84	0.69	12.21	1.92
1912	7.92	4.92	3.00	13.18	1.98
1913	−9.45	4.85	−14.30	11.93	1.69
1914	−3.13	5.37	−8.50	11.56	1.55
1915	33.90	5.01	28.89	15.48	2.00
1916	8.39	4.98	3.41	16.78	2.07
1917	−25.05	5.62	−30.67	12.57	1.43
1918	23.91	7.82	16.09	15.58	1.66
1919	20.31	7.24	13.07	18.75	1.88
1920	−17.93	5.75	−23.68	15.38	1.43
1921	13.43	6.13	7.30	17.45	1.54
1922	26.56	6.49	20.07	22.09	1.85
1923	3.39	5.80	−2.41	22.83	1.80
1924	24.52	5.94	18.58	28.43	2.14
1925	28.64	5.87	22.77	36.58	2.63

SOURCE: Alfred Cowles, *Common Stock Indexes, 1871–1937*, Bloomington, Ind.: Principia Press, 1938. Reprinted with permission of the Cowles Foundation for Research in Economics.

Table 8-3. New York Stock Exchange Value-Weighted Annual Returns (1926–1990)

Year	Total return (%)	Income return (%)	Capital appreciation return (%)	Year-end total return index	Year-end capital appreciation index	Aggregate value ($ billion)
1925				1.00	1.00	27.35
1926	9.62	5.85	3.77	1.10	1.04	30.95
1927	33.30	6.27	27.03	1.46	1.32	42.49
1928	38.93	5.34	33.59	2.03	1.76	58.96
1929	−14.56	3.15	−17.71	1.73	1.45	55.22
1930	−28.37	3.30	−31.67	1.24	0.99	41.31
1931	−44.43	3.25	−47.68	0.69	0.52	21.57
1932	−9.25	6.02	−15.27	0.63	0.44	18.52
1933	57.90	6.54	51.36	0.99	0.66	28.16
1934	4.30	4.20	0.10	1.03	0.67	28.92
1935	44.45	5.85	38.60	1.49	0.92	40.46
1936	32.38	5.69	26.69	1.97	1.17	52.45
1937	−34.62	3.48	−38.10	1.29	0.72	32.98
1938	28.22	5.43	22.79	1.65	0.89	40.83
1939	2.00	4.77	−2.77	1.69	0.86	39.83
1940	−7.48	5.24	−12.72	1.56	0.75	35.00
1941	−9.50	6.11	−15.61	1.41	0.64	29.86
1942	16.10	7.62	8.48	1.64	0.69	32.51
1943	28.05	6.39	21.66	2.10	0.84	40.30
1944	21.40	5.91	15.49	2.55	0.97	46.91
1945	38.35	5.52	32.83	3.53	1.29	63.16
1946	−6.00	3.82	−9.82	3.32	1.16	60.20
1947	3.38	5.60	−2.22	3.43	1.13	60.67
1948	2.32	6.23	−3.91	3.51	1.09	59.15
1949	20.25	7.99	12.26	4.22	1.22	68.32
1950	29.86	8.20	21.66	5.48	1.49	85.70
1951	20.87	6.67	14.20	6.62	1.70	101.73
1952	13.33	5.94	7.39	7.50	1.83	112.24
1953	0.33	5.41	−5.08	7.53	1.73	109.26
1954	50.26	7.06	43.20	11.31	2.48	162.54
1955	25.31	5.03	20.28	14.17	2.99	200.79
1956	8.41	4.21	4.20	15.37	3.11	217.31
1957	−10.54	3.73	−14.27	13.75	2.67	194.27
1958	44.81	5.53	39.28	19.91	3.72	276.48
1959	13.10	3.61	9.49	22.51	4.07	309.25
1960	0.86	3.40	−2.54	22.71	3.96	307.71
1961	27.44	3.74	23.70	28.94	4.90	388.05
1962	−9.96	2.99	−12.95	26.05	4.27	337.15
1963	21.42	3.79	17.63	31.64	5.02	401.64
1964	16.38	3.44	12.94	36.82	5.67	462.92
1965	14.07	3.37	10.70	42.00	6.28	523.84
1966	−8.84	2.99	−11.83	38.29	5.54	469.07
1967	26.84	3.82	23.02	48.56	6.81	585.17
1968	12.75	3.28	9.47	54.75	7.45	662.42
1969	−9.78	2.77	−12.55	49.40	6.52	598.70

Table 8-3. New York Stock Exchange Value-Weighted Annual Returns (1926–1990) (Continued)

Year	Total return (%)	Income return (%)	Capital appreciation return (%)	Year-end total return index	Year-end capital appreciation index	Aggregate value ($ billion)
1970	1.29	3.60	−2.31	50.04	6.37	605.26
1971	15.85	3.43	12.42	57.97	7.16	705.06
1972	17.65	3.16	14.49	68.20	8.20	836.13
1973	−16.91	2.59	−19.50	56.66	6.60	681.10
1974	−26.80	3.26	−30.06	41.48	4.62	480.24
1975	37.67	5.71	31.96	57.10	6.09	650.57
1976	26.24	4.96	21.28	72.09	7.39	816.57
1977	−4.84	4.40	−9.24	68.60	6.70	765.45
1978	7.33	5.46	1.87	73.63	6.83	793.49
1979	21.87	6.34	15.53	89.73	7.89	923.14
1980	32.64	6.67	25.97	119.02	9.94	1204.96
1981	−4.15	4.72	−8.87	114.08	9.06	1112.97
1982	20.99	6.71	14.28	138.02	10.35	1273.60
1983	22.76	5.30	17.46	169.44	12.16	1538.96
1984	5.80	4.87	0.93	179.26	12.27	1549.37
1985	32.16	5.82	26.34	236.91	15.50	1950.33
1986	18.47	3.84	14.63	280.67	17.77	2278.24
1987	5.23	3.20	2.03	295.35	18.13	2332.00
1988	16.81	4.40	12.41	345.00	20.38	2647.94
1989	31.49	4.23	27.26	453.64	25.94	3260.15
1990	−3.17	3.41	−6.58	439.26	24.23	2833.91

SOURCE: Center for Research in Security Prices, Graduate School of Business, University of Chicago. 1985 to 1990 return data represent the S&P 500 and are from *Stocks, Bonds, Bills, and Inflation 1991 Yearbook*™, Ibbotson Associates, Inc., Chicago (annually updates work by Roger G. Ibbotson and Rex A. Sinquefield).

Figure 8-1 shows the growth of a dollar invested in a U.S. stock market total return index, a capital appreciation index, and an index of inflation over the period 1789 to 1990. The remarkable property of this figure is the constancy of the slope of the line representing stock market total return. From the bicentennial vantage point, equity risk seems to disappear. The only blip that is clearly visible is the Great Crash of 1929 to 1932. It is important to remember, when taking this grand perspective, that the shorter-run poor returns did happen and that fortunes were lost and lives ruined in the Great Depression and other short-term calamities.

As Figure 8-1 suggests, NYSE returns and their associated risks have both been astonishingly stable over the past 2 centuries. To examine the market's performance over subperiods, the years from 1790 to 1990 are divided into four periods of a half-century each (the last period is 51 years). Statistics for these subperiods are shown in Table 8-4. Interestingly, average returns are

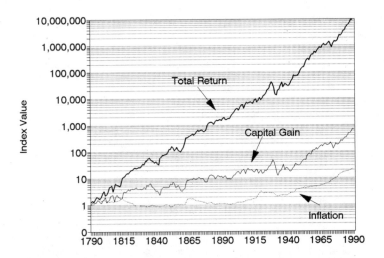

Figure 8-1. U.S. equity returns and inflation: 1790–1990 (year-end 1789 = 1.00). *(Source: Tables 8-1, 8-2, 8-3, and 12-3.)*

similar for all four subperiods. In nominal terms, the exceptional subperiod was 1940 to 1990, in which returns impounded high inflation. In real (inflation-adjusted) terms, the subperiod 1890–1939, containing 2 depressions, was the only one to deviate significantly from the long-run average. But most remarkable is the consistency of the market's standard deviation over almost 2 centuries.

Looking at the best and worst years within each half-century provides an intuitive appreciation for the short-term volatility of the U.S. stock market. For the 1790–1839 period the best calendar year was 1814 (up 74 percent); this was also the best of the full 201 years. The early years also had sharp declines: the 1807 return of −41 percent was the worst of the century. The Great Depression of the 1930s included the worst year for equities in U.S. history, 1931 (down 44 percent). The recovery from the Depression included the best year of the twentieth century, 1933 (up 58 percent). More recently the best year was 1954 (up 51 percent) and the worst was 1974 (down 27 percent).

The serial correlation (first-order autocorrelation) of returns over the 50-year intervals is also reported in Table 8-4. The serial correlation of returns measures the relation of one period's return to the next period's return. Perfectly related series have a correlation of 1.00, unrelated series a correlation of 0.00, and perfectly negatively related series a correlation of −1.00. The serial correlations in Table 8-4 are all statistically indistinguishable from zero. Over the whole 201-year period the serial correlation was

Table 8-4. Summary Data on U.S. Equity Total Returns by Subperiod (1790–1990)

Period	Compound annual return (%)	Arithmetic mean return (%)	Standard deviation (%)	Serial correlation
	Whole period			
1790–1990				
Nominal	8.3	10.1	19.6	−0.01
Real	6.6	8.5	19.9	−0.01
	Half-centuries			
1790-1839				
Nominal	7.5	9.4	19.8	−0.11
Real	7.6	9.7	20.9	−0.06
1840–1889				
Nominal	7.9	9.4	19.0	0.12
Real	7.5	9.1	19.1	0.09
1890–1939				
Nominal	6.3	8.6	21.6	−0.01
Real	4.8	7.2	22.0	−0.02
1940–1990				
Nominal	11.5	12.8	16.6	−0.08
Real	6.7	8.1	17.4	−0.02

SOURCE: Tables 8-1, 8-2, 8-3, and 12-3.

almost exactly zero, −0.01. These results indicate that the returns from one period are not related to returns in the next period. This suggests that investors cannot forecast returns (except as a probability distribution) by knowing past returns. In other words, U.S. equity total and excess returns from period-to-period appear to be independently and identically distributed (cumulative returns follow a random walk).[5] The apparent random walk of cumulative total returns is an artifact of the fact that the volatility of equity excess returns dominates the volatility of total returns. We believe that a random walk accurately describes cumulative equity excess returns.[6]

---

[5]Excess return as measured is the return to equities in excess of inflation or risk-free government bills as the data permit.

[6]Although a serial correlation of annual returns very close to zero suggests that stock returns are not forecastable, not all researchers concur. Variables other than past returns,

Table 8-5 contains decade-by-decade nominal and real returns for the past 201 years. Note that nearly all of the real return over the period comes from the reinvestment of dividends. The real capital appreciation index has increased only about thirtyfold in 201 years.

Bull and Bear Markets in the United States

Table 8-6 identifies the four severe bear markets (defined here as periods in which investors lost at least 45 percent of their wealth in real terms). The most severe bear market was from 1929 to 1932, during which stocks declined by 83 percent on a month-end basis. Precursors of the Great Crash were the bear markets of 1836 to 1842, with a 48 percent nominal decline, and 1853 to 1859, when losses amounted to 37 percent in nominal terms. More recently, the years 1973–1974 saw a stock market loss of 43 percent, exacerbated by the high inflation rate during that time. Less severe bear markets, conventionally defined as a 15 to 20 percent decline, have been much more frequent.

Bull markets are defined here as periods when real stock prices at least doubled, without a major interruption. Such markets have occurred 10 times since 1790, as shown in Table 8-7. There were unusually rapid advances that occurred in the late 1920s, during the 1932 to 1937 recovery from the Great Crash, in the explosive postwar period from 1949 to 1966, and in the 1980s.

Bear and bull markets reflect major changes in the general level of stock prices. Yet these labels are after-the-fact characterizations and do not imply that stock returns follow trends. As the French statistician Louis Bachelier first showed in 1900, the serial correlation of equity returns is practically zero.[7] More specifically, stock returns in excess of the riskless rate are close to a random process. This means that no one can predict next year's excess returns by knowing this year's. A random process, however, can produce results which visually resemble a trend and which, over the "trendy" periods, greatly affect investors' wealth.

---

one year. See Robert P. Flood, Robert J. Hodrick, and Paul D. Kaplan, "An Evaluation of Recent Evidence on Stock Market Bubbles," in *Policy Switching*, MIT Press, forthcoming; James A. Poterba and Lawrence M. Summers, "Mean Reversion in Stock Prices: Evidence and Implications," *Journal of Financial Economics*, October 1988; and three papers by Eugene F. Fama and Kenneth R. French: "Permanent and Transitory Components of Stock Prices," *Journal of Political Economy*, April 1988, "Dividend Yields and Expected Stock Returns," *Journal of Financial Economics*, October 1988, and "Business Conditions and Expected Returns on Stocks and Bonds," *Journal of Financial Economics*, November 1989.

[7]Louis Bachelier, "Theory of Speculation," reprinted in Paul Cootner, editor, *The Random Character of Stock Market Prices*, MIT Press, Cambridge, Mass., 1964.

Table 8-5. U.S. Stock Market Compound Nominal and Real Total and Capital Appreciation Returns (1790–1990)

| | Nominal | | | | Inflation | | Real | | | | |
| | Capital appreciation returns | | Total returns | | | | Capital appreciation returns | | Total returns | | |
Period	Decade compound annual return	End of decade index value	Decade compound annual return	End of decade index value	Decade mean	End of decade index value	Decade compound annual return	End of decade index value	Decade compound annual return	End of decade index value
1789		1.00		1.00		1.00		1.00		1.00
1790–1799	5.1	1.68	10.4	2.68	3.9	1.47	1.2	1.12	6.2	1.83
1800–1809	3.8	2.42	9.0	6.36	-0.6	1.38	4.4	1.73	9.7	4.60
1810–1819	3.9	3.59	9.1	15.19	-0.2	1.35	4.1	2.60	9.3	11.22
1820–1829	1.7	4.30	6.8	29.38	-3.6	0.94	5.5	4.43	10.8	31.21
1830–1839	-2.4	3.31	2.5	37.53	0.0	0.94	-2.4	3.48	2.5	39.86
1840–1849	3.9	4.92	9.1	89.90	0.6	1.00	3.3	4.83	8.5	90.16
1850–1859	-3.7	3.27	1.1	100.32	0.4	1.04	-4.1	3.17	0.7	96.52
1860–1869	10.4	9.18	15.9	440.05	4.5	1.62	5.6	5.49	10.9	272.11
1870–1879	2.0	11.26	8.1	955.77	-3.5	1.14	5.6	9.50	11.9	840.01
1880–1889	0.8	12.17	5.7	1,661.67	-0.1	1.12	0.9	10.42	5.8	1,481.98
1890–1899	1.3	13.80	5.5	2,829.03	-0.3	1.09	1.5	12.11	5.7	2,588.23
1900–1909	5.5	23.58	9.7	7,153.35	3.0	1.46	2.5	15.44	6.6	4,882.71
1910–1919	-1.4	20.42	4.1	10,673.98	7.0	2.88	-7.9	6.79	-2.7	3,813.89
1920–1929	7.3	39.65	13.0	36,114.12	-0.3	2.80	7.6	14.18	13.3	12,912.62
1930–1939	-5.1	23.61	-0.3	35,129.04	-2.0	2.27	-3.1	10.38	1.8	15,445.07
1940–1949	3.6	33.49	9.6	87,815.28	5.4	3.85	-1.8	8.69	4.0	22,794.08
1950–1959	12.8	111.30	18.2	468,735.92	2.2	4.49	10.3	23.24	15.7	97,891.90
1960–1969	4.8	178.37	8.2	1,028,509.70	2.5	6.14	2.2	29.04	5.5	167,422.54
1970–1979	1.9	215.86	6.2	1,868,234.75	7.4	12.51	-5.1	17.26	-1.1	149,344.98
1980–1990	10.7	662.95	15.5	9,145,780.43	5.2	21.81	5.3	30.40	9.8	419,348.56

SOURCE: Tables 8-1, 8-2, 8-3, and 12-3.

Table 8-6. Great Bear Markets in the United States (1790–1990)

Period	Percent decline during bear market		Percent advance in first year after bear market	
	Nominal (%)	Real (%)	Nominal (%)	Real (%)
1836–1842	−48.3	−47.8	77.1	76.9
1853–1859	−36.9	−50.9	23.0	24.0
Sept. 1929–June 1932	−83.4	−78.7	162.9	181.6
Jan. 1973–Sept. 1974	−42.6	−52.2	38.1	28.2

SOURCE: Tables 8-1, 8-2, 8-3, and 12-3.

Table 8-7. Great Bull Markets in the United States (1790–1990)

Period	Percent advance during bull market		Compound annual return during bull market	
	Nominal (%)	Real (%)	Nominal (%)	Real (%)
1790–1800	239.0	105.0	11.8	6.7
1813–1818	210.7	237.6	20.8	22.5
1843–1845	129.8	119.6	32.0	30.0
1860–1863	226.9	174.2	34.5	25.4
1897–1905	212.1	163.1	13.5	11.4
1924–Aug. 1929	369.7	375.0	31.4	31.7
July 1932–Feb. 1937	414.6	395.2	42.1	40.9
May 1942–May 1946	210.0	171.3	31.9	27.7
July 1949–Jan. 1966	1260.9	921.7	17.1	15.0
Aug. 1982–Sep. 1987	273.1	216.6	29.6	25.5

SOURCE: Tables 8-1, 8-2, 8-3, and 12-3.

War and the Market

Whether war is good or bad for stock markets is an unsettled question. Because wars mandate high production and consumption of goods, they might benefit the economy and thus the stock market. On the other hand, the goods produced are generally destroyed and detract from both private consumption and investment. When one blows up one's stock of goods, even though the money used to buy the goods remains in the economic system, it makes intuitive sense that this would affect wealth negatively and have disastrous effects on the market. The effect of war on the market can be mitigated somewhat by holding as much of a country's wealth in a safe haven. For example, in late 1990 and early 1991, Iraq destroyed much of Kuwait's infrastructure, but because the bulk of Kuwait's financial assets were held overseas, much of Kuwait's wealth was preserved.

Table 8-8. U.S. Stock Market Returns during War (1790–1990)

War	Years	Mean nominal return (%)	Mean real return (%)
War of 1812	1812–1814	26.75	18.64
Mexican War	1846–1848	4.32	0.40
Civil War	1861–1865	26.32	14.26
Spanish-American War	1898	22.70	19.57
World War I	1917–1918	−0.57	−18.01
World War II	1942–1945	26.01	21.81
Korean War	1950–1953	16.15	12.86
Vietnam War	1966–1973	4.87	0.08
All war years		15.13	7.74
All peacetime years		9.17	8.60
All years		10.06	8.55

SOURCE: Tables 8-1, 8-2, 8-3, and 12-3.

U.S. equity returns during wartime do not support either hypothesis. Total returns during war years appear in Table 8-8. In nominal terms, wartime markets appear quite healthy, with an average return of 15 percent compared to 9 percent during peacetime. However, after adjusting for the high inflation associated with wars, American investors on average earned the same return during wars as during peacetime.

Investors on the winning side of wars, of course, fare differently from those backing the losers. Because the United States has won every major war in its history that involved an attack on domestic wealth, it is not surprising that U.S. wartime returns are generally positive.[8] War, along with hyperinflation, has often destroyed the wealth and capital markets of defeated countries.

U.S. Presidential Elections and the Market

Because politicians affect a country's business and economic climate, political changes affect the stock market. Total returns for presidential election years, reported in Table 8-9, have been substantially better than in nonelection years.[9] Perhaps investors are optimistic when a new or reelected presi-

[8]The wars in Vietnam and Korea did not involve attacks on U.S. domestic wealth.

[9]The standard error of the mean for election years was 3.4 percent and 2.8 percent for nonelection years. Thus the means (both nominal and real) are separated by approximately 2 standard errors, suggesting that the difference of means is significant near the 95 percent level, assuming normally distributed, stationary returns for both series.

dent begins a new term with a fresh agenda. But more likely, the election-year returns are superior because political campaigns provide information about the future business climate and as a result some uncertainty is resolved.

Detailed analysis of the results suggests no "November effect," or jump in returns immediately after the election. Furthermore, returns seem unrelated to the party of the winner; the market favors neither Republicans nor Democrats.

Table 8-9. U.S. Stock Market Returns in Presidential Election Years (1900–1988)

Year	Nominal total return (%)	Real total return (%)
1900	17.23	14.46
1904	30.41	28.18
1908	42.88	38.81
1912	7.92	4.20
1916	8.39	0.76
1920	−17.93	−29.15
1924	24.52	24.27
1928	38.93	40.28
1932	−9.25	1.17
1936	32.38	30.80
1940	−7.48	−8.36
1944	21.40	18.89
1948	2.32	−0.38
1952	13.33	12.34
1956	8.41	5.40
1960	0.86	−0.61
1964	16.38	15.01
1968	12.75	7.66
1972	17.65	13.77
1976	26.24	20.45
1980	32.64	18.01
1984	5.08	1.08
1988	16.81	11.87
Mean total return in election years	14.86	11.79
Mean total return in nonelection years	10.00	6.50

SOURCE: Tables 8-1, 8-2, 8-3, and 12-3.

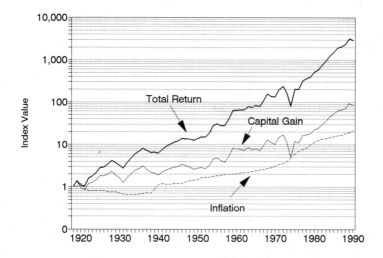

Figure 8-2. U.K. equity returns and inflation: 1919–1990 (year-end 1918 = 1.00). *(Source: Data through 1988 is from Peter Thompson, Jeffrey Thompson, Bryan Allworthy, and David Roden, BZW Equity-Gilt Study, Barclays de Zoete Wedd, London, 1989. Data since 1988 is from Morgan Stanley Capital International.)*

Stock Market Returns in the United Kingdom

Figure 8-2 is a summary of the performance of the U.K. equity market from 1919 to the present. The data used to construct Figure 8-2 are in Table 8-10. The 1920s were good years for British equities; with the exception of sharp contractions in 1920 and 1929, the stock market showed a positive real return in every year. As in the United States, 1929 signaled the beginning of a depression, but the stock market decline was not as severe as in the United States. In fact, the 1929 to 1932 decline in the United Kingdom was less severe than that country's crash of 1973 to 1974.[10]

Stocks bounced back in the 1932 to 1936 period (in real terms, 1936 was the market peak until 1954), but World War II and the subsequent decline of Britain as an economic power caused the market to drift for 3 decades, with only a 4.8 percent real compound annual total return from 1937 to

[10]The U.S. crash affected Britain because the British, ever the multinational investors, held substantial quantities of U.S. stocks. According to Peter Thompson et al., *BZW Equity-Gilt Study*, Barclays de Zoete Wedd, London, 1989, "Overseas railway stocks . . . accounted for a larger share of the London equity market than UK industrials; although U.S. Railways did not suffer as badly as some groups, they nevertheless lost 70 percent of their value between 1929 and 1932" (p. 20).

Table 8-10. U.K. Equity Market Annual Returns (1919–1990)

Year	Capital gain (%)	Dividend yield (%)	Total return (%)	Total return index
1918				1.00
1919	35.5	4.8	42.0	1.42
1920	−30.8	9.5	−24.2	1.08
1921	−9.6	8.9	−1.6	1.06
1922	41.4	6.0	49.9	1.59
1923	5.1	6.4	11.8	1.78
1924	15.6	5.4	21.8	2.16
1925	25.7	4.8	31.7	2.85
1926	−2.1	5.4	3.2	2.94
1927	11.9	4.9	17.4	3.45
1928	15.5	4.6	20.8	4.17
1929	−17.3	6.1	−12.3	3.66
1930	−17.1	6.7	−11.5	3.24
1931	−20.9	6.8	−15.5	2.73
1932	29.1	4.7	35.2	3.70
1933	26.2	3.9	31.1	4.85
1934	19.9	3.8	24.5	6.03
1935	9.9	3.7	14.0	6.87
1936	15.1	3.4	19.0	8.18
1937	−16.7	4.6	−12.9	7.13
1938	−14.9	5.5	−10.2	6.40
1939	−3.1	5.4	2.1	6.54
1940	−10.2	6.3	−4.5	6.24
1941	16.8	5.2	22.9	7.67
1942	12.9	4.4	17.9	9.04
1943	7.1	4.1	11.5	10.07
1944	8.3	3.8	12.4	11.33
1945	2.0	3.8	5.9	11.99
1946	13.9	3.5	17.9	14.14
1947	−6.3	4.3	−2.2	13.83
1948	−7.7	4.3	−3.8	13.30
1949	−10.3	5.0	−5.7	12.54
1950	5.6	5.0	10.8	13.90
1951	3.0	5.4	8.5	15.08
1952	−5.9	6.1	−0.1	15.07
1953	17.8	5.4	24.2	18.72
1954	42.4	4.4	48.6	27.81
1955	5.8	4.8	10.9	30.83
1956	−13.9	5.7	−9.0	28.05
1957	−7.0	6.3	−1.2	27.72
1958	41.1	4.8	47.9	41.01
1959	49.5	3.6	54.8	63.48

(*Continued*)

Table 8-10. U.K. Equity Market Annual Returns (1919–1990)
(Continued)

Year	Capital gain (%)	Dividend yield (%)	Total return (%)	Total return index
1960	−2.6	4.5	1.7	64.57
1961	−3.0	4.8	1.7	65.67
1962	−4.4	5.0	0.4	65.91
1963	14.8	4.1	19.5	78.76
1964	−10.6	5.2	−5.9	74.12
1965	6.8	5.2	12.4	83.32
1966	−10.8	5.9	−5.4	78.80
1967	32.5	4.2	38.0	108.72
1968	37.0	3.4	41.6	153.98
1969	−15.1	4.0	−11.7	136.02
1970	−6.2	4.6	−1.9	133.49
1971	40.5	3.4	45.3	193.94
1972	18.1	3.1	21.7	236.11
1973	−34.9	4.4	−32.1	160.35
1974	−54.7	11.8	−49.4	81.20
1975	136.1	5.7	149.6	202.64
1976	−7.9	7.4	−1.0	200.53
1977	49.1	5.4	57.2	315.27
1978	6.1	5.6	12.1	353.33
1979	2.7	6.8	9.6	387.31
1980	26.7	5.8	34.1	519.44
1981	6.0	5.9	12.3	583.18
1982	22.4	5.2	28.8	751.20
1983	22.7	4.7	28.5	965.13
1984	24.2	4.5	29.8	1252.58
1985	16.7	4.2	21.5	1522.43
1986	21.4	4.1	26.4	1924.88
1987	3.8	4.4	8.4	2085.73
1988	7.6	4.8	12.8	2352.31
1989	32.0	4.1	36.6	3213.26
1990	−11.4	3.6	−7.8	2962.62

SOURCE: Data through 1988 is from Peter Thompson, Jeffrey Thompson, Bryan Allworthy, and David Roden, *BZW Equity-Gilt Study*, Barclays de Zoete Wedd, London, 1989. Data since 1988 is from Morgan Stanley Capital International.

1972, a peak-to-peak period. The 1954 and 1958 bull markets mirrored those of the United States in the same years.

In 1973 and 1974, the reality of high inflation, the first oil price shock, union strife, and the election of a Labour government brought about the worst crash of modern U.K. stock market history. From November 1972 to November 1974, the market fell 64.5 percent. The largest single-year gain in the twentieth century occurred in 1975, with a return of 143.6 percent. Stock prices bounced back from extremely depressed levels, and legislative measures were taken that would protect British firms from the most sustained inflationary period of the century.

From 1976 to 1981 the market posted consistent gains in nominal terms, but inflation remained very high, diluting the gains. With the reduction in inflation rates, the 1982 to 1989 period was one of the strongest, sustained expansions ever and is sometimes referred to as the British economic miracle. Prime Minister Margaret Thatcher's free-market policies boosted investor confidence and worker productivity. In 1990, as Thatcher left office, inflation was again an issue as were the dampening economic effects of the restrictive monetary actions (resulting in higher interest rates) used to fight it.

Interestingly, while the United States gained in power and influence over the period and Britain fell from world leadership, the U.K. stock market beat the U.S. stock market in local currency terms. Over the 1919 to 1990 period the compound annual return on British stocks was 11.74 percent compared with 10.10 percent for the United States. This higher return in the United Kingdom came at the expense of greater volatility and higher inflation. In real terms and after converting returns to a common currency, returns in the two countries are approximately the same.

Figure 8-3 shows the cumulative capital gain returns to an index of London Stock Exchange stocks from 1700 to 1918.[11] The magnitude of gain is fairly slight, which highlights the tremendous importance of reinvested dividends. A similar effect is observed when viewing U.S. equity returns over a similar time period.

---

[11]This data series was created by Columbia University Professor William Goetzmann ("Accounting for Taste: An Analysis of Art Returns Over Three Centuries," working paper, March 1990), who spliced together several independent series:

1700–1810: Philip Mirowski, "The Rise (and Retreat) of a Market: English Joint Stock Shares in the Eighteenth Century," *Journal of Economic History*, September 1981.

1812–1850: Arthur Gayer, W.W. Rostow, and Anna Schwartz, *The Growth and Fluctuation of the British Economy*, vol. 1, Oxford, 1953.

1851–1866: The Haekel Index quoted by Gayer, Rostow, and Schwartz.

1867–1914: K.C. Smith and F.G. Horne, "An Index Number of Securities 1867–1914," *London and Cambridge Economic Service*, Special Memorandum No. 37.

1915–1918: *Bankers Magazine*.

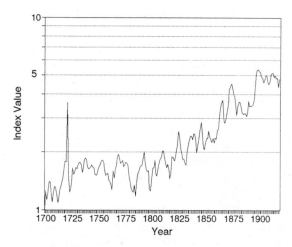

Figure 8-3. U.K. equity capital gains: 1700–1918 (year-end 1699 = £1.00). *(Source: William N. Goetzmann, "Accounting for Taste: An Analysis of Art Returns Over Three Centuries," working paper, March 1990.)*

Survivorship Bias in Measuring World Equity Returns

When countries are stable and the relations between interacting countries are also stable, investing abroad has about the same flavor as investing domestically. The major differences lie in the business mix of the foreign countries. Other differences, already documented, include exchange risk and information costs.

When countries or international relations are unstable, however, additional risks arise. A healthy business can have poor, or even catastrophic, returns to shareholders if the country where the business is located undergoes a revolution or loses a war. A parallel but different risk is that cross-border investors will lose their claims to an asset because of enmity between the investors' home country and the country they have invested in. As we noted earlier, this circumstance creates an investment risk that is not inherent in the asset.

Consider the case of a multinational investor contemplating the Japanese equity market in the late 1800s. In 1867 the Meiji restoration brought a procapitalist government into power and opened Japan to world trade. Japanese equity returns were high, like those of other high-growth nations of the time, such as the United States, Great Britain, and Argentina. Our investor would have fared quite well. By the end of World War II, however, most claims by non-Japanese investors to Japanese assets were void. To participate in the growth of Japan in the postwar period would have required the investor to pony up more capital after 1945. Even in economically "winning" countries with high returns, then, cross-border investors face the risk of losing their equity claims and not participating in the high returns.

A nineteenth-century investor who bet on the United States, Canada, or the United Kingdom would have been a prodigious forecaster of the world economy. Investors cannot ordinarily expect to have such foresight. In 1900, an international investor might well have bought Argentine, Austro-Hungarian, Russian, or German stocks instead of American, British, or Canadian issues. The Argentine stocks would have plummeted in value, as the development of that country, considered a rival of the United States at the turn of the century, unwound in later years. The Austro-Hungarian equities would have lost all their value by the end of World War I; Russian equity values disappeared shortly after the October 1917 revolution; and whatever German equities survived World War I did not make it reliably through World War II. Even if the economy survives a social upheaval, there is no guarantee that the market will survive. To achieve the high returns during a recovery may necessitate a reinvestment of capital. These stories illustrate vividly that although long-term investors may expect growth in the overall world economy, if they do not diversify, they run a substantial risk of choosing a "losing" country. Figure 8-4 schematically represents some actual outcomes for investors.

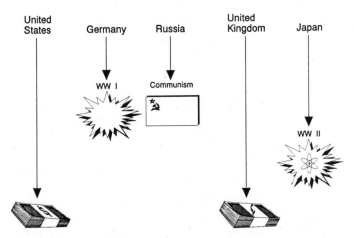

Figure 8-4. Outcomes of a diversified global portfolio of promising investments in 1900.

For these reasons, there is a definite survivorship bias in the returns presented in this book. Even the lowest-returning countries over the primary period studied, 1970–1990, have provided investors with the uninterrupted opportunity to try to make money in the market. In no case was all of an investor's money simply taken away by nonmarket forces. Moreover, the longer series, for the United States and United Kingdom, represent market results for two of the most successful countries in the history of the world.

This observation suggests that the return to all investors is lower than the returns shown here. The failures and confiscations simply did not make it into the data. A corollary observation is that the *expected* return on world assets, including failures and confiscations not foreseeable at this time, is somewhat lower than we would infer from the market results presented here.

9
Analyzing the World Equity Market: The Search for Higher Returns

Three Approaches to Analyzing Markets

Most investors try to achieve high returns by identifying and acquiring undervalued securities. Benjamin Graham and David Dodd provided rules for ascertaining value that have become the basis for traditional security analysis.[1] This approach, which we call *classical value theory*, assumes that because of the market's pricing inefficiency, an asset's market price fluctuates around its true value. A few renowned investors, like Lord Keynes, relied on psychological interpretation of market movements to take advantage of such fluctuations, whereas others, such as Warren Buffett, use their unusual insights about current and future economic value. Implicitly, these quests are attempts to assign a true value to a security, business, property, or activity.

The *efficient market hypothesis* provides a second approach. By emphasizing efficient markets and risk, modern portfolio theory has shifted some investors from value analysis to risk diversification. According to its most literal interpretation, skill at identifying value cannot be acquired. Except by luck, no investor can gain an advantage over others. Instead, investors should buy and hold a diversified set of securities. Market analysis consists of identifying the

---

[1]Benjamin Graham and David L. Dodd, *Security Analysis*, McGraw-Hill, New York, 1934.

investment opportunity set; ascertaining the risks, expected rewards, and other attributes of asset classes and the correlations among them; and matching portfolio choices to investor needs (see Chapters 3 and 4).

Many tenets of modern portfolio theory have been found to be consistent with the data. Few economists question that there are gains from diversification or that taking risk is rewarded on average. However, some economists doubt that *all* securities are priced appropriately. Because investors incur different costs and because capital markets are imperfect (see Chapter 3), the security prices may depart from their underlying values. In such cases, more knowledgeable investors can expect to outperform less knowledgeable ones.

We merge these two approaches, recognizing the existence of mispriced securities, but believe that because most markets are largely efficient, bargains are the exception rather than the rule. Furthermore, investors may need special skills to identify such securities. The cost of acquiring the skills and information necessary to identify bargain securities must be compared with the expected profits from transacting in these securities. Finally, this strategy emphasizes that investors must recognize the characteristics that make their situation unique and tailor their portfolios accordingly (see Chapter 3).

In our approach to investment analysis, identification of *groups* of securities that behave in unusual ways is thought to be more fruitful than studying stocks one by one. The best-known example is that stocks in small companies have had very different returns than those in larger companies. On average, the returns on small stocks have been higher, but the salient characteristic of these returns is not their excellence—there have been long periods of underperformance—but their relative independence. Our approach to analyzing securities emphasizes such differences among groups of stocks.

Securities Markets and the Scientific Method

In the classic treatise on the philosophy of science, *The Structure of Scientific Revolutions,* Thomas Kuhn noted that the basic assumptions describing the way the world works remain relatively fixed over long periods of time.[2] He calls such a set of assumptions a *paradigm.* The classical value approach to investing, in which it is taken for granted that securities are mispriced, is a scientific paradigm. A *paradigm shift* occurs when development

---

[2] Second edition, University of Chicago Press, Chicago, 1970.

of an alternative theory coincides with mounting empirical evidence that the paradigm is inappropriate. Modern portfolio theory is a paradigm; and the gradual acceptance of the basic tenets of modern portfolio theory (as compared to classical value theory) over the past generation, was a paradigm shift.

Kuhn refers to a piece of empirical evidence that contradicts a paradigm as an *anomaly* with respect to that paradigm. Systematic departures from the results predicted by modern portfolio theory are, consequently, anomalies with respect to that theory. While no competing theory exists that would cause us to reject modern portfolio theory, numerous anomalies with respect to the efficient market hypothesis and other tenets of modern portfolio theory have been documented in recent years.[3] This chapter reviews the principal anomalies that have been observed in markets around the world.

Valuation Anomalies

Cash Flow/Value Ratio

Many studies show an excess return from investing in stocks that appear underpriced from the standpoint of cash flows, earnings, or some other accounting-based measure of current corporate income. The low price/earnings ratio (P/E) effect is the best known of these effects. To better isolate the effect, we sorted the largest half of all NYSE stocks into quintiles each year over the period 1963 to 1988 according to their *cash flow/value* ratios. The numerator, cash flow, is constructed by adding deferred taxes back (because they are not a cash expense) to earnings before extraordinary items. We do not add back depreciation.[4] Because all company assets are required to generate the cash flows in the numerator, we use the market value of the stock plus debt (equivalent to the market value of the assets) as the denominator.

---

[3] The body of anomalous evidence against the efficient market hypothesis in particular, and modern portfolio theory in general, has caused some to characterize the current period as one of crisis in financial theory—the beginning of another paradigm shift. See Andrei Shleifer and Lawrence H. Summers, "Crowds and Prices: Toward a Theory of Inefficient Markets," Working Paper 282, University of Chicago, December 1989; and Simon M. Keane, "Paradox in the Current Crisis in Efficient Market Theory," *The Journal of Portfolio Management,* Winter 1991.

[4] Many researchers add back depreciation to earnings to arrive at cash flow. We do not, because doing so unrealistically assumes that the cash expense associated with the deterioration of physical assets is zero. To avoid deterioration, one must spend cash on maintenance of assets that eventually deteriorate anyway. Accounting depreciation assumes that the cash expense is distributed over all of the years in which the asset is used (up to some cutoff date), rather than when the cash expense is actually incurred. This is also unrealistic, but is a better representation of reality than assuming that depreciation is zero.

Table 9-1 shows the cash flow/value quintile returns. The high quintile—where current cash flows were purchased cheapest—had by far the highest returns. While the cash flow/value effect is quite consistent over time, some years (most notably 1969, 1980, and 1982) showed poor performance for the high cash flow/value quintile.

Price/Earnings Ratio

The earnings/price (E/P) ratio is analogous to the cash flow/value ratio, in that the numerator is a measure of a company's profits and the denominator is a measure of the cost required to obtain them. The price/earnings (P/E) ratio—the E/P ratio's reciprocal—is perhaps the most commonly used statistic for comparing the market's valuation of companies.[5] It is calculated by dividing a stock's price by its earnings per share over the last year.

Over the last two decades, P/E ratios had a direct relationship to return. Table 9-2 shows returns on deciles of NYSE stocks sorted according to their P/E ratios. Stocks with the lowest ratios were placed in the first decile; those stocks with the highest ratio, as well as those with undefined or negative ratios, were placed in the tenth decile. Stocks with low P/E ratios greatly outperformed the others during the period studied. As with the cash flow/value effect, high returns on low P/E stocks did not occur in all years.[6]

Table 9-1. Summary Statistics of NYSE Stocks Sorted into
Cash Flow/Value Quintiles (1963–1988)

Quintile	Compound annual return (%)	Standard deviation (%)	Ending index value
1 (lowest)	7.99	18.95	$7.37
2	8.91	18.02	9.21
3	10.35	18.73	12.96
4	13.33	18.46	25.88
5 (highest)	15.98	20.11	47.15

NOTE: Index = $1.00 at end of 1962.
SOURCE: Ibbotson Associates, Inc., Chicago, 1991.

[5]E/P ratios are easier to use than P/E ratios because the denominator of the E/P ratio is never zero or negative; prices are always positive numbers. To conform to convention, however, we focus on the P/E (not E/P) ratio in our discussion.

[6]For a fuller review of the P/E effect, see Roger G. Ibbotson, "Price-Earnings Ratios," in *The New Palgrave Dictionary of Money and Finance,* Macmillan, New York, 1992.

Table 9-2. Summary Statistics of NYSE Stocks Sorted into P/E Ratio Deciles (1967–1988)

Decile	Compound annual return (%)	Standard deviation (%)	Ending index value
1 (lowest)	16.26	21.63	$27.53
2	15.76	19.48	25.04
3	13.14	20.80	15.12
4	13.11	17.58	15.02
5	10.70	17.54	9.37
6	9.83	17.55	7.87
7	10.06	18.56	8.23
8	9.01	17.26	6.68
9	7.02	16.46	4.45
10 (highest)	6.64	27.13	4.11

NOTE: Index = $1.00 at end of 1966.

SOURCE: Ibbotson Associates, Inc., Chicago, 1991.

Dividend Yield

Table 9-3 displays the returns of NYSE stocks sorted into deciles according to their dividend yields. Stocks with the lowest dividend yields are sorted into the first decile, and stocks with the highest into the tenth decile, with all stocks being sorted at year-end. The value-weighted total return on each of these decile portfolios is then calculated.

Table 9-3. Summary Statistics of NYSE Stocks Sorted into Dividend-Yield Deciles (1927–1987)

Decile	Compound annual return (%)	Standard deviation (%)	Ending index value
1 (lowest)	9.80	37.09	$299.76
2	7.74	31.21	94.59
3	7.63	28.34	88.76
4	7.45	22.05	80.22
5	9.40	22.96	239.97
6	9.90	22.41	317.39
7	10.92	21.64	558.09
8	11.22	22.71	657.09
9	11.68	25.20	842.61
10 (highest)	10.51	28.23	443.88

NOTE: Index = $1.00 at end of 1926.

SOURCE: Ibbotson Associates, Inc., Chicago, 1991.

For the entire 1927 to 1987 period, there is a weak positive relation between dividend yield and total return. For certain periods, (1937–1950 and 1968–1977, in particular) the relation was much stronger. But since 1978 a stock's dividend yield has had no direct relation to its return. It is difficult to draw a conclusion about a process that varies so much over time.

In Chapter 8 we indicated that most equity return comes from the reinvestment of dividends. This is largely because corporations have traditionally paid large dividends to satisfy shareholders' desires for cash flows. Economically, it does not matter whether the corporation or the investor reinvests the dividend. If the corporation does so, the investor can expect a capital gain. For investors subject to personal tax, capital gains are preferable to dividends because capital gains can be deferred and realized when the investor chooses.[7] Investors in high-tax brackets should thus tend to avoid high-dividend stocks. Since dividends are double-taxed in the United States,[8] it is unclear why any dividends are paid. One common explanation is "signaling"—that is, by paying a dividend (and typically increasing the amount of the dividend), the corporation communicates its financial strength and confidence to investors. But the payment of a dividend may also be interpreted as telling investors that they have better opportunities to invest money than the corporation does!

An alternative explanation for the persistence of dividends in the face of high taxes is investors' need for current income. It may be very costly for small investors to sell shares of stock to create "homemade" dividends. Thus they prefer high-dividend stocks; that is, there is a clientele for dividends. Finally, Shefrin and Statman argue that investors simply have an irrational preference for cash dividends.[9]

Market/Book Ratio

Fundamental stock analysts often compare a firm's market value to its true, or economic, value. If the accounting measure of book value is related to true value, then the market/book ratio may indicate which stocks are over- and undervalued.[10] To test this, NYSE stocks are sorted into deciles accord-

---

[7]The attractiveness of capital gains is increased if capital gains are taxed at a lower rate than dividends.

[8]Dividend payments are not deductible for determination of income subject to the corporate income tax; then they are taxable as personal income to the recipient.

[9]Hersh Shefrin and Meir Statman, "Explaining Investor Preference for Cash Dividends," *Journal of Financial Economics,* June 1984.

[10]See Barr Rosenberg, Kenneth Reid, and Ronald Lanstein, "Persuasive Evidence of Market Inefficiency," *Journal of Portfolio Management,* Spring 1985 and Eugene F. Fama and Kenneth R. French, "The Cross Section of Expected Stock Returns," *Journal of Finance,* June 1992.

Table 9-4. Summary Statistics of NYSE Stocks Sorted into
Market/Book Value Ratio Deciles (1967–1987)

Decile	Compound annual return (%)	Standard deviation (%)	Ending index value
1 (lowest)	16.01	17.12	$22.61
2	17.11	21.47	27.58
3	14.68	21.12	17.75
4	12.84	20.31	12.64
5	11.08	18.69	9.09
6	9.77	17.69	7.08
7	10.88	19.06	8.75
8	9.32	20.61	6.49
9	7.94	17.26	4.98
10 (highest)	7.75	17.58	4.80

NOTE: Index = $1.00 at end of 1966.
SOURCE: Ibbotson Associates, Inc., Chicago, 1991.

ing to their market/book ratios. As shown in Table 9–4, stocks with low market/book ratios had substantially higher returns than high market/book ratios over the past decade.

Other Cross-Sectional Anomalies

The lengthy list of real or supposed anomalies seems only limited by the imagination of the investigators who continue to search for them. Among the characteristics that appear to be associated with excess returns are:[11]

- Neglect (a lack of wide following by security analysts)
- Low price/sales ratio
- Low absolute price
- Lack of earnings consensus by analysts
- Increase in consensus earnings expectations
- Earnings surprises (realizations very different from consensus expectations)

[11]Many of the following anomalies, in addition to those previously mentioned, were tested by Bruce Jacobs and Kenneth Levy, "Disentangling Equity Return Regularities: New Insights and Investment Opportunities," *Financial Analysts Journal*, May/June 1988. In addition, their article contains a comprehensive bibliography of the original works identifying these anomalies.

Market Capitalization and Return

United States

By far the most notable and well-documented anomaly in the stock market is the size effect. Much of a stock's return can be explained statistically by firm size, or more specifically, market capitalization. Rolf Banz first observed the small-stock effect for the United States when he sorted NYSE stocks into quintiles based on their market capitalization and calculated total returns for a value-weighted portfolio of the stocks in each quintile.[12] His results, covering the years 1926 to 1980, indicate that returns from the smallest quintile surpassed all other quintiles, as well as the S&P 500 and other large stock indexes. A dollar invested in the largest quintile grew to only about $109 after 55 years, while the same dollar invested in the smallest quintile grew to $524.

This 5-to-1 ratio of ending wealth did not hold up over the 1980s. Beginning in mid-1983, small stocks dramatically underperformed larger issues, causing the small-stock effect to be questioned by many market observers. It should be noted, however, that underperformance by small stocks has occurred over long periods before, in 1926–1931, 1951–1957, and 1969–1973. Thus the size effect is best described as small stocks behaving *differently* from large stocks, with serial correlation (an indication of pre-dictability) being the difference. The small-stock premium, or differential return between small and large stocks, has a serial correlation of .38, higher than that of almost every other capital market return series. This means that the premium has had lengthy "runs" of winning and losing years relative to large stocks. We also believe, despite the experience of the 1980s, that there is a positive premium (that small stocks outperform on average over the long run). Figure 9-1 illustrates how $1 invested in small and large (S&P 500) U.S. stocks at the end of 1925 grew over the subsequent 65 years. The small stock investment finished 1990 at $1277.45, while the S&P 500 portfolio ended the period at $517.50.[13] The year-by-year small stock premium is charted in Figure 9-2.

[12]Rolf W. Banz, "The Relationship Between Market Value and Return of Common Stocks," *Journal of Financial Economics*, November 1981.

[13]For the 1926 to 1981 period, small stocks are represented by Banz's historical series, where small stocks are those comprising the lowest quintile of NYSE stocks as ranked by equity market capitalization. Starting in 1982, the small stock return is the total return achieved by the

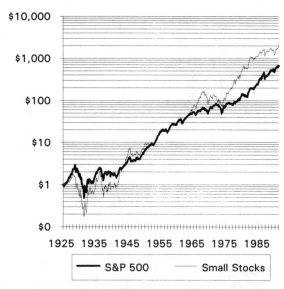

Figure 9-1. Growth of $1 invested in large and small U.S. stocks: January 1926 to September 1991. (*Source:* Stocks, Bonds, Bills, and Inflation 1991 Yearbook™, *Ibbotson Associates, Inc. Chicago [annually updates work by Roger G. Ibbotson and Rex A. Sinquefield].)*

Europe

The size effect is not limited to the United States. For the United Kingdom, Elroy Dimson and Paul Marsh found that the compound annual return for small stocks exceeded that of large stocks by 7 percent per year over the 1955 to 1984 period.[14] Mario Levis has determined that, much like the U.S. small-stock premium, the U.K. premium is quite volatile.[15]

In Continental Europe, studies of the size effect have been conducted for the major markets. Bergstrom, Frashure, and Chisholm report a large size

---

Dimensional Fund Advisors Small Company Fund. This fund is constructed by purchasing in market-value-weighted proportions all of the stocks in the ninth and tenth deciles (i.e., the lowest quintile) of the NYSE plus AMEX and OTC stocks with the same or less capitalization as the upper bound of the ninth NYSE decile. Stocks are sold if they become larger than the largest stock in the *eighth* NYSE decile. Stocks that are below $10 million in market value or in bankruptcy are not purchased, but they are not sold if they fall under $10 million or become bankrupt.

[14]Elroy Dimson and Paul R. Marsh, "Risk, Return, and Company Size Effects on the London Stock Exchange: The Thirty Year Record," working paper, London Business School.

[15]Mario Levis, "Are Small Firms Big Performers?", *The Investment Analyst,* 1985.

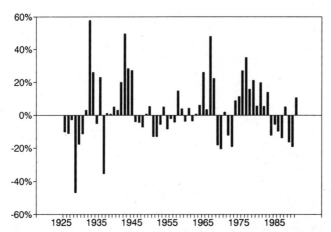

Figure 9-2. U.S. yearly small-stock premium: 1926 to 1991. (*Source:* Stocks, Bonds, Bills, and Inflation 1991 Yearbook™, *Ibbotson Associates, Inc., Chicago [annually updates work by Roger G. Ibbotson and Rex A. Sinquefield].)*

effect for France but not for Germany.[16] Specifically, over the period 1975 to 1989, French small-company stocks returned 32.3 percent per year, compared with 23.5 percent for large companies. For Germany, small stocks edged out larger issues by a margin of 22.7 to 22.1 percent over the same period.

Japan

Yasushi Hamao studied the size effect in Japan over the period 1971 to 1988. Over this period the compound annual return for all large (Tokyo Stock Exchange section I) stocks was 18.6 percent, while the smallest quintile of section I stocks returned 23.7 percent.[17] However, section II stocks, which are described as small, young, or troubled companies, did not perform well. This result suggests that characteristics other than size cause section II stocks to behave differently from the small stocks listed on section I of the TSE.

Figure 9-3 shows the growth of an investment of ¥100 at the end of 1970 in large (all TSE-I) and small (smallest-quintile TSE-I) Japanese stocks. This

[16]Gary L. Bergstrom, Ronald D. Frashure, and John R. Chisholm, "Stock Return Anomalies in Non-U.S. Markets," in Robert Z. Aliber and Brian R. Bruce, eds., *Global Portfolios*, Richard D. Irwin, Inc., Homewood, Ill. 1991.

[17]Yasushi Hamao, "Japanese Stocks, Bonds, and Inflation, 1973–1987," *The Journal of Portfolio Management*, Winter 1989; updated in Yasushi Hamao and Roger G. Ibbotson, *Stocks, Bonds, and Inflation Japan 1989 Yearbook*, Ibbotson Associates, Chicago, 1989.

Figure 9-3. Growth of ¥100 invested in large and small Tokyo Stock Exchange section I stocks: January 1971 to September 1990. (*Source: Yasushi Hamao and Roger G. Ibbotson,* Stocks, Bonds, and Inflation Japan 1989 Yearbook, *Ibbotson Associates, Chicago, 1989. Updated by I/IDEAS Stocks, Bonds, and Inflation Japan data module, Ibbotson Associates, Inc., Chicago, 1991.*)

investment grew to ¥1410 in large stocks and ¥3839 in small stocks by September 1990. Because of the appreciation of the yen against most other currencies over this period, a non-Japanese (say, U.S.) investor in either of these categories would have done substantially better.

Investing in Small Stocks

One explanation for the higher returns of small stocks is that investors must be compensated for the higher costs associated with finding information with which to evaluate small stocks, and their higher transaction costs. Investors can avoid information costs, however, by buying no information about stocks except their size. A diversified, index-like portfolio of small stocks would then be expected to beat the market.[18] Several mutual fund

[18]For a discussion of small-company diversification in an international context, see Rex A. Sinquefield, "The Gains from International Small-Company Diversification," in Robert Z. Aliber and Brian R. Bruce, eds., *Global Portfolios*, Richard D. Irwin, Inc., Homewood, Ill., 1991.

groups offer diversified portfolios of small-company stocks in the United States, the United Kingdom, Japan, and Continental Europe. [19]

Seasonality of the Size Effect

Much of the excess return on small stocks has been earned in the first few trading days of January of each year. Donald B. Keim of the University of Pennsylvania divided stocks on both the NYSE and AMEX into quintiles based on market capitalization.[20] The quintile with the smallest companies had large positive premiums in January, compared with negative premiums for large stocks. After adjusting for risk, Keim concludes that in January, small stocks generally had earned a 15 percent premium, defined as the average excess return per day, multiplied by the number of trading days in the month. Since this premium is larger than the premium for the whole year, Keim concludes that the *entire* small stock effect has been a January effect. Ibbotson Associates, studying a longer time period and not adjusting for risk, found that more than all of the small stock premium has occurred in January and February.[21] It is possible that some of the small-stock excess return that actually occurred in January was measured in February because of infrequent trading.[22] Figure 9-4 shows the average returns on small and large stocks for each month of the year for the 1926 to 1990 period.

According to Marc Reinganum, the January effect on small stocks may be limited to the first five trading days of the year—a "turn of the year" effect. He finds that the first trading day in January usually has provided the holder of the smallest quintile of stocks a 4 percent premium, the second day a 2.5 percent premium, and the third day a 1.75 percent premium.[23] These

[19]While it is sometimes alleged that small stocks do not earn their higher returns after accounting for investor costs, Rex A. Sinquefield ("Are Small Stock Returns Achievable?," *Financial Analysts Journal*, January/February 1991) points out that actual, small-stock based portfolios do achieve the returns of their benchmarks. Differences in these actual returns appear to be related to management style. Portfolios that attempt to maintain perfect index-like composition have the lowest returns while those that attempt to minimize trading costs at the expense of perfect composition have the highest returns.

[20]Donald B. Keim, "Size-Related Anomalies and Stock Return Seasonality: Further Empirical Evidence," *Journal of Financial Economics*, March 1983.

[21]*Stocks, Bonds, Bills and Inflation: 1991 Yearbook*, Ibbotson Associates, Chicago, 1991, Exhibit 46 (p. 114). The period studied is 1926 to 1990.

[22]Consider the extreme example of a stock that trades once a month, on the first day of each month. The return from December 1 to January 1 is called the return for January, because the January 1 quote is the closing quote for the month of January. The return from January 1 to February 1, which contains the small-stock premium for January, is correspondingly called the return for February.

[23]Marc R. Reinganum, "The Anomalous Stock Market Behavior of Small Firms in January: Empirical Tests for Tax-Loss Selling Effects," *Journal of Financial Economics*, June 1983.

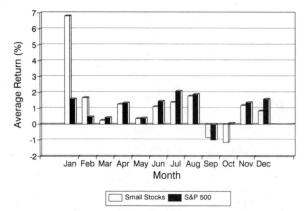

Figure 9-4. U.S. small-stock seasonality: average monthly return, 1926 to 1990. (*Source:* Stocks, Bonds, Bills, and Inflation 1991 Yearbook™, *Ibbotson Associates, Inc., Chicago [annually updates work by Roger G. Ibbotson and Rex A. Sinquefield].*)

magnitudes of single day premiums are almost unbelievable. Analysts are unsure why small stocks have behaved this way. Some attribute the effect to measurement error or a statistical artifact of some kind. Others believe that investors sell stocks at year-end to realize tax losses and repurchase the shares in January, forcing prices up.

The discovery of seasonal anomalies in the United States has set off a surge of activity to locate similar effects in foreign markets. Brown, Keim, Kleidon, and Marsh examined small stock returns for Australia.[24] They found two seasonalities—one corresponding to the end of the Australian tax year, which occurs in June, and the other in January, corresponding to the end of the U.S. tax year and apparently attributable to American investors in Australian stocks. Reinganum and Shapiro looked at the United Kingdom and encountered seasonalities in April (the end of the U.K. tax year), and also in January.[25] Berges, McConnell, and Schlarbaum found a January effect in Canada, including one in years prior to 1972 when Canada did not have a capital gains tax.[26] Again, this may be attributable to the year-end tax behavior of U.S. investors.

[24]Philip Brown, Donald B. Keim, Allan W. Kleidon, and Terry A. Marsh, "Stock Return Seasonalities and the Tax-loss Selling Hypothesis: Analysis of the Arguments and the Australian Evidence," *Journal of Financial Economics*, June 1983.

[25]Marc R. Reinganum and Alan C. Shapiro, "Taxes and Stock Return Seasonalities: Evidence from the London Stock Exchange," *Journal of Business*, April 1987.

[26]Angel Berges, John J. McConnell, and Gary G. Schlarbaum, "The Turn-of-the-Year in Canada," *Journal of Finance*, March 1984.

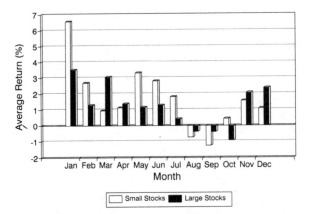

Figure 9-5. Japan small-stock seasonality: average monthly return, 1971 to 1990. *(Source: I/IDEAS Stocks, Bonds, and Inflation Japan data module, Ibbotson Associates, Inc., Chicago, 1991.)*

In Japan, small-stock returns are abnormally high in January, February, May, June, July, and October. Figure 9-5 shows the average returns on Japanese small and large stocks for each month of the year for the 1971 to 1990 period.[27]

Seasonalities in the General Market

Unlike small stocks, large stocks have not exhibited a January effect in any major country. However, other peculiarities in the timing of stock returns have been observed.

Mean returns on the market have been negative on Monday, but positive on all other days. In the United States this effect has been documented for both S&P stocks and actively traded OTC stocks.[28] The frequency with which this result has been replicated in U.S. markets has inspired other researchers to look at other exchanges around the world. Condoyanni,

---

[27]Data used to construct Figure 9-5 are from Yasushi Hamao and Roger G. Ibbotson, *Stocks, Bonds, and Inflation Japan 1989 Yearbook,* Ibbotson Associates, Chicago, 1989, updated by the authors. The seasonality of the Japanese size effect was first documented in Kiyoshi Kato and James S. Schallheim, "Seasonal and Size Anomalies in the Japanese Stock Market," *Journal of Financial and Quantitative Analysis,* 1985.

[28]Frank Cross, "Price Markets on Fridays and Mondays," *Financial Analysts Journal,* November/December 1973; Donald B. Keim and Robert F. Stambaugh, "A Further Investigation of the Weekend Effect in Stock Returns," *Journal of Finance,* July 1984.

O'Hanlon, and Ward document the effect in Australia, Canada, France, Japan, Singapore, and the United Kingdom.[29] Other seasonalities, including time-of-the-month and intraday effects, have been noted by researchers.

Initial Public Offerings

United States

When privately held firms want to raise capital from the public, they retain an investment banker to issue the new security in a public offering; this security is called an *unseasoned new issue,* or *initial public offering* (IPO). New issues are potentially profitable to investors because there are periods in which these securities have predictable high returns in the initial period (measured until the end of the first calendar month) after the stock "goes public." Figure 9-6 shows the monthly average excess return of new issues from 1960 to 1987. These excess returns are a measure of the amount by which new issues are underpriced.

Figure 9-7 shows the number of IPOs occurring each month over the same period. New issues occur in giant waves lasting several years ("hot issue markets"), interspersed with periods having almost no new issues ("cold issue markets"). Three large waves are evident in the Figure 9-7: 1960 to 1962, 1967 to 1972, and 1980 to 1987. After the 1987 crash, the IPO market entered a cold phase, but it has heated up again recently.

If Figures 9-6 and 9-7 are compared, one can see that IPO volume has lagged underpricing by roughly 6 to 12 months. Table 9-5 contains the year-ly data for both the number of issues and average initial return. One expla-nation for this lag is that companies prefer to offer their stock when they believe the market is expecting IPOs to be underpriced and is therefore eager to invest in IPOs. Roger G. Ibbotson and Jeffrey Jaffe have argued that it is better to issue in cold markets because the issue price is more likely to be closer to its after-market price.[30]

Many ideas have been offered to explain the underpricing phenomenon. Table 9-6 breaks all the issuing firms down by annual sales and illustrates that smaller firms are more likely to offer higher returns. Smaller-firm stock prices are generally priced below $3 per share and are usually quite risky, thus implying that underpricing is a form of risk compensation.

---

[29]Leda Condoyanni, John O'Hanlon, and Charles Ward, "Weekend Effects in Stock Market Returns: International Evidence," in Elroy Dimson, ed., *Stock Market Anomalies,* Cambridge University Press, Cambridge, 1988.

[30]Roger G. Ibbotson and Jeffrey F. Jaffe, "Hot Issue Markets," *Journal of Finance,* September 1975.

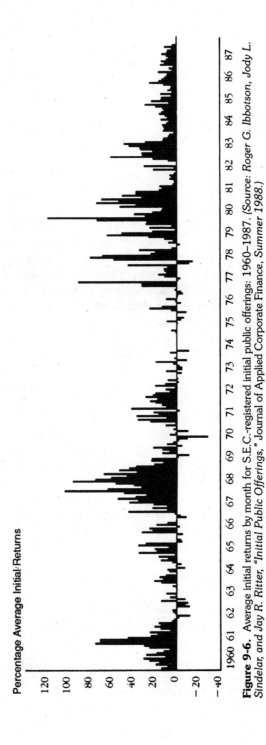

Figure 9-6. Average initial returns by month for S.E.C.-registered initial public offerings: 1960–1987. (Source: *Roger G. Ibbotson, Jody L. Sindelar, and Jay R. Ritter, "Initial Public Offerings," Journal of Applied Corporate Finance, Summer 1988.*)

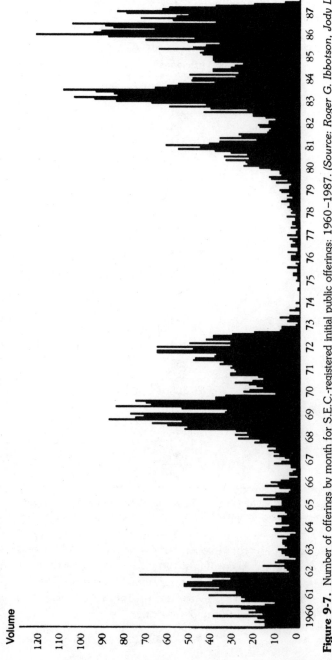

Figure 9-7. Number of offerings by month for S.E.C.-registered initial public offerings: 1960–1987. (*Source: Roger G. Ibbotson, Jody L. Sindelar, and Jay R. Ritter, "Initial Public Offerings," Journal of Applied Corporate Finance, Summer 1988.*)

Table 9-5. Initial Public Offerings: Yearly Volume and Average Initial Returns (1960–1987)

Year	Number of offerings	Average initial return (%)
1960	269	17.83
1961	435	34.11
1962	298	−1.61
1963	83	3.93
1964	97	5.32
1965	146	12.75
1966	85	7.06
1967	100	37.67
1968	368	55.86
1969	780	12.53
1970	358	−0.67
1971	391	21.16
1972	562	7.51
1973	105	−17.82
1974	9	−6.98
1975	14	−1.86
1976	34	−2.90
1977	40	21.02
1978	42	25.66
1979	103	24.61
1980	259	49.36
1981	438	16.76
1982	198	20.31
1983	848	20.79
1984	516	11.52
1985	507	12.36
1986	953	9.99
1987	630	10.39
Total	8668	16.37

SOURCE: Roger G. Ibbotson, Jody L. Sindelar, and Jay R. Ritter, "Initial Public Offerings," *Journal of Applied Corporate Finance,* Summer 1988.

Kevin Rock suggests that insiders have a better idea of a new stock's true value than outsiders.[31] Accordingly, the underwriting investment bank allocates the new issues among insiders and outsiders without knowing who is in what group, but insiders know to line up for the relatively underpriced issues, leaving outsiders with the poorer ones.

[31]Kevin Rock, "Why New Issues are Underpriced," *Journal of Financial Economics,* March 1986.

Table 9-6. Initial Public Offerings Annual Sales and Average Initial Returns (1975–1984)

Annual sales	Number of offerings	Average initial return (%)
$0	386	42.9
$1–999,999	678	31.4
$1,000,000–4,999,999	353	14.3
$5,000,000–14,999,999	347	10.7
$15,000,000–24,999,999	182	6.5
$25,000,000 and larger	493	5.3
All	2439	20.7

SOURCE: Roger G. Ibbotson, Jody L. Sindelar, and Jay R. Ritter, "Initial Public Offerings," *Journal of Applied Corporate Finance,* Summer 1988.

If there are not enough insiders to go around, underwriters depend on outsiders to buy up the remaining total of the new issues. Outsiders demand a competitive return and get stuck with the less desirable issues. These relatively bad issues must be at least fairly priced to attract outsiders. If the bad issues are fairly priced at issuance, then the good issues must be underpriced, making the whole market underpriced on average. This hypothesis may explain why average new issues are underpriced at the start and, therefore, have had good initial performance. It does not explain why firms would willingly issue such underpriced securities, although possibly they have a strong desire to bring their offerings to a successful completion.

Richard Carter and Steven Manaster extend Rock's work by positing that investors allocate their information gathering resources to analyzing the riskiest of IPOs; therefore, these IPOs have the largest concentration of "smart" money. As a result, there is a positive correlation between the proportion of informed investor participation and the degree of underpricing. Since underpricing harms the issuer, low-risk firms will try to communicate their relative risk standing by selecting prestigious underwriters who do not need to underprice aggressively to bring an IPO to a successful conclusion.[32]

IPOs Over the Long Run

The University of Illinois's Jay Ritter has continued the research into the peculiar performance of IPOs by examining their behavior over the period

[32]Richard Carter and Steven Manaster, "Initial Public Offerings and Underwriter Reputation," *Journal of Finance,* September 1990.

from the close of trading on their first day of public trading to their 3-year anniversaries.[33] He finds that issuing firms typically have underperformed a matching portfolio during this 3-year window, with companies going public during the "hottest" years faring the worst over the long run. He concludes that investors are periodically overly optimistic about IPOs, and firms take advantage of these situations.

IPOs Outside the United States

Many of the anomalies discussed in this chapter were first identified in the U.S. market, which is the most heavily researched equity market in the world. Such discoveries have inspired scholars to look at other markets to see if similar effects can be unearthed. Jay Ritter compiled IPO performance statistics for several of the world's equity markets, as reported in Table 9-7.[34]

He points out that government regulation in some countries has forced firms to issue equity at a lower price than the company otherwise would. In some privatizations or denationalizations (most notably in the United Kingdom under former Prime Minister Margaret Thatcher), governments deliberately sell state assets at a low price to encourage a broad individual shareholder base.

Performance of Newly Exchange-Listed Stocks

Yet another set of anomalies concerns the performance of newly exchange-listed stocks. The stock returns of companies have been abnormally high in the 52-week period prior to the announcement of an impending listing on an exchange, during the announcement week, and during the period between announcement and actual listing.[35] A further peculiarity is that in the month following an exchange listing, stocks have had a reversal, or neg-

---

[33]Jay R. Ritter, "The Long-Run Performance of Initial Public Offerings," *Journal of Finance*, March 1991.

[34]Jay R. Ritter, "IPO Underpricing Around the World," in Stephen A. Ross, Randolph W. Westerfield, and Bradford D. Jordan, *Fundamentals of Corporate Finance*, Richard D. Irwin, Inc., Homewood, Ill., 1991, p. 417. See also Roger G. Ibbotson and Jay R. Ritter, "Initial Public Offerings," in Robert A. Jarrow, Vojislav Maksimovic, and William T. Ziemba, eds., *North-Holland Handbooks of Operations Research and Management Science: Finance*, North-Holland, Amsterdam, forthcoming.

[35]Gary C. Sanger and John J. McConnell, "Stock Exchange Listing, Firm Value, and Security Market Efficiency: The Impact of NASDAQ," *Journal of Financial and Quantitative Analysis*, March 1986.

Table 9-7. International Initial Public Offering Performance

Country	Sample size	Time period	Average initial return (%)
Canada	100	1971–83	9.3
France	131	1983–86	4.2
Germany	97	1977–87	21.5
Hong Kong	34	1979–85	10.5
Japan	114	1979–84	51.9
Korea	103	1988	163.5
Malaysia	34	1979–84	149.3
Singapore	43	1978–84	38.1
Sweden	55	1983–85	40.5
United Kingdom	297	1965–75	9.7
	54	1986	6.9
United States	8668	1960–87	16.4

SOURCE: Jay Ritter, "IPO Underpricing Around the World," in Stephen A. Ross, Randolph W. Westerfield, and Bradford D. Jordan, *Fundamentals of Corporate Finance*, Richard D. Irwin, Inc., Homewood, Ill., 1991.

ative return. John McConnell and Gary Sanger find that stocks declined 0.78 percent in the month following listing and declined 1.45 percent after adjusting for the performance of the market.[36] This behavior may have been due to temporary demand for the stock as it became eligible for inclusion in certain types of portfolios that held only exchange-listed stocks. A related effect is the S&P inclusion effect, which is the abnormal return on stocks as they are brought into the S&P 500 index. It is not known whether this effect is followed by a reversal. There is also some evidence that S&P 500 stocks have outperformed comparable stocks that are not in the S&P 500, owing (it is thought) to demand from a growing pool of index funds.[37]

Conclusion

This chapter has catalogued the search for exceptions to strict efficiency in the stock market. In particular, we have surveyed the literature for systematic stock selection strategies that have a reasonable expectation of beating

[36]John J. McConnell and Gary C. Sanger, "The Puzzle in Post-Listing Common Stock Returns," *Journal of Finance*, March 1987.

[37]A review of the literature on the S&P inclusion effect is in Roger G. Ibbotson and Reid W. Click, "The S&P Inclusion Effect: A New Assessment," Ibbotson Associates working paper, Chicago, 1990.

the market and do not require exposure to large costs. We conclude with three observations. First, any team of investigators with a history of financial data will find some systematic rule that would have beat the market. Whether this finding is repeatable in the future or in another market is an entirely different issue. Second, when regular anomalies are found, the market will incorporate that information and investors will begin implementing strategies designed to exploit that anomaly. While it may be possible to beat the market for a while, this behavior will serve to reduce the magnitude of the anomaly. Third, if an anomaly is found and persists, it may be due to market inefficiency, or alternatively, to unidentified costs that inhibit or prevent investors from exploiting the opportunity. Despite these caveats, it is rational and potentially very rewarding for active equity investors to continue the search for higher returns.

PART 4

The Fixed-Income Market

10
Bond Markets Around the World

The writhing silhouettes were the arms and torsos of young men, few of them older than forty. They had their suit jackets off. They were moving about in an agitated manner and sweating early in the morning and shouting, which created the roar. It was the sound of well-educated young white men baying for money on the bond market.[1]

Today's bond market, as described in Tom Wolfe's colorful prose, is one of the most active, carefully analyzed, and finely tuned markets of any kind. Although lending to corporations, governments, and homeowners does not sound intrinsically fascinating, the remarkable mathematical properties of bonds make the bond business the most quantitative of the capital market disciplines.

How times have changed. About 70 years ago, another literary character, the narrator of F. Scott Fitzgerald's *The Great Gatsby*, "decided to go East and learn the bond business." But what about the market attracted him? A young man must work even if he is rich, but the work should be dignified and easy and, above all, safe. And it was so in the spring of 1922. No business was safer than bonds, whose yields moved only within the astonishingly narrow range of three-tenths of 1 percent from 1922 to 1929. The bond business did not require much technical expertise, but it was very important to have a good tennis arm.

Today, bonds are often as volatile as stocks during some periods. It is a dull *month* when long-term bond yields move only three-tenths of 1 percent.

---

[1] Excerpt from *The Bonfire of the Vanities* by Tom Wolfe. © 1987 by Tom Wolfe. Reprinted by permisson of Farrar, Straus, & Giroux, Inc.

The capitalization of the world bond market and the diversity and complexity of instruments is huge and continues to grow. The aggregate world bond market value has grown from $700 billion in 1966 to $11 trillion today, a growth rate of 12 percent per year. All of this growth comes from net new issues, unlike the equity market in which much of the capitalization growth comes from capital appreciation of existing shares. Finally, because of the size and number of countries participating, Tom Wolfe's depiction of Wall Street is recreated around the world as traders swarm about bond trading floors, arbitraging tiny price discrepancies.

Bond Theory

Despite the complexity associated with the bond market, a bond itself is simple and on the surface might appear a bit dull when compared with stocks. A share of stock, after all, represents a piece of a company's wealth. After subtracting the company's debt, this implies that an evaluation of a stock's worth involves an evaluation of the entire company's worth. An ordinary bond is a decidedly unexotic agreement that merely entitles one party to make and another to receive a series of cash flows.[2] Yet while differences among forms of equity are small, there is a plethora of bond types; innovative financial engineers are creating new fixed-income securities almost faster than lawyers can prepare the prospectuses.

The reason for the variety of bond types lies in their cash flow structure. Investors have strong preferences for specific levels and timing of cash flows. Knowing this, financial intermediaries buy securities, carve up their cash flows, and resell the pieces to those investors who value them most. Intermediaries make money from this activity because the pieces can be sold for more than the whole. For example, in the mortgage market intermediaries buy securities backed by the payments from a pool of mortgages and issue new interest-only and principal-only securities called *IOs* and *POs*, respectively. The IO holder is entitled to only the interest portion of the payments made by the homeowners while the PO holder is entitled to only the principal portion of the payments. These securities will be examined in

---

[2]Fixed-rate bonds, when classified by cash flow structure, can be divided into three categories: *Coupon bonds* pay a fixed dollar amount of interest called the *coupon rate*. Coupon payments are made to bondholders periodically according to a schedule, until maturity, at which time the principal is repaid. *Zero coupon*, or original-issue discount, bonds are issued below par value, or at a discount. The income return on a "zero" comes from the increase in principal value resulting from the specified accrual of interest. *Annuities*, for example, home mortgages, have level payments over a finite term and do not have a "balloon" payment of principal at maturity. This payment structure results in each payment consisting of both principal and interest.

more detail later, but suffice it to say at this point that these are very different securities designed to satisfy different investor preferences. Issuers are also getting into the act (cutting out the intermediaries) by selling a wide variety of fixed-income instruments directly to the same clienteles. The existence of so many fixed-income forms is testimony to the wide variety of investor demand for different cash flow streams.

To get a feel for the tremendous depth of analysis possible on a bond, let's start from the simple proposition that a bond's market price is usually not equal to its face value. This occurs because a bond's market price is the discounted (present) value of its future cash flows, where the discount rate is the current market yield and thus is usually different from the bond's coupon rate. A bond sells for face value when the discount rate, or yield, is equal to the coupon rate; more than face value when the yield is lower than the coupon rate; and less than face value when the yield is higher. (Thus zero-coupon bonds always sell below face value until they mature.) From this set of simple facts we can derive a number of remarkable properties.

Expected Return

As suggested above, a bond's yield is its internal rate of return, or the discount rate that equates the present value of future promised income to the bond's current market price.[3] The yield measures the expected total return—including both income and capital gain or loss—on the overall investment.[4] No other financial instrument has such an easily observed or intuitively understandable expected return.

Duration

Bond mathematics also provides an accurate measure of the sensitivity of a bond's price to movements in its current market yield. This measure is related to the bond's *duration,* which is the present-value-weighted average time that bond holders have money owed to them, taking into account both coupon and principal payments. The weight of each time-to-receipt is the present value of each cash flow expected to be received as a percentage of the present value of the bond as a whole. Since duration is a measure of time, it is usually denominated in years (to receipt of one's money). For a given coupon rate and bond price, the duration increases much more slowly than the maturity in years. Also, other things being equal, a bond has a

---

[3]The term yield is used throughout to refer to yield-to-maturity.

[4]Strictly speaking, this holds only if there is no possibility of default, interest rates are constant through time, and the same rate is used to discount all payments. In fact, bondholders may demand different rates over different future periods.

shorter duration the higher its coupon rate. This is because large coupons have larger weights relative to the principal amount.

Since the extent to which bond prices are affected by changes in the associated interest rates depends on the length of time investors have their funds committed, duration (when properly modified) also measures the interest rate sensitivity of a bond. Modified duration, or the interest rate sensitivity of bond price, is duration divided by the quantity 1 plus the bond yield.

Like all tools of measurement, duration must be used carefully. Since a bond's duration falls as its yield rises, it overestimates the fall in bond prices as interest rates rise and underestimates the rise in prices when interest rates fall. This property, known as *convexity*, needs to be accounted for when interest rates change by more than a small amount. Stated another way, the convexity of a bond is the extent to which the *duration* changes with interest rates. An ordinary bond has positive convexity: *rising* interest rates shorten the duration. Mortgages and callable bonds have negative convexity: borrowers are motivated to prepay the loan when interest rates fall so they can refinance their borrowing at a lower rate. To the holder of negatively convex bonds, *falling* interest rates shorten the duration. The difficulty presented by mortgages is that the rate of prepayment is unknown. Mortgages are prepaid for a variety of reasons that have proven to be difficult to model. Consequently, the degree of negative convexity is a source of risk in mortgage-backed securities.

Factors Influencing Yield

The amazing (or confounding) property of a bond's yield is that it summarizes, in one number, many disparate economic influences. Consequently, bonds with identical yields can be otherwise very different. This section looks at the effects various variables have on a bond's yield.

Term Structure of Interest Rates

Because long-term bonds typically have a greater duration and consequently larger price fluctuations than shorter bonds, one might guess that long-maturity bonds would provide a risk premium relative to shorter bonds, that is, a higher yield. Empirically, investors on average demand a higher yield on longer bonds when the bonds are identical in all other respects. The yield curve, or term structure of interest rates, describes the way that rates vary with duration or time to maturity. Yield curves on securities with no default risk typically have three shapes:

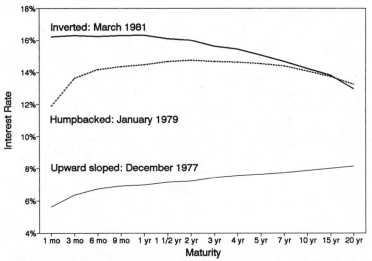

Figure 10-1. Yield curve shapes. *(Source: Thomas S. Coleman, Lawrence Fisher, and Roger G. Ibbotson, U.S. Treasury Yield Curves, Moody's Investors Service, New York, 1989.)*

1. Upward sloping (the most common), where long-term rates exceed short-term rates

2. Downward sloping or inverted, where short-term rates exceed long-term rates

3. Humpbacked, where intermediate-term rates exceed both short- and long-term rates

Examples of each shape (using actual month-end yields) are graphed in Figure 10-1.

Three major hypotheses have been proposed to explain these yield-curve shapes. The pure expectations hypothesis states that short- and long-term bond portfolios are perfect substitutes. The differences in their yields represent a forecast, by investors, of changes in the future level of interest rates.[5]

The expectations theory is challenged by proponents of the liquidity preference and preferred habitat hypotheses, who argue that there are well-identified clienteles for different maturities of bonds, so that short- and long-term bonds are imperfect substitutes.

[5]Peter S. Spiro, in *Real Interest Rates and Investment and Borrowing Strategy*, Quorum Books, New York, 1989, pp. 96–101, notes that the yield curve typically sloped downward throughout the nineteenth century, and in the twentieth century until 1930. Such behavior is consistent with investors expecting declining inflation on average over time, in the context of the pure expectations hypothesis.

The liquidity preference hypothesis asserts that the price risk of longer bonds is more burdensome to investors than the reinvestment risk of rolling over short-term bills and that the higher yields of long bonds are a market-determined compensation for this burden. This hypothesis predicts that even if interest and inflation rates were expected to remain unchanged, the yield curve would slope upward. Cases of yield curve inversion are thus a strong indication that the market expects rates to decline.

The preferred habitat hypothesis is a version of the liquidity preference hypothesis that asserts that the market is dominated by investors with very specific maturity preferences. Investors can only be induced to hold bonds outside their preferred habitat by offering them a substantially higher yield. If yields for a particular maturity are abnormally low (that is, bond prices are high), then a strong demand for instruments of that maturity is implied.

Credit Risk

Other than time to maturity, credit or default risk is usually the most important characteristic of a bond. Bonds with default risk must have yields high enough to cover the probability of default and provide compensation for being exposed to the risk. Since U.S. government bonds are considered to be default-free, the difference in yield between a bond subject to default risk and a U.S. government bond with otherwise identical characteristics is typically taken as the market's assessment of that default risk. The difference in yields (yield spread) between these two bonds may thus be regarded as a default premium.

Tax Status

Not all bonds receive identical tax treatment by governments. Since taxable investors are obviously concerned with after-tax returns, a bond's tax status will influence its price and yield. For example, in the United States, corporate bond income is typically treated as ordinary income at the federal, state, and local levels; municipal (state and local) government bond income is exempt from federal tax; and federal bond income is exempt from state and local taxes. With equal risk considerations, the tax-exempt status of municipal bonds makes them attractive to investors in high tax brackets and the market thus prices them to have lower before-tax yields.

Option Provisions

Some bonds are issued with the provision that the issuer may pay back the principal or "call" the bonds prior to maturity. Bonds are likely to be called if the issuer observes that interest rates have dropped dramatically and that a new issue at a lower rate would substantially reduce interest expense. Thus, *callable* bonds have higher yields (lower prices) than those of comparable, noncallable bonds to compensate bondholders for the risk that bond proceeds might have to be reinvested at lower rates before maturity.[6]

A mortgage may be thought of as a callable bond issued by a homeowner. Any number of conditions may cause a homeowner to prepay (or call). For example, if interest rates fall enough, it will pay for the homeowner to incur refinancing costs in order to lock in lower interest payments. A family that is moving is likely to sell their house and pay off the mortgage, regardless of the interest rate environment. These prepayments motivated by individual behavior such as moving often make it much more difficult to value this option than the call option embedded in some corporate debt.

Convertible bonds are corporate bonds that may be exchanged by the holder at a specified price for a specified number of the issuer's common shares. The value of a convertible bond is the present value of the expected coupon and principal payments (or straight bond portion) plus the value of the option to purchase the firm's shares. Since a call option has unlimited upside potential, the convertible's value will rise with the price of the corporation's stock. If the stock declines so far as to render the option effectively worthless, the convertible is still worth as least as much as other identical straight debt instruments of the same issuer. While convertibles offer an attractive package to some investors, there is no such thing as a free lunch, and convertibles sell at higher prices (lower yields) than comparable, nonconvertible bonds.

Factors Influencing Bond Risk across Countries

When investors purchase bonds denominated in a currency other than the currency in which they intend to buy goods, they are exposed to exchange rate risk. Thus, in addition to yield, investors must consider potential appreciation or depreciation of the bond's currency against their home currency. Investors may hedge the currency risk of bonds denominated in a currency other than their own (Chapters 2 and 5).

From the point of view of U.S. investors, bonds issued in foreign markets, even if issued in U.S. dollars and not subject to currency risk, are exposed to political risks such as sovereign risk and repatriation-of-funds risk, while U.S.

---

[6]An exception is that bonds likely to be called in the near future (that is, with a coupon greater than or nearly equal to the current coupon and a short term to the call date) typically trade as cash equivalents, so that their yields may be lower than those of noncallable bonds.

dollar domestic bonds are not.[7] Likewise, the German investor finds deutschemark bonds issued outside Germany exposed to political risk, while deutschemark bonds issued within Germany are not.

World Bond Markets: A Brief Tour

Figures 10-2 and 10-3 show the composition of the world bond market by issuer in 1966 and 1989, respectively. While the market has grown tremendously in size, the relative size of the primary categories of bonds has not changed much.

Government bonds have been a fast-growing segment of the world bond market. In 1967, their worldwide market value summed to about $400 billion. Today this value is $6.6 trillion, representing a 13 percent annual growth rate. (As noted earlier, growth in bond market size typically comes from net new issues, not capital gains such as those which propel the capitalization growth in the stock market.) Figure 10-4 presents the current distribution of the global market for government bonds by country.[8] This segment is currently dominated by the United States, with significant participation by Japan, Italy, France, Germany, and the United Kingdom. Interestingly, Japan was not a leading government bond issuer until rela-

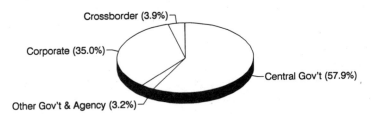

Figure 10-2. Global distribution of bonds by type: 1966 market capitalization = $633.65 billion. *(Source: Roger G. Ibbotson, Laurence B. Siegel, and Kathryn S. Love, "World Wealth: U.S. and Foreign Market Values and Returns," The Journal of Portfolio Management, Fall 1985.)*

---

[7]The division of political risk into parts is somewhat arbitrary, but the following definitions are sometimes used. Sovereign risk is the risk of a government's refusing to honor its debts. Repatriation-of-funds risk is the risk of a government's blocking payment of interest and principal to foreign creditors. Other political risks may exist.

[8]For the present purpose, government bonds include both central government and other governmental and related issues, as well as issues bearing government guarantees and bonds issued by government agencies.

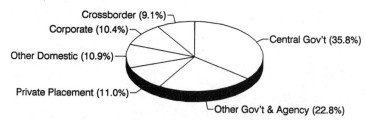

Figure 10-3. Global distribution of bonds by type: 1989 market capitalization = $11,647 billion. *(Source: "How Big is the World Bond Market?—1990 Update", Salomon Brothers, International Bond Market Analysis, 1990.)*

tively recently because until 1966 the central government was constitutionally forbidden to issue debt.

The market for corporate bonds, although not as large as that for governments, is significant and rapidly growing. In 1966, corporate bonds comprised 35 percent of the U.S. bond market. Since then this market has grown at a slower rate than governments', so that today corporate bonds occupy 24 percent of the U.S. market. Figure 10-5 shows the distribution by country for the major participants in the global corporate bond market.

The well-publicized mountain of corporate debt, then, is overshadowed by an even larger mountain of government debt. Debt has always been considered a necessary and prudent part of the capital structure of corporations. Government indebtedness, however, has historically been motivated by wartime needs. The current high level of worldwide government debt in peacetime reflects public tolerance of such indebtedness and demand for services provided by governments that are not financed by current taxation.

The most rapidly growing segment of the world bond market is the market for *crossborder* bonds. These are bonds issued by the government of a

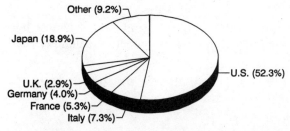

Figure 10-4. Global distribution of government bonds: 1989 market capitalization = $6821 billion. Note: included are bonds issued by central, state, and local governments, bonds guaranteed by governments, and those issued by governmental agencies. *(Source: "How Big is the World Bond Market?—1990 Update," Salomon Brothers, International Bond Market Analysis, 1990.)*

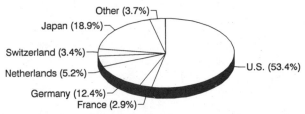

Figure 10-5. Global distribution of corporate and private placement bonds: 1989 market capitalization = $2492 billion. Note: private placement bonds are typically issued by corporations in the United States and governments in the rest of the world. *(Source: "How Big is the World Bond Market?—1990 Update," Salomon Brothers, International Bond Market Analysis, 1990.)*

country or by a corporation resident in that country, in the currency of another country and/or primarily held by residents of another country. Crossborder bonds can be divided into "Eurobonds" and traditional foreign bonds. Eurobonds, irrespective of currency denomination, are unregistered bonds that trade in the international over-the-counter market; thus they trade in a different market, but not necessarily a different currency, from that of the issuer.[9]

Traditional foreign bonds are denominated in a currency other than that of the issuer. These bonds appeal to investors who seek a fixed income stream and also anticipate appreciation of the bond's currency relative to the investor's home currency. Foreign bonds are also a valuable diversification tool. Examples include:

- Yankee bonds, denominated in dollars and issued by non-United States borrowers to investors in the United States. Unlike Eurobonds, Yankees are registered with the U.S. Securities and Exchange Commission, and U.S. investors may purchase them in the original issue market.

- Samurai and Shogun bonds, both issued in Japan by non-Japanese borrowers. Samurais are denominated in yen and Shoguns are denominated in non-yen currencies.

- Bulldog bonds, denominated in pounds sterling and issued in the United Kingdom by non-British borrowers.

---

[9]The Eurobond market started to flourish after the imposition of the Interest Equalization Tax (1963) by the United States. After the tax was repealed a decade later, the market did not die, but flourished even more. One reason for the market's durability is that by avoiding the time-consuming and costly registration procedure, Eurobond issues can be brought to market more quickly and cheaply. However, U.S. investors are permitted to buy unregistered bonds such as Eurobonds only in the secondary market, not at original issue.

In 1967, the first year for which a meaningful market capitalization can be compiled, the crossborder bond market accounted for only $27 billion. By 1989 it had reached $1063 billion, having grown at a 17 percent annual rate. Figure 10-6 shows the distribution by currency for bonds issued in the crossborder market. Eurodollar bonds make up the largest component of the Eurobond market. Euroyen bonds, denominated in yen and issued outside Japan, and Eurosterling bonds, denominated in sterling and issued outside the United Kingdom, are also large components. The market value of Eurodeutschemark bonds is not tracked separately from that of other deutschemark foreign bonds, but it is large.

Because world bond markets are more similar to each other than world equity markets, we will not review the institutional facts of each country's bond market as we did with world equity markets in Chapter 6. Instead we will concentrate on two large markets: the United States and Japan.

U.S. Domestic Bond Market

In this section we fill in some of the institutional details of the government (federal and agency), municipal (state and local), and corporate bond markets in the United States. In addition, we explore the unique characteristics of the mortgage-backed market and other structured financing markets.

Government and Agency Bonds

The debt issues of the federal government and its agencies are the largest sector of the U.S. bond market and are the largest parcel of government indebtedness in the world. These securities have had minuscule default risk because both principal and interest are guaranteed by the U.S. government.

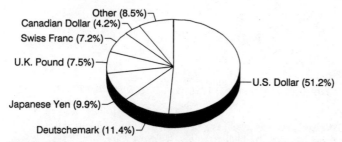

Figure 10-6. Crossborder bonds by currency: 1989 market capitalization = $1063 billion. Note: Crossborder bonds include both traditional foreign bonds and Eurobonds. *(Source: "How Big is the World Bond Market?— 1990 Update", Salomon Brothers, International Bond Market Analysis, 1990.)*

The monetizing power of the government makes the guarantee practically ironclad in nominal, if not real, terms. Federal debt issues are exempt from state and local tax, but not federal income tax.

The principal U.S. government debt issues are bills, notes, and bonds. U.S. Treasury bills, or "T-bills," are short-term zeros with original maturities up to 1 year and are quoted on a discount rate basis. Treasury notes have original maturities ranging from 2 to 10 years. Treasury bonds have original maturities of 10 years or longer. STRIPS (Separate Trading of Registered Interest and Principal of Securities) are the Treasury's attempt to allow trading of the interest and principal of T-bonds separately. The principal and interest portions are, in effect, zero-coupon bonds. These issues are highly liquid because security dealers maintain an active secondary market.

The government debt consists of the market capitalization of Treasury issues. While current discussions of policy focus intensively on both the growth and level of U.S. government debt, these discussions frequently lack historical perspective. Figure 10-7 provides such perspective. The figure indicates that while federal debt as a proportion of GNP is at an all-time high for peacetime years, it is far lower than during major wars. This suggests that while the current level of debt is survivable (since we have sur-

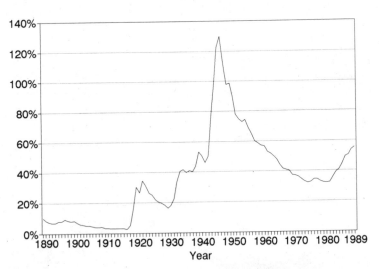

Figure 10-7. U.S. federal government debt as a percentage of GNP: 1889–1989. (*Sources:* Historical Statistics of the United States, Colonial Times to 1970, Bicentennial edition, part 2, *U.S. Department of Commerce, Bureau of the Census, Washington D.C., 1975;* Statistical Abstract of the United States: 1988, 108th ed. U.S. Department of Commerce, Bureau of the Census, Washington D.C., 1987; Survey of Current Business, *various issues, U.S. Department of Commerce, Bureau of Economic Analysis, Washington D.C., 1990.*)

vived the financial consequences of wars), it may be inappropriately high considering that a war is not being fought.[10] Taking another tack, Milton Friedman has suggested that the size of the government (that is, spending relative to GNP), not the size of the debt used to finance it, is the driving force behind the government's impact on the economy—less government being better.

Several federally sponsored credit agencies also issue securities, with various degrees of government backing. Within the U.S., agency securities are second only to those of the U.S. government in safety. The principal agencies issuing securities are those involved with the mortgage market.[11] The following agencies had a combined $750 billion in debt securities outstanding in 1990:

- Federal National Mortgage Association (FNMA or "Fannie Mae") is, after the Treasury, the largest borrower in U.S. capital markets. Fannie Mae buys privately issued mortgages and holds them in its portfolio. The portfolio is funded (leveraged) by Fannie Mae's issuance of bonds. Fannie Mae also repackages and sells mortgage portfolios in the form of mortgage-backed securities with Fannie Mae guaranteeing both principal and interest payments.

- Government National Mortgage Association (GNMA or "Ginnie Mae") purchases mortgages insured by the Veterans Administration and Federal Housing Administration and repackages and sells them as guaranteed pass-through securities.

- Federal Home Loan Mortgage Corporation (FHLMC or "Freddie Mac") is similar to Fannie Mae but tends to sell the mortgages it guarantees, rather than holding them in its portfolio.

Municipal Bonds

State and local governments, and other nonfederal governmental entities such as airport and highway authorities, also issue debt. Such debt bears the general name of *municipal bonds*. All income from municipal bonds, notes, and other such instruments is exempt from federal personal income tax.

---

[10]A revealing discussion of the federal government debt is in Robert L. Heilbroner and Peter L. Bernstein, *The Debt and the Deficit*, W.W. Norton, New York, 1989.

[11]A comprehensive treatment of the mortgage-backed securities market can be found in Frank J. Fabozzi, ed., *The Handbook of Mortgage-Backed Securities*, 3rd edition, Probus Publishing, Chicago, 1992.

General obligation bonds are unsecured instruments backed by the "full faith and credit" of the governmental unit. These securities are thus a general lien on the unencumbered revenues of the government body. Other municipal securities are simply a "moral obligation" of the government. Still others, called *revenue bonds*, are repayable only from designated funds, such as public utility revenues.

State and local bonds are subject to default risk and bondholders cannot sue bankrupt issuers, even municipal or state governments. To lower the interest rate required by investors, municipal bond issuers often buy insurance, called *credit enhancement*, to protect buyers against default.

State and local bonds are usually issued in serial form, meaning that some are redeemed each year until all are retired. These bonds may also be callable at specific dates and prices. The issuing agency is sometimes required to contribute to a sinking fund to retire bonds or guarantee that resources will exist to repay bondholders at maturity.

Corporate Bonds

Most corporates are coupon bonds, although some firms issue zero-coupon bonds. Because default risk is greater for firms than for most governments, corporate bonds tend to have higher yields. Various restrictive covenants, like sinking fund requirements, exist to protect bondholders from loss of principal.

Most short-term corporate bonds are backed by issuers' guarantees alone, and consequently, yields depend on the firms' credit ratings. Such unsecured bonds, called *debentures*, have as collateral the corporation's revenues. Secured bonds, which are more common than unsecured bonds for longer maturities, have additional collateral in the form of a pledge of specific property.

The 1980s saw the rapid expansion of the so-called junk or high-yield bond market. While this market existed prior to 1980, it took off primarily because the investment firm of Drexel Burnham Lambert was willing to make a market in these previously illiquid securities. With a marketplace full of buyers hungry for high yields, firms were more than willing to issue junk bonds rather than submit to the scrutiny that comes with a bank loan. Apparently, these buyers believed that the yield spread on these bonds was fair compensation for the increased default risk. Initial academic findings supported this view. In 1987 Edward Altman and Scott Nammacher reported that junk bonds had an annual default rate of 1 to 3 percent.[12] More

[12]Edward I. Altman and Scott A. Nammacher, *Investing in Junk Bonds,* John Wiley & Sons, Inc., New York, 1987.

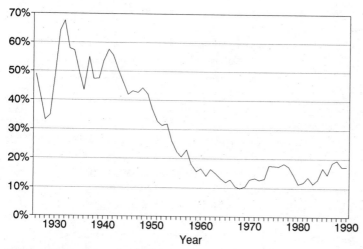

Figure 10-8. U.S. corporate leverage: 1926 to 1990. *(Source: Ibbotson Associates, Inc., Chicago, 1991.)*

recent work by Asquith, Mullins, and Wolff shows that these bonds have much higher default rates over long holding periods.[13] They found that for bonds outstanding for 2 to 4 years, the cumulative default rates are 3 to 9 percent. These cumulative rates are consistent with the high end of the annual default rates estimated by Altman and Nammacher. The rate rises, however, to 34 percent for bonds outstanding 10 to 11 years.

Although corporate debt grew mightily in the 1980s, and there were celebrated instances of excessive leverage, the data show surprising stability in the leverage of corporate America in the recent past. Figure 10-8 shows the debt-to-capitalization ratio of U.S. corporations in aggregate over the period from 1926 to 1990. The first half of the period was characterized by high leverage, especially after the stock market collapse of 1929 to 1932. The second half of the period has exhibited much less leverage, with only a modest increase in the 1980s; like debt, equity market capitalization grew very fast in that decade, keeping the ratio moderate.

Structured Finance

Structured finance is a catchall term denoting bonds and bondlike securities created by repackaging cash flows from other sources.[14] This process, also

[13]Paul Asquith, David W. Mullins, Jr., and Eric D. Wolff, "Original Issue High Yield Bonds: Aging Analyses of Defaults, Exchanges, and Calls," *Journal of Finance*, September 1989.

[14]These securities are also referred to as *asset-backed securities*.

known as *securitization*, while most prevalent in the United States, is spreading to the rest of the world.

The key economic concept behind securitization is that many cash flow streams, which investors would not touch in original form, can be recut (structured) so that the pieces are more valuable to the market than the whole. Financial guarantees (credit enhancement), overcollateralization, and other techniques are used to make the more predictable pieces of the cash flow streams behave like riskless bonds, which are sold to more risk-averse investors. The capital gain potential of the less predictable pieces is attractive to less risk-averse buyers. Clienteles appear to exist for the in-between pieces too. Ultimately, the success of structured financing as a way to make investments that would otherwise go unmade depends on the sustained existence of clienteles for the wide variety of payoffs offered.

In the United States, the oldest and most familiar structured instruments are U.S. government agency (Fannie Mae and so forth) bonds, most of which are issued to obtain funding for home mortgages. In the 1980s, more complex structures arose, such as interest only (IO) and principal only (PO) securities, collateralized mortgage obligations (CMOs), and real estate mortgage investment conduits (REMICs).

Each mortgage payment is composed of an interest payment and a principal payment. IOs represent the interest portion of the cash flow generated by a pool of mortgages. An IO is subject to prepayment risk because the cash flow decreases as mortgages prepay. IO holders prefer a stable interest rate environment because that will reduce the number of prepayments.

POs represent the principal portion of the cash flow generated by a pool of mortgages. POs are also subject to prepayment risk, but unlike IOs, benefit from a declining interest rate environment. This result occurs because as prepayments occur, PO holders receive their funds back faster.

CMOs break up the cash flows from mortgages into categories called *tranches*. The tranches are differentiated by the priority they receive when principal payments are received from the mortgage pool. The "fast-pay tranches" receive all principal payments until that tranche is paid off. Subsequent principal payments go to the second tranche until that tranche is paid off. This process is repeated until all tranches have received their payoffs. The investor may buy any tranche, or combination of tranches, so that investors can carefully control their exposure to the various risks inherent in mortgages. For example, an investor who wants exposure to mortgages, but requires front-loaded cash flows, would prefer the most senior tranches while investors who are comfortable with more uncertain cash flows can purchase more subordinated tranches. The breaking up of a set of cash flows into pieces with well-defined risk and return characteristics—with tranches ranging from practically riskless bonds to speculative residual claims—represents a leap in the completeness of asset markets.

The issuance of REMICs was sanctioned by the Tax Reform Act of 1986. REMICs resemble CMOs in that they enable mortgage cash flows to be cut into various pieces, each (ideally) playing into the needs or desires of some clientele. They differ from CMOs in their tax treatment as well as in the exact form of the securities.

The phenomenal success of real estate-related structured financings has spawned a flood of additional structured financings, or securitizations, of assets other than mortgages. Assets recently securitized include bank loans, high-yield corporate bonds, and consumer receivables such as automobile loans and credit card balances, to name only the most prominent examples.

The Japanese Bond Market

The last 15 years have seen both an explosion in the types of instruments available (for both domestic and foreign investors) and a dramatic reduction in restrictive Ministry of Finance regulations. The result has been a revolution for the Japanese bond market.

Government Bonds

The Japanese government is second only to the U.S. government in amount of debt outstanding and dominates the Japanese bond market. As reliance on deficit financing has increased, the government bond market is becoming less regulated and offers a broader range of instruments. For example, foreign security firms were allowed to participate in government bond underwriting syndicates starting in 1984.[15] The Japanese equivalent of U.S. Treasury bills first became available in 1986. Currently, the Japanese market offers a broad range of securities ranging from short-term bills up to a maximum maturity of 20 years.[16]

---

[15]In April 1989, the distribution of Japanese government bonds was revamped. Under the new regime, 60 percent of each issue would be distributed on a fixed-share basis, in which each underwriter would receive a fixed percentage of the issue and 40 percent would be distributed at competitive auction. In the United States, almost all government securites are distributed at competitive auction.

[16]The 10-year bond is most popular. T-bills are less popular than in the United States. A number of reasons account for this: (1) they are only issued quarterly, (2) only six month maturities are issued, (3) holders are subject to an 18 percent withholding tax, and (4) the minimum size is ¥50 million (about $400,000) as opposed to $10,000 for U.S. T-bills.

Corporate Bonds

Historically, the Japanese corporate bond market has been unimportant because of the reliance of corporations on banks for their financing, a rising stock market, and strict government regulation. As of March 1990, there were only $58 billion in domestic corporate bonds, two-thirds of which were issued by electric utilities.[17] But bank loans and equity are becoming less dominant sources of capital for Japanese firms. To fill this gap, the Japanese corporate bond market is developing more fully.

As of 1992 banks worldwide must comply with the capital standards of the Bank for International Settlements (BIS). Currently, many Japanese banks are in violation of those standards and must either raise new capital or restrict loan growth. Given the impact that recent volatility of the Japanese stock market has had on bank capital, restricting loan growth appears to be the path of least resistance.

Prior to 1990, firms that could not slake their thirst for capital via bank loans could always turn to the equity market. In an era where Japanese stocks were on a seemingly endless upward path, investors were more than willing to snatch up equity as soon as it hit the market. In this environment, convertible bonds were also popular. The equity market free-fall of 1990–1992 has made investors less sanguine about accepting these offerings.

With so many firms relying on banks and equity for financing, the restrictive Ministry of Finance regulations on corporate debt were not especially burdensome.[18] Now that corporations are hungry to issue bonds, they have lobbied successfully for liberalization of governmental policy in this area.

Despite liberalization of the market, several institutional floodgates continue to hold back more corporate issues: registration requirements that can delay an issue for three months, fixed underwriting fees, and a so-called fixed pricing system that does not allow the price of an issue to fluctuate between the time the deal is priced and when the issue is actually put up for sale.

Additional Highlights of the World Bond Market

We conclude this chapter by reviewing segments of the world fixed-income securities market that have unusual or noteworthy attributes.

---

[17] *The Economist*, November 24, 1990, p. 89.

[18] For example, until 1974 Japanese firms were prohibited from floating debt securities abroad. While firms, thereafter, could issue unsecured debt, the standards were so strict that as of 1979 only two firms met them.

Cash Equivalents

Short-term interest-bearing securities (with maturities one year or less) are regarded as the functional equivalent of cash. Historically, the real rate of return on government-backed cash equivalents was near zero, but lately, it has been significantly positive. Thus, investors have altered their conception of cash equivalents, thinking of them now as investments rather than a "parking place" for funds not yet invested. Cash returns are highly correlated with inflation, making them an inflation hedge. Finally, cash is safe; because of its short duration, returns on cash have been far less volatile than those of either stocks or bonds.

Since most institutional investors are tax-exempt, they seek those cash equivalents that would be highly taxable to taxpaying investors. These include securities like Treasury bills, commercial paper, bankers' acceptances, and jumbo certificates of deposits issued by banks in denominations of $100,000 or greater.

Investors seeking the highest real yields shop the world cash market, the most internationally integrated of all capital markets. A special category of foreign bank deposits, called *Eurodeposits,* allow investors to open accounts in foreign banks that are denominated in different currencies.[19] This unregulated market can offer competitive yields because banks are not required to hold reserves against Eurodeposits. Some countries (the Bahamas and the Cayman Islands are examples) offer the additional incentive of favorable tax treatment of interest on deposits.

An attractive alternative for the taxable investor (such as a taxpaying corporation) is variable-rate preferred stock. This type of stock pays a dividend that is tied to an interest rate benchmark; hence it is cashlike, offering inflation protection. From a U.S. tax perspective, interest income from a bond is taxable, but 85 percent of dividend income is excluded from taxation for corporations.

There is substantial evidence that of cash equivalents, the longer-term issues offer the best risk-return combination. Empirical work done by the University of Chicago professor Eugene Fama shows that securities with around 6 months to 1 year to maturity and short-term bonds with 1 to 5 years to maturity have higher returns than very short-term money-market instruments, with little additional risk.[20]

---

[19]Eurodeposits are not only offered in Europe. The term only denotes the historical origin of these markets. Accounts are available in any of the major currencies. Dollar-denominated accounts happen to comprise the bulk of the market.

[20]Eugene F. Fama, "The Information in the Term Structure," *Journal of Financial Economics,* December 1984; Eugene F. Fama, "Term Premiums and Default Premiums in Money Markets," *Journal of Financial Economics.* November 1986.

We find that a diversified portfolio of commercial cash instruments provides returns superior to government cash instruments with little additional risk. From 1927 to 1991, U.S. commercial paper had a compound annual return of 4.52 percent and a standard deviation of 3.57 percent. T-bills had a 3.71 percent return and 3.39 percent standard deviation. Defaults tend to cluster, however, so that in case of a severe economic downturn, a diversified portfolio of commercial paper might not perform well. The relatively high returns on commercial paper reflect the fact that defaults have not been a serious problem, but their high yield suggests that the market attaches a substantial risk premium to them.

High-Yield Sovereign Bonds

High-yield sovereign bonds are the central government issues of countries that are perceived by the market as having substantial default risk. This market is small, but thriving as of this writing. Central governments sell bonds directly to investors in an attempt to bypass the reluctance of banks to make risky loans and the burdensome restrictions attached to loans from agencies like the International Monetary Fund and the World Bank. Bonds may be issued in the currency of the likely investor (say, the U.S. dollar) or in the issuer's home currency. The market is small ($11 billion in 1989), but is significant enough for Merrill Lynch to compile an index which tracks the most popular bonds issued by countries like Argentina, Brazil, Mexico, and Venezuela.

Why would investors consider high-yield sovereign bonds? First, the risks are reflected in higher yields. Second, the larger issuers have an unsullied payment record. Eastern Europe is a likely target for expansion of this market in the near term. As marginally creditworthy countries become more developed, the market for high-yield sovereign bonds can be expected to grow in the future.

11

World Bond Markets: Historical Returns and Yields

This chapter reviews bond yields and returns around the world.[1] As we saw in Chapter 10, yields are expected returns: they are the market's forecast (subject to some simplifying assumptions) of what the actual return will be. However, the market sometimes makes very inaccurate forecasts. Early in the twentieth century, British investors priced perpetual and long-maturity gilts (British Treasury bonds) to have yields around 5 percent. These investors were in for a rude surprise. Counting principal only, a hypothetical £1 investment in long-term gilts at the end of 1918 rose to £1.56 by 1934 as interest rates fell. After that the bond market first slowly declined, then collapsed until, by 1974, only £0.31 of the investor's original £1 principal was left. By 1988, gilts had recovered somewhat and our investor had £0.51. The bloodbath is much worse when stated in inflation-adjusted terms: £1 invested in 1918 shrank to a minuscule £0.03 by 1988.[2]

[1]Portions of this chapter appeared in Roger G. Ibbotson and Laurence B. Siegel, "The World Bond Market," *Journal of Fixed Income,* June 1991.

[2]Peter Thompson, Jeffrey Thompson, Bryan Allworthy, and David Roden, *BZW Equity-Gilt Study,* Barclays de Zoete Wedd, London, 1989.

Yields, Inflation, and Real Interest Rates in Seven Major Markets

As we noted in Chapter 10, a bond's yield summarizes in a single number the numerous economic factors that influence bond value. In this section we study the historical relationships among real interest rates, inflation, and yields for long-term bonds and short-term bills. To facilitate comparison across both time and location, we use the yields on government bonds of developed countries because of their relatively comparable credit risk.

Nominal interest rates have an embedded expectation of inflation.[3] (See Chapter 2.) We separate the inflation component from the real interest rate component. Figures 11-1 through 11-7 depict ex-post real interest rates (yields adjusted for *actual* inflation) on long-term bonds and short-term bills, along with inflation rates, for seven countries over the 1961 to 1990 period. Real interest rates are constructed as the nominal interest rate as of the *end* of the year indicated minus the inflation rate measured *over* the year. This imperfect match between the timing of the two variables used to construct real interest rates is unavoidable.

These measures of real interest rates were quite stable throughout the 1960s in the markets studied. Then, starting about 1970, real rates on both long- and short-term bonds fell in almost every country as inflation rates rose faster than nominal interest rates. By 1975 all seven countries had experienced negative real interest rates, with the extreme being the United Kingdom with a −14.2 percent rate. Of the countries studied, only Germany avoided high inflation and interest rates during this period.

In most countries, the extreme inflation rates of 1974 and 1975 (associated with the first oil price shock) would not be seen again, although Japan was the only country to entirely avoid the second oil-related surge in the late 1970s. In the United States, however, inflation rates reached a new high in the 1979 to 1980 period, and real interest rates in the United States turned sharply negative again. Finally, during the 1980s inflation rates fell in every country, but nominal interest rates did not fall as fast. Real interest rates consequently rose to high levels.

As measured, real interest rates are seen to differ markedly among countries at a given point in time. Also, they are not low and stable as the data from the 1960s and earlier suggested. Their instability across time and the variation between countries may be due to measurement problems, includ-

---

[3]Measures of these expectations are not available, but will be approximated with the actual inflation data. The reader should keep this expedient in mind when interpreting the historical record presented in this chapter.

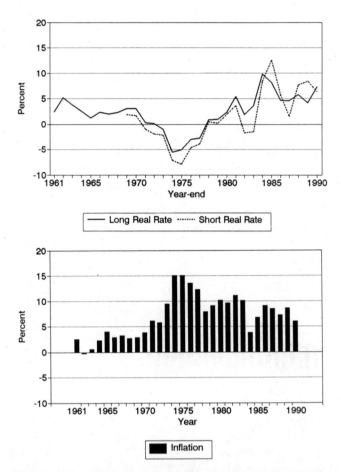

Figure 11-1. Australia: real interest rates and inflation. (*Source: Roger G. Ibbotson and Laurence B. Siegel, "The World Bond Market: Market Values, Yields, and Returns," Journal of Fixed Income, June 1991.*)

ing difficulties in estimating expected inflation rates and inexact comparability between bond markets, or they may indicate investment opportunities in the international bond market.

Returns in the World Bond Market

While yields measure expected returns, investors prosper and suffer with actual returns. As before, for comparability across both location and time,

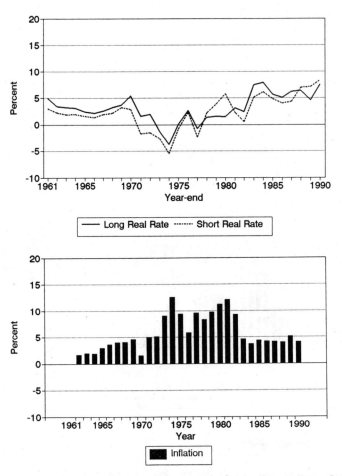

Figure 11-2. Canada: real interest rates and inflation. (*Source: Roger G. Ibbotson and Laurence B. Siegel, "The World Bond Market: Market Values, Yields, and Returns," Journal of Fixed Income, June 1991.*)

we use the returns on government bonds of developed countries because of their low credit risk.[4]

Summary statistics of the returns in major long-term government bond markets over the 1961 to 1990 period appear in local-currency terms in Table 11-1 and in United States dollar terms in Table 11-2. Over this period,

---

[4]Summary statistics of returns on corporate and crossborder bonds are presented, along with the appropriate caveats, by Robert A. Brown and Laurence B. Siegel, "Introduction to International Bonds," in Brian R. Bruce, ed., *Quantitative International Investing*, Probus, Chicago, 1990.

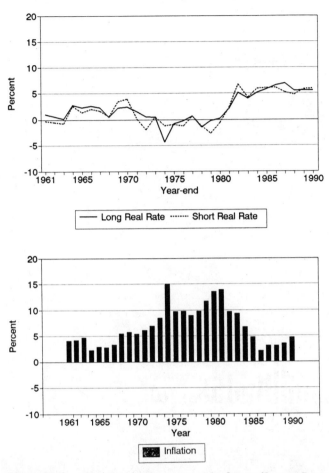

Figure 11-3.   France: real interest rates and inflation. (*Source: Roger G. Ibbotson and Laurence B. Siegel, "The World Bond Market: Market Values, Yields, and Returns," Journal of Fixed Income, June 1991.*)

local-currency compound annual returns range from 4.1 percent in Switzerland to 9.1 percent in Italy. In line with Irving Fisher's hypothesis, countries with low inflation rates tend to have the lowest nominal returns.[5]

Currency movements cause United States dollar-translated returns to be very different from local currency returns. For example, because Switzerland has had low inflation and Italy high inflation, Swiss interest rates were materially lower than Italian rates and the lira depreciated

---

[5]Irving Fisher, *The Theory of Interest,* Macmillan, New York, 1930.

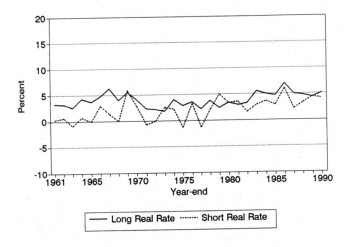

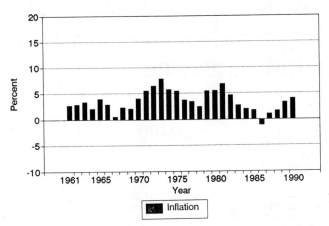

Figure 11-4.   Germany: real interest rates and inflation. (*Source:
Roger G. Ibbotson and Laurence B. Siegel, "The World Bond Market: Market Values, Yields, and Returns,"* Journal of Fixed Income, *June 1991.*)

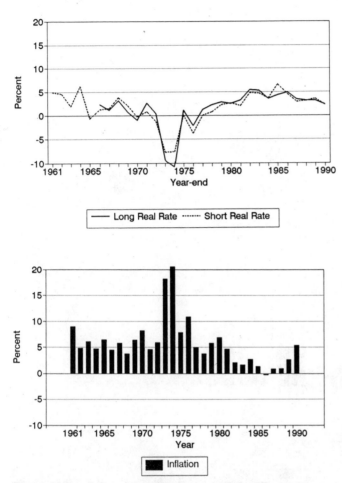

Figure 11-5. Japan: real interest rates and inflation. (*Source: Roger G. Ibbotson and Laurence B. Siegel, "The World Bond Market: Market Values, Yields, and Returns,"* Journal of Fixed Income, *June 1991.*)

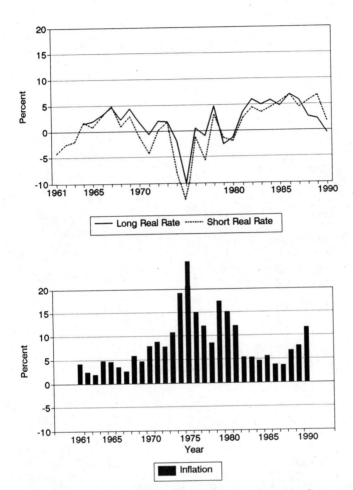

Figure 11-6. United Kingdom: real interest rates and inflation. (*Source: Roger G. Ibbotson and Laurence B. Siegel, "The World Bond Market: Market Values, Yields, and Returns,"* Journal of Fixed Income, *June 1991.*)

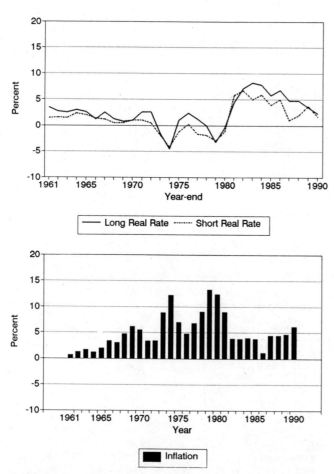

Figure 11-7. United States: real interest rates and inflation. (*Source: Roger G. Ibbotson and Laurence B. Siegel, "The World Bond Market: Market Values, Yields, and Returns," Journal of Fixed Income, June 1991.*)

Table 11-1. Long-Term Government Bonds
Summary Statistics of Annual Returns in Local Currency

	Period	Compound return (%)	Arithmetic mean (%)	Standard deviation (%)
Australia	1961–1990	7.35	7.93	11.38
Canada	1961–1990	7.41	7.72	8.62
France	1961–1990	7.68	8.06	9.23
Germany	1961–1990	6.81	7.03	7.05
Italy	1961–1990	9.06	10.10	15.65
Japan	1967–1990	6.96	7.17	6.84
Netherlands	1965–1990	6.87	7.10	7.31
Switzerland	1965–1990	4.10	4.28	6.30
United Kingdom	1961–1990	8.45	9.46	15.79
United States	1961–1990	6.18	6.69	10.99

SOURCE: *International Financial Statistics,* International Monetary Fund, and/or *Financial Statistics Part I,* Organization for Economic Cooperation and Development.

Table 11-2. Long-Term Government Bonds
Summary Statistics of Annual Returns in United States Dollars

	Period	Compound return (%)	Arithmetic mean (%)	Standard deviation (%)
Australia	1961–1990	6.03	6.74	12.70
Canada	1961–1990	6.87	7.21	9.03
France	1961–1990	7.54	8.53	15.27
Germany	1961–1990	10.53	11.36	14.00
Italy	1961–1990	6.92	8.80	21.52
Japan	1967–1990	11.42	12.77	17.76
Netherlands	1965–1990	10.03	10.93	14.71
Switzerland	1965–1990	9.10	10.30	16.70
United Kingdom	1961–1990	7.11	8.86	20.88
United States	1961–1990	6.18	6.69	10.99

SOURCE: *International Financial Statistics,* International Monetary Fund, and/or *Financial Statistics Part I,* Organization for Economic Cooperation and Development.

accordingly against the Swiss franc. On balance, United States dollar returns on Swiss government bonds were actually higher than on Italian bonds: 9.1 percent versus 6.9 percent. In U.S. dollar terms, the range of compound annual returns over the 1961 to 1990 period is from 6.0 percent (Australia) to 11.4 percent (Japan). In general, countries with low inflation rates had appreciating currencies, boosting United States dollar-translated bond returns. Japan and Germany had the highest U.S. dollar returns, due entirely to the appreciation of the yen and deutschemark against the dollar during this time period; these two countries had only average returns measured in local currency.

The risk of government bonds, as measured by standard deviation, also differs across countries. In local currency terms, Swiss bonds were the safest while British issues were the most volatile. Translated to United States dollars, however, United States bonds were the second least volatile (Canada's were safer) while Italian bonds were the riskiest. The standard deviations of bond returns were also higher for every foreign country when measured in U.S. dollars than when measured in local currency. This observation highlights the importance of exchange risk as an element of global bond performance.

Returns by Five-Year Periods

By examining period-by-period data, we can better understand the world bond market's changing character. Table 11-3 presents compound annual total returns for 1961 through 1990 in six successive 5-year periods, for seven major countries. Returns are presented in both local-currency and U.S. dollar-translated form and in both nominal and real (inflation-adjusted) terms. To better understand bond returns in the context of two of the major forces that affect them — inflation rates and exchange rates — Table 11-3 also presents these latter series. The Inflation column gives the compound annual rate of inflation in each country over each 5-year period. The FOREX column shows the return to a U.S. investor holding the currency of the country named.[6] Thus, under FOREX for Japan for 1986 to 1990, the 7.5 percent return signifies that a United States investor holding a yen-denominated bond would have realized a 7.5 percent compound annual return from appreciation of the yen against the dollar from 1986 to 1990.

In general, inflation and nominal bond yields rose slowly in the 1960s, then dramatically in the 1970s only to fall again in the 1980s. Total returns, consequently, were low in the 1960s and 1970s as yields rose and capital losses offset high income (yield) returns. In the 1980s, falling yields produced very high returns on bonds.

---

[6]The return shown is for a non-interest-bearing position in the currency. Interest-bearing accounts denominated in the currency earned higher returns. For each month, we calculated the FOREX return as the change in the dollar price of a foreign currency over the month, divided by the previous month-end price. We linked (compounded) monthly returns to form annual and longer-period returns.

Table 11-3.
Compound Annual Total Returns of Long-Term Government Bonds,
in Percent, Five-Year Periods (1961–1990)

Period	Nominal (local)	Nominal (US$)	Real (local)	Real (US$)	Inflation (local)	FOREX (vs. US$)
			Australia			
1961 – 65	5.12	5.09	3.25	3.22	1.81	−0.03
1966 – 70	1.56	1.50	−1.51	−1.57	3.12	−0.06
1971 – 75	1.71	4.18	−7.74	−5.50	10.24	2.37
1976 – 80	5.98	4.66	−4.16	−5.36	10.58	−1.26
1981 – 85	11.13	−0.46	−2.64	−8.06	8.27	−11.64
1986 – 90	19.66	22.72	10.91	13.74	7.89	2.49
			Canada			
1961 – 65	5.04	3.44	3.30	1.73	1.68	−1.54
1966 – 70	4.37	5.66	0.79	2.04	3.55	1.22
1971 – 75	4.45	4.35	−3.47	−3.56	8.20	−0.10
1976 – 80	6.03	2.66	−2.65	−5.75	8.92	−3.29
1981 – 85	16.76	13.16	9.37	5.99	6.76	−3.19
1986 – 90	8.31	12.42	3.78	7.72	4.36	3.66
			France			
1961 – 65	4.95	4.96	1.28	1.29	3.62	0.00
1966 – 70	2.40	0.01	−2.06	−4.34	4.55	−2.41
1971 – 75	7.30	11.85	−1.76	2.41	9.22	4.07
1976 – 80	4.16	4.02	−5.94	−6.07	10.74	−0.14
1981 – 85	18.40	6.80	8.81	−1.85	8.81	−10.86
1986 – 90	9.61	18.64	6.45	15.22	2.97	7.61
			Germany			
1961 – 65	4.06	4.90	1.02	1.83	3.01	0.81
1966 – 70	6.71	8.73	4.26	6.23	2.35	1.85
1971 – 75	8.81	16.23	2.49	9.48	6.17	6.39
1976 – 80	6.32	12.71	2.13	8.27	4.10	5.67
1981 – 85	12.13	7.12	8.32	3.48	3.52	−4.67
1986 – 90	3.10	13.92	1.91	12.60	1.17	9.50
			Japan			
1971 – 75	6.06	9.48	−4.70	−1.63	11.29	3.13
1976 – 80	7.45	16.58	0.98	9.56	6.41	7.83
1981 – 85	11.75	12.03	9.04	9.31	2.49	0.25
1986 – 90	3.01	11.36	1.97	10.24	1.02	7.50
			United Kingdom			
1961 – 65	4.69	4.68	1.01	1.00	3.64	−0.01
1966 – 70	1.76	−1.41	−2.99	−6.02	4.90	−3.21
1971 – 75	3.41	−0.01	−9.34	−12.34	14.06	−3.42
1976 – 80	15.26	19.12	1.52	4.92	13.53	3.23
1981 – 85	17.77	6.53	10.50	−0.05	6.58	−10.55
1986 – 90	8.82	15.31	3.17	9.32	5.48	5.63

(Continued)

Table 11-3.

Compound Annual Total Returns of Long-Term Government Bonds, in Percent, Five-Year Periods (1961–1990) (Continued)

Period	Nominal (local)	Nominal (US$)	Real (local)	Real (US$)	Inflation (local)	FOREX (vs. US$)
		United States				
1961–65	2.63	2.63	1.28	1.28	1.33	n/a
1966–70	−0.02	−0.02	−4.36	−4.36	4.54	n/a
1971–75	6.16	6.16	−0.69	−0.69	6.90	n/a
1976–80	1.68	1.68	−6.89	−6.89	9.21	n/a
1981–85	16.83	16.83	11.43	11.43	4.85	n/a
1986–90	10.75	10.75	6.86	6.86	3.64	n/a

SOURCE: Roger G. Ibbotson and Laurence B. Siegel, "The World Bond Market: Market Values, Yields, and Returns," *Journal of Fixed Income,* June 1991.

Correlations of World Bond Returns

A recurring theme of this book is the importance of diversification. An asset's diversification value depends on the correlation of its return with those of other assets. Table 11-4 shows the correlation coefficients of annual bond returns, measured in U.S. dollar terms, for 10 countries studied over the 30-year period from 1961 to 1990.

Correlations of the U.S. market with foreign markets (except Canada) are generally low. Continental Europe (with an exception for Italy) contains the highest correlations, particularly among Germany, Switzerland, and the Netherlands. Japan has moderately high correlations with all European countries represented in the table, but quite low with Australia, Canada, and the United States. Canada has low correlations with all countries in the table (with the exception of the United States), as does Australia.

The correlations in Table 11-4 suggest gains available to the investor from global bond diversification. The benefits of a globally diversified government bond portfolio can also be quantified by comparing returns on diversified and undiversified portfolios. Table 11-5 compares long-term United States government bonds with equally weighted global portfolios of like maturity, rebalanced monthly. The unhedged global portfolio return is an equally weighted combination of the U.S. dollar returns on long-term government bonds in the 10 countries studied in Table 11-1. The hedged global portfolio return is an equally weighted combination of the same countries' local currency returns; it represents the returns that a hypothetical perfectly and costlessly hedged U.S. dollar investor would have achieved.

The unhedged global portfolio had a higher mean return than the U.S. portfolio, reflecting the dollar's historical decline against many of the leading currencies. The standard deviation of the unhedged global portfolio is

Table 11-4. Correlations of Annual Total Returns for Long-Term Government Bonds in U.S. Dollars (1961–1990)

	Australia	Canada	France	Germany	Italy	Japan	Nether- lands	Switzer- land	United Kingdom	United States
Australia	1.00									
Canada	.18	1.00								
France	.30	.18	1.00							
Germany	.12	.15	.69	1.00						
Italy	.38	.12	.73	.45	1.00					
Japan	.29	−.08	.56	.59	.44	1.00				
Netherlands	.13	.29	.77	.93	.49	.54	1.00			
Switzerland	.11	−.10	.68	.88	.37	.67	.86	1.00		
United Kingdom	.37	.09	.39	.41	.32	.60	.42	.41	1.00	
United States	.08	.80	.44	.36	.35	.04	.50	.14	.15	1.00

NOTE: Netherlands data begin in 1965, Japan in 1967, and Switzerland in 1965. For each pair of countries, correlations are estimated over the longest period for which data are available for both countries.

SOURCE: *International Financial Statistics*, International Monetary Fund, and/or *Financial Statistics Part 1*, Organization for Economic Cooperation and Development.

Table 11-5. Summary Statistics of Annual Returns on U.S. and Global Bond Portfolios in U.S. Dollars (1961–1990)

Portfolio	Geometric mean (%)	Arithmetic mean (%)	Standard deviation (%)
United States	6.18	6.69	10.99
Global (unhedged)	8.27	8.72	10.35
Global (hedged)	7.20	7.42	7.11

NOTE: The global portfolio returns are equally weighted combinations of bond returns in the 10 countries identified in Table 11-1. The unhedged return is in U.S. dollars (returns are from Table 11-2). The hedged return assumes a perfect and costless hedge to U.S. dollars (returns are from Table 11-1).

SOURCES: Roger G. Ibbotson and Laurence B. Siegel, "The World Bond Market: Market Values, Yields, and Returns," *Journal of Fixed Income*, June 1991.

lower than that of the U.S. portfolio, reflecting gains from diversification. The hedged portfolio's return was lower than the unhedged portfolio's return because it avoided the gain from the dollar's decline, but it still beat the U.S. portfolio; its volatility was dramatically less than that of either the U.S. or unhedged global portfolios.

Figure 11-8 graphically presents the U.S. dollar results from Table 11-5. One U.S. dollar is invested at the end of 1960 in each of the three bond portfolios. The global portfolios beat the U.S. portfolio substantially, with a dollar growing to $10.86 (unhedged) and $8.16 (hedged) over the 30-year period, compared to $6.05 for U.S. bonds alone.

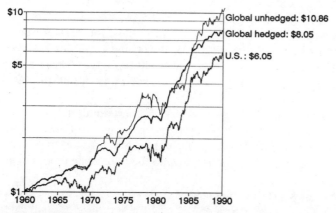

Figure 11-8. U.S. and global bond portfolios: growth of $1 invested at year-end 1960. (*Source: Roger G. Ibbotson and Laurence B. Siegel, "The World Bond Market: Market Values, Yields, and Returns,"* Journal of Fixed Income, *June 1991.*)

Long-Run Bond Yields and Returns in the United States

Historical Returns

The value of a dollar invested in 1789 in government bonds grew to over $9767.24 by the end of 1991.[7] (Over approximately the same period, a $1 investment in the United States stock market grew to over $9 million.) All of this growth, and then some, comes from income returns (coupon payments), since an investor would have suffered a capital loss over the period studied. Over the two centuries, inflation pushed consumer prices up 21-fold. Thus bond investors would have beat inflation by 3.15 percent per year.

Historical Yields

Yields tell a different and perhaps more interesting story. In Figure 11-9, we see only a loose relation between long-term bond yields and short-term inflation rates over most of U.S. history.[8] Long-term yields moved less than yearly inflation rates because the yield represents the market's inflation expectation over the life of the bond, not just over the current year. For example, during the Civil War, yearly inflation rates exceeded 30 percent, but long-term yields rose only to 7 percent because investors expected inflation to decrease, or perhaps turn negative. Consumer prices did in fact fall every year from 1869 to 1879.

For the first 150 years of post-Revolutionary American history, bond yields rose in wartime, corresponding to the inflationary character of such periods. Yields peaked during the War of 1812, the Civil War, and World War I. (These peaks do not show up in Figure 11-9 because only decennial averages are graphed until 1926.) Each peak was below the previous one, indicating the increasingly good credit of the government and/or lowered inflation expectations. Although there were wide swings in yields over time, the general trend was downward, producing capital gains (a bull market) for holders of long-term bonds.

Interestingly, World War II, the largest military effort ever undertaken by the United States, was not associated with an increase in long-term bond yields, even though there was substantial inflation during the war. Investors appeared to anticipate low or negative inflation rates beyond the immediate time frame.

---

[7]This result assumes reinvestment of cash flows at prevailing yields, and excludes taxes (which were negligible for most of the period) and transaction costs. Returns are assumed to equal yields from 1790 to 1925. Since yields decreased on average over this period, the return is understated.

[8]For the period 1790 to 1925, only decennial average yields were available. The yields for individual years were estimated by interpolation.

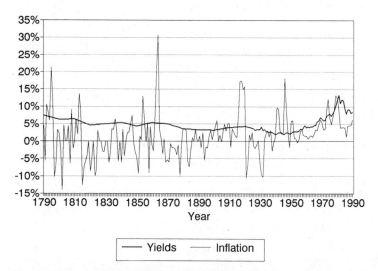

Figure 11-9. U.S. government bond yields and inflation, 1790–1990. (*Source: pre-1926 government bond yields are from Sidney Homer,* A History of Interest Rates. *Copyright © 1963, 1977 by Rutgers, the State University. Reprinted with permission of Rutgers University Press. Post-1926 yields are from I/IDEAS U.S. Capital Markets data module, Ibbotson Associates, Inc., Chicago, 1991. Inflation statistics are from Table 12-3.*)

After World War II, yields started to rise. The rise was considerable in the 1950s, larger still in the 1960s, and astounding in the 1970s. By September 1981, the yield on a long-term government bond had passed 15 percent. The practically unbroken rise in yields from 1945 to 1981 represented the most sustained bond bear market in history. Investors who maintained a constant 20-year-maturity portfolio would have lost two-thirds of their principal due to falling bond prices over that period. Inflation further eroded their principal, so that a dollar invested in 1945 in the constant 20-year maturity portfolio fell to *6 cents* in real terms by 1981, counting principal only. Coupon income caused the total real returns on bonds to be somewhat less disastrous.

The bear market, or rise in yields, was due to the unprecedented peacetime inflation that accelerated almost continuously over the same years. In previous inflations, investors had anticipated a return to price stability or deflation within the life of long-term bonds, keeping long-term bond yields under 8 percent even in the most inflationary years of the nineteenth century. In the postwar inflation, investors eventually learned from bitter experience that inflation was not only durable, but likely to accelerate over a long-term bond's life. Yields soared and bond prices crashed.

The great bond bear market ended suddenly in 1981. By the middle of 1982, yields were falling even more rapidly than they had risen. Bond prices skyrocketed, but since they were rising from extremely depressed levels, most investors were simply recovering a portion of what they had lost. The lucky few who bought bonds when yields were at their highest enjoyed a real bonanza. By 1986, yields had fallen to about 8 percent and have remained near there ever since. This level is roughly the maximum level reached over the country's history until late in the previous decade.

A different perspective on the history of U.S. interest rates can be obtained by examining changes in yield curves over time. Thomas Coleman, Lawrence Fisher, and Roger G. Ibbotson estimated *spot* yield curves from 1926 to 1989.[9] Figure 11-10 is a graph of their estimates of year-end spot yield curves from 1971 to 1989. The figure illustrates that the 1970s and 1980s were a period of extreme volatility not only in overall interest rate levels but also in yield curve shapes.

Real Interest Rates

We have already seen the movement in real interest rates since 1960, but what about prior years? In Figure 11-11 the short-term U.S. real riskless interest rate from 1926 to 1990 is displayed. For the entire period, it averages 0.61 percent, practically indistinguishable from zero.

During the deflationary 1920s and early 1930s, real interest rates climbed to great heights as Treasury yields approached zero but rarely dipped below it.[10] Investors do not buy securities with negative yields when they can leave cash in their checking accounts and avoid a negative return. That is, if cash investments earn a near zero (but not negative) interest rate, deflation causes the cash to be worth more over time, producing high real rates of interest.

Later, in the 1940s, real interest rates were persistently negative because the government fixed Treasury bill yields below the high inflation rates of the war and postwar years. Then, beginning with the Treasury–Federal

---

[9]A spot yield curve is constructed by estimating the spot rates for various maturities, the spot rate being the interest rate for a single payment at a specified time. For a more detailed explanation of the procedure used to estimate spot rates see Thomas S. Coleman, Lawrence Fisher, and Roger G. Ibbotson, *U.S. Treasury Yield Curves,* Moody's Investors Service, New York, 1989.

[10]The negative yields observed in the data do not indicate that investors bought bills with a guaranteed negative return. Rather, Treasury bills of that era sometimes contained a provision which made them exchangeable for other bonds or bills with positive yields. The value of this option provision occasionally resulted in bills being quoted above par, producing a spurious negative yield in the data. For further information see Steven G. Cecchetti, "The Case of the Negative Nominal Interest Rates," *Journal of Political Economy,* December 1988.

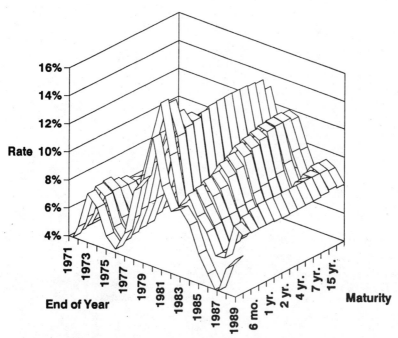

Figure 11-10. Spot yield curves: 1971–1989. (*Source: Thomas S. Coleman, Lawrence Fisher, and Roger G. Ibbotson,* U.S. Treasury Yield Curves, *Moody's Investors Service, New York, 1989.*)

Reserve accords of 1951, Treasury bill yields were deregulated and tracked inflation very closely. Since real interest rates were low and stable, around 1 percent, some academics came to believe that the "natural" real riskless rate was 1 percent.

Again, in the 1970s, the financial winds shifted. While inflation rates soared, expectations and thus nominal interest rates were slower to react. Ex-post real interest rates plunged to sharply negative levels. But the negative real rates on short-term bills were often smaller (and thus better) than the negative real returns on stocks and longer-term bonds. In the 1980s, returns on stocks and bonds both picked up again; cash, too, performed well relative to the moderate inflation rates of the period. By this time, nominal interest rates were very high and they were slow to react to disinflation. Setting aside deflationary periods, the real riskless rate was at record high levels for most of the 1980s. The latter part of the 1980s and the early 1990s have seen a gradual decline in the real interest rate, while remaining above its historical average.

Over the short term, then, Treasury bill yields have deviated substantially from the inflation rate, producing real returns that were markedly positive or

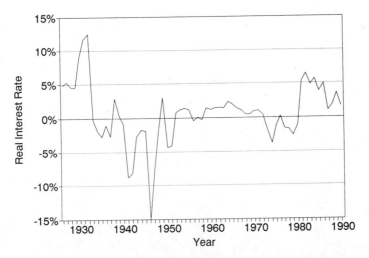

Figure 11-11. U.S. short-term real interest rates: 1926–1990. (*Source:* Stocks, Bonds, Bills, and Inflation 1991 Yearbook™ *(annually updates work by Roger G. Ibbotson and Rex A. Sinquefield), Ibbotson Associates, Inc., Chicago.*)

negative. Some persons claim that the variation of real interest rates occurs because investors incorrectly forecast near-term inflation. If this were so, lenders, as investors, must have accepted negative real rates in 65 out of 93 months from January 1973 to September 1980. Similarly, borrowers, or Treasury bill and commercial paper issuers, must have paid positive real rates to investors in 112 of the 123 months from October 1980 to December 1990. Rational borrowers and lenders would not behave in this way. One plausible explanation of the trends in real interest rates is that short-term inflation is persistently mismeasured; in addition, real interest rates may reflect a varying time value of money as well as varying expectations of inflation.

Yields from the Distant Past

Business enterprises have existed for thousands of years and bond yields are available anecdotally back to the preclassical period of history. Bond or loan yields from the distant past provide evidence of early economic activity and the interest rates that lenders charged. The rates in this section are provided only to give a long-term perspective. More recent returns, on the other hand, are typically measured more accurately to set standards for investment performance. Thus, a continuous series of returns is unnecessary.

Table 11-6. Long-Term Bond Yields from Medieval Times to 1799
Minimum Rates on Best Credits by Half Century

Date	England	France	Nether-lands	Germany	Switzer-land	Italy
1200–1249	—	—	8.00	—	—	—
1250–1299	—	14.00	8.00	—	—	6.62
1300–1349	—	—	8.00	—	—	4.88
1350–1399	—	—	8.00	—	—	5.25
1400–1449	—	10.00	8.00	—	—	6.00
1450–1499	—	10.00	8.00	5.00	—	5.00
1500–1549	10.00	8.33	4.00	4.00	—	4.00
1550–1599	10.00	8.33	4.00	4.00	—	4.00
1600–1649	8.00	8.33	5.00	—	—	—
1650–1699	4.00	5.00	3.00	—	—	—
1700–1749	3.05	5.00	3.00	4.00	5.00	4.00
1750–1799	3.13	5.00	2.50	4.00	4.00	4.00

SOURCE: Sidney Homer, *A History of Interest Rates.* Copyright © 1963, 1977 by Rutgers, the
State University. Reprinted with permission of the Rutgers University Press.

The economist Sidney Homer finds that bond yields in ancient times
formed a bow-shaped pattern over time.[11] These yields reached a low of
about 10 percent in Babylon, 6 percent in Greece, and 4 percent in Rome,
at the time of each empire's economic heyday. From these patterns, he the-
orizes that as trust between business participants increases and as economies
mature, interest rates decrease. One reason is that creditworthiness
becomes easier to evaluate, so that borrowers with the best credit pay closer
to the true riskless rate. When trust decreases with political and economic
disruptions, and when information becomes unreliable, interest rates
increase correspondingly. Inflation is also impounded in these rates, and it
is likely that prices were most stable at the high-water mark of each empire.

More continuous information on bond markets exists from the thirteenth
century on. Such quotes, shown in Table 11-6 (covering A.D. 1200 to 1799)
and Table 11-7 (1800 to the present), indicate which countries were most
active economically. Before 1500, these were Italy and the Netherlands; after
that date, economic activity is evident throughout Europe. In the nineteenth
and twentieth centuries, bonds are issued as business activity picks up in the
United States and Canada.

[11]Sidney Homer, *A History of Interest Rates,* Rutgers University Press, 1977.

Table 11-7. Long-Term Bond Yields from 1700 to 1989
Decennial Averages

Date	England	France	Nether-lands	Germany	Sweden	Switzer-land	Italy	United States
1700–1709	7.00	—	—	—	—	—	—	—
1710–1719	6.00	—	—	—	—	—	—	—
1720–1729	3.40	—	—	—	—	—	—	—
1730–1739	3.05	—	—	—	—	—	—	—
1740–1749	3.22	—	—	—	—	—	—	—
1750–1759	3.13	—	—	—	—	—	—	—
1760–1769	3.59	—	—	—	—	—	—	—
1770–1779	3.75	—	—	—	—	—	—	—
1780–1789	4.64	—	—	—	—	—	—	—
1790–1799	4.54	14.00	6.42	—	—	—	—	7.49
1800–1809	4.80	8.66	—	—	—	—	—	6.23
1810–1819	4.57	7.29	5.95	5.45	—	—	—	6.39
1820–1829	3.72	4.21	4.79	4.91	—	—	—	4.55
1830–1839	3.40	4.06	5.11	4.05	—	—	—	4.95
1840–1849	3.26	4.14	4.53	3.84	—	—	—	5.41
1850–1859	3.16	4.45	4.02	4.08	4.64	—	—	4.33
1860–1869	3.27	4.37	4.21	4.03	5.41	—	—	5.34
1870–1879	3.19	4.71	4.17	4.29	4.91	—	—	4.98
1880–1889	2.97	3.68	3.55	3.82	3.73	—	—	3.60
1890–1899	2.47	3.03	2.93	3.53	3.68	—	—	3.23
1900–1909	2.79	3.06	3.20	3.64	3.74	3.68	—	3.17
1910–1919	3.81	4.06	4.00	4.72	5.10	4.52	—	3.93
1920–1929	4.63	5.22	4.50	7.25	4.72	5.20	5.68	4.26
1930–1939	3.54	3.98	3.50	6.26	3.48	3.94	4.74	3.34
1940–1949	3.06	3.60	3.24	3.84	3.04	3.31	4.16	2.31
1950–1959	4.31	5.68	3.52	4.08	3.65	2.96	6.12	2.99
1960–1969	6.53	5.39	5.30	4.03	5.16	3.84	5.70	4.51
1970–1979	12.18	9.69	8.18	4.29	8.72	5.19	11.18	7.60
1980–1989	11.16	11.65	8.03	7.41	12.21	4.63	14.38	10.39

SOURCE: Sidney Homer, *A History of Interest Rates.* Copyright © 1963, 1977 by Rutgers, the State University. Reprinted with permission of Rutgers University Press. Updated by the authors.

Conclusion

In a hypothetical perfectly integrated and efficient world capital market, real interest rates should be equal across countries. Evidence from the last 40 years contradicts this belief. The opportunity to obtain high real returns while simultaneously diversifying one's portfolio leads us to conclude that foreign bonds are an appropriate and desirable portion of an institutional investment portfolio.

PART 5

Inflation and Other Assets

12

Inflation Around the World

Inflation is a "sustained increase in the general price level over time."[1] Like death and taxes, inflation today is typically regarded as a certainty — not a matter of whether, but merely of when and how much. This has not always been the case, however. Until the second half of the twentieth century, sustained inflation in peacetime was almost unknown. In the United Kingdom, where records of prices have been kept longer than in any other country, inflation averaged a minuscule 0.35 percent per year from 1260 to 1914.

More than all of this increase, which amounts to a tenfold price rise in the better part of a millennium, came during wars and in the sixteenth century, when gold importation from the New World greatly increased the European monetary supply. During the interim periods, prices trended slowly *downward*.[2] The trend of prices was relatively flat because commodities (typically gold and/or silver) were widely used as money, and the aggregate stock of these commodities was relatively fixed. Responsible governments used fiat (unbacked) money only temporarily as a matter of desperation, such as in time of war. Less responsible governments, the prototype being the French

---

[1] Robert J. Barro, *Macroeconomics,* John Wiley & Sons, 1984.

[2] The primary source of the antiquarian inflation data for the United Kingdom is E. H. Phelps Brown and Sheila V. Hopkins, "Seven Centuries of the Prices of Consumables, Compared with Builders' Wage Rates," *Economica,* November 1956. An updating and interpretive study of this series, and a comparison with other countries' inflation experience, is in Michael Jefferson's classic paper, "A Record of Inflation," in Michael Jefferson, Andrew D. White, Thomas Mann, and Walter W. Rostow, *Inflation,* Riverrun Press, New York, 1978.

revolutionary regime,[3] issued fiat money as a matter of course. The rule of those governments was generally short, however, and they left behind no price series for study.

The general replacement of commodity-related money by fiat money began with the breakdown of gold convertibility arrangements in the 1920s and 1930s, as noted in Chapter 2. By the early 1970s, exchange rates were floating (more or less) relative to each other and floating unconditionally relative to gold; the official dominance of fiat money was complete. Central banks now manage the growth of the national money supplies. The inflation that started after World War II, in stark contrast to the deflations that followed earlier wartime inflations, is testimony to the fact that these newer institutions have not worked particularly well to achieve stability of prices.[4]

The Great Inflation

As we have noted, prices continued to rise after World War II, in contrast to earlier periods. In some countries, by the 1970s, prices were escalating at an even faster pace than during wartime. Throughout the world, inflation appeared to be a permanent fixture in the global economy. This environment of steadily increasing prices can be called the *great inflation*, and its occurrence internationally is unprecedented. In Table 12-1, decade-by-decade consumer inflation rates are presented for nine developed countries over 64 years.[5]

The great inflation did not arrive simultaneously in all countries. While the U.S., German, and Swiss inflation rates settled in at about 1 percent in the 1950s, the United Kingdom suffered 4 percent annual inflation in that decade, France was at 6 percent, and Japan recorded 2.5 percent. While these rates of price increase seem moderate by today's standards, they were a sign of more trouble to come because prices were rising, not falling, after a wartime inflation.

---

[3]Andrew Dickson White's 1876 article, "The Fiat Money Inflation In France," in Michael Jefferson, et al., *Inflation*, Riverrun Press, New York, 1978, describes this episode in detail.

[4]In most countries, the public demand for government services, as expressed through the legislature or parliament if the country is a democracy, typically exceeds the ability or willingness of the public to pay for these services through current taxation. Under such circumstances, inflation (through monetization of government debt) is the only form of taxation available to render the government solvent if the discipline to limit spending is lost.

[5]Consumer prices are used throughout this chapter because of data availability. For a discussion of the limitations of consumer price indexes as a proxy for the general level of prices see Armen A. Alchian and Benjamin Klein, "On a Correct Measure of Inflation," *Journal of Money, Credit, and Banking*, February 1973.

Table 12-1. International Consumer Price Indexes (1926–1989)
(Year-end 1925 = 1.00; Germany, 1948 = 1.00)

Decade	Annual rate of change(%)	End-of-period index	Annual rate of change (%)	End-of-period index	Annual rate of change (%)	End-of-period index
	Canada		France		Germany	
1926–29	0.18	1.01	8.52	1.39	0.33	—
1930–39	−1.80	0.84	3.08	1.88	−1.96	—
1940–49	4.52	1.31	31.48	29.02	—	—
1950–59	2.36	1.65	6.40	53.97	1.05	1.11
1960–69	2.59	2.13	3.78	78.17	2.47	1.42
1970–79	7.54	4.41	9.09	186.66	5.02	2.32
1980–89	6.23	8.07	6.88	363.09	2.77	3.05
	Italy		Japan		Sweden	
1926–29	−2.82	0.89	−4.46	0.83	−0.98	0.96
1930–39	0.24	0.91	2.11	1.03	0.10	0.97
1940–49	47.72	45.19	66.80	171.17	4.10	1.45
1950–59	2.65	58.69	2.42	217.50	4.39	2.23
1960–69	3.66	84.09	5.51	371.97	3.52	3.15
1970–79	12.88	282.43	8.94	876.08	8.72	7.27
1980–89	10.72	781.94	2.32	1101.92	7.66	15.21
	Switzerland		United Kingdom		United States	
1926–29	−1.05	0.96	−1.68	0.93	−1.09	0.96
1930–39	−1.53	0.82	−0.41	0.90	−2.05	0.78
1940–49	4.76	1.31	5.69	1.56	5.41	1.32
1950–59	1.08	1.46	4.36	2.39	1.02	1.64
1960–69	3.20	1.99	3.68	3.44	2.52	2.10
1970–79	4.99	3.25	13.04	11.71	7.37	4.28
1980–89	3.34	4.51	6.96	22.95	5.10	7.04

SOURCE: Starting in 1960, *International Financial Statistics* (various issues), International Monetary Fund, Washington, D.C.; DRI-FACS, a service of DRI/McGraw-Hill, Lexington, Mass. Prior to 1960, the authors collected government statistics from diverse sources.

In the 1920s and 1930s, inflation rates were negative or near zero in most countries. Monetization of government deficits associated with World War II caused inflation rates to rise from the previous decade in every country shown in Table 12-1, with France, Italy, and Japan showing spectacularly high rates.[6]

For the most part, inflation accelerated modestly in the 1950s and 1960s. France, Sweden, and the United Kingdom actually saw a reduction in inflation rates from the 1950s to the 1960s. For the 1950s, France had the highest rate at 6.4 percent, with Germany, Switzerland, and the United States approximately tied for the lowest rate at about 1 percent. For the 1960s,

[6]Germany had high inflation during World War II as well, but the exact rates are unknown. In 1948 the worthless reichsmark was officially replaced by the deutschemark.

Japan had the highest rate, 5.5 percent, and Germany, the United States, and Canada had the lowest rates, about 2.5 percent.

In the 1970s, inflation accelerated spectacularly around the world. Of the nine countries in Table 12-1, only Switzerland had a compound annual inflation rate below 5 percent; seven had rates over 7 percent; and two were over 12 percent. All nine countries had higher inflation rates in the 1970s than in any other peacetime decade shown in Table 12-1.

The global inflation surge in the 1970s was initiated by a nonmonetary force—the monopoly pricing activity of OPEC. The oil price shocks had permanent effects on the *level* of world prices, as the wealth of the oil-consuming nations was reduced. However, in many countries, this one-time price level boost was translated into sustained increases in the *rate of change* of prices. Among these major countries, only Germany, Japan, and Switzerland maintained control of their domestic monetary policies and began to make progress in reducing the trends of their inflation rates in the late 1970s. For the others, including the United States, money growth remained excessive into the 1980s and progress in slowing inflation was delayed until the decade was well underway.

Inflation decelerated dramatically from 1982 to 1986 in most of the countries, but the rates as of the early 1990s, while low by the standards of the last two decades, are still high by historical peacetime standards. Figure 12-1 compares inflation rates in five leading countries during the period from 1961 to 1990, and Figure 12-2 shows the cumulative indexes of these inflation rates, with year-end 1960 set equal to 1.00.

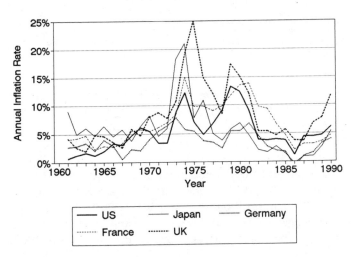

Figure 12-1. World inflation rates: 1961–1990. (*Source:*I/IDEAS U.S. and World Capital Markets *data modules, Ibbotson Associates, Inc., Chicago, 1991.*)

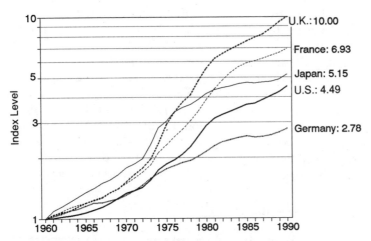

Figure 12-2. World inflation indexes: 1961–1990. (*Source: I/*IDEAS U.S. and World Capital Markets *data modules, Ibbotson Associates, Inc., Chicago, 1991.*)

The arithmetic of compounding illustrates the magnitude of the great inflation. Prices increasing by 4 percent per year will double every 18 years and rise 50-fold in a century. At a 10 percent inflation rate, prices double every 7 years and rise a staggering 14,000-fold in a century.

Effect of Inflation on Capital Market Returns

Inflation affects the returns on different assets in different ways. To illustrate these differing effects, returns on major asset classes are regressed on the inflation rate of that country and the results are displayed in Table 12-2. Gold and silver are regressed on U.S. inflation.

Assets with an inflation beta of 1 have kept up with inflation; such assets are obvious candidates for consideration as inflation hedges. Returns on assets with a zero beta are unrelated to inflation. Assets with betas greater than 1 have rates of return very sensitive to the inflation rate. During inflationary periods, particularly when inflation is unexpected, investors would expect to make money holding assets with inflation betas over 1 (ignoring tax effects). Holding assets with inflation betas of less than 1 or assets with negative inflation betas, investors would expect to lose real value during periods of inflation.

As shown in Table 12-2, virtually all world equity markets have negative (but not significant) betas when regressed on inflation. It is not surprising to find that the relation between equity returns and inflation is weak, as indicated by the low R^2's (which measure the amount of variability of the asset return that is related to variability in inflation) of the regressions. While equities are sometimes observed to react negatively in the short run to increases in inflation rates, there is also evidence that over the long run, equity returns impound inflation rates (having stable long-term real returns). These two effects may be offsetting each other.

While bonds should be expected to be very sensitive to changes in long-run inflation expectations, such expectations are unobservable. The regressions in Table 12-2 measure the reaction of bonds to changes in short-term inflation, which is weak, as indicated by the R^2's near zero. In fact, there is strong evidence from earlier periods that changes in short-run inflation do

Table 12-2. Annual Asset Returns Regressed on Home Country Annual Inflation

Dependent variable	Period	Alpha (%)	Beta	Beta t-statistic	Adjusted R^2
Equities	1970–1990				
United States		22.15	−1.61	−1.48	0.06
Japan		30.24	−2.23	−1.78	0.10
United Kingdom		0.98	1.84	1.24	0.03
Germany		20.63	−2.59	−0.91	−0.01
France		30.16	−1.84	−1.05	0.00
Canada		17.39	−0.81	−0.65	−0.03
Australia		−0.42	1.50	0.71	−0.03
Long-term gov't. bonds	1961–1990				
United States		11.37	−0.90	−1.53	0.04
Japan	1967–1990	9.22	−0.36	−1.31	0.03
United Kingdom		7.31	0.26	0.48	−0.03
Germany		8.51	−0.42	−0.63	−0.02
France		9.68	−0.24	−0.51	−0.03
Canada		8.84	−0.20	0.41	−0.03
Australia		6.04	0.27	0.52	−0.03
Treasury bills	1961–1990				
United States		3.73	0.54	4.49	0.40
Japan		5.89	0.29	3.35	0.26
United Kingdom	1965–1990	7.74	0.26	2.57	0.18
Germany		2.92	0.75	3.95	0.33
France		4.22	0.66	4.92	0.44
Canada		4.45	0.69	3.64	0.30
Australia	1970–1990	11.25	−0.03	−0.09	−0.05
Real Estate	1960–1989				
U. S. business		3.96	0.96	4.95	0.45
U. S. residential		6.97	0.73	4.51	0.40
U. S. farmland		4.45	1.16	2.81	0.19
Metals					
Gold	1972–1990	−21.54	6.07	2.58	0.24
Silver	1971–1990	−53.29	11.48	2.19	0.17

NOTE: Annual inflation rate for Australia is an average of quarterly rates.
SOURCE: Ibbotson Associates, Inc., Chicago, 1991.

not affect bond returns. During both the Civil War and World War II in the United States, long bond yields remained very low during periods of high short-term inflation, presumably because market participants believed the inflation would be reversed by postwar deflation.

Treasury bills, which might be expected to react to short-term inflation rate changes, are seen in Table 12-2 to have highly significant positive inflation betas; the bills were good, but imperfect inflation hedges. The United Kingdom and Japan showed a weaker relation than other countries, and in Australia, bills failed to hedge against inflation. The Australian result is probably due to the annual inflation rate being an average of quarterly rates.

Real estate was the most effective hedge against U.S. inflation over the period studied. This advantage over T-bills was earned at the expense of considerable volatility in the *real* return on real estate, which was positive on average (note the high alphas). Gold and silver were, statistically, "super" inflation hedges—with very large inflation betas—but their overall performance was below that of other assets (note the extremely negative alphas) as these assets fell in price with the deflation of the 1980s.

Causes of Inflation

Many economists believe that the *quantity theory of money* provides a paradigm for explaining inflation. According to this theory, inflation results from increases in the money supply in excess of increases in the amount of goods that the money can buy.[7] An example often given is an island economy consisting only of mangoes and dollars. Given a fixed supply of both dollars and mangoes, the exchange rate between dollars and mangoes (i.e., the dollar price of a mango) remains stable. Assume that an airplane drops a sack of dollars on the island. Because dollars are now more plentiful and mangoes are not, the dollar price of mangoes rises. (The magnitude of the price rise is related to the size of the sack.) In other words, the exchange rate between real goods and money changes in proportion to the quantity of money.

In more complex economies, however, the supply of goods is neither fixed nor homogeneous. There are many goods, and the supply of each grows or shrinks at varying rates. Moreover, the money supply is not clearly defined, with many different instruments used as money or quasi money. Therefore,

---

[7]To be precise, inflation results from an increase in the money supply in excess of increases in the amount of money demanded. Attempts of individuals to dispose of excess money bids up the price of goods and services to a point where *real* money balances are in equilibrium. The driving force is typically presumed to be excessive money creation, with the demand for money being stable.

the observed relation between money and prices is not nearly as precise as in the mango-dollar economy. Nonetheless, empirical evidence from different countries and time periods suggests a direct causal relation between trends in various measures of the money supply and trends in the inflation rate.

A few economists cite other causes of inflation. Some claim that disequilibrium in goods or labor markets causes demand-pull or cost-push inflation, independent of monetary considerations. Others have formulated expectations hypotheses, which suggest that today's inflation is caused by anticipation of future inflation and can be lowered by altering people's expectations about the future.

Measuring Inflation

Consumer Price Index

In most countries, a consumer price index (CPI) is typically the most accessible and consistent measure of aggregate price changes. Despite its limited coverage, the CPI is accepted as a reliable indicator of inflation trends. A CPI is an index of reported prices of a "market basket" of consumer goods. Wage contracts, pension agreements, business contracts, and social security legislation often contain clauses requiring price or wage adjustments based on changes in the CPI. Thus, investors should understand the characteristics and limitations of this frequently used index.

As an inflation measure, the CPI has four main problems:

1. Short-run substitutability
2. Long-run substitutability
3. Changes in the quality of goods for which costs are measured
4. Limited coverage

In the short run, say week to week, the prices of goods that are close substitutes may fluctuate relative to one another. The relative prices of chicken and fish, for example, commonly change by 20 percent or more on a weekly basis. The CPI does not capture this week-to-week fluctuation. Any shopper can beat the index (since it assumes a constant consumption basket) simply by buying more chicken than fish when chicken is relatively cheaper, and vice versa.

Substitutability of goods in the long run is even more difficult to incorporate in the index. For example, scientific calculators fell in price from about $800 in 1970 to about $100 in the 1980s for a similar, but better model. Less powerful calculators, now selling for a few dollars, did not even exist in

1970. The U.S. CPI began to include calculators in the mid-1970s, after most of the price decline had already occurred. This is appropriate because the CPI should reflect the market basket of typical consumers, not only mechanical engineers. Nevertheless, the CPI missed the dramatic 5-year drop in the price of a calculation. Judgment is necessary to determine when goods or services become cheap enough to be part of a typical market basket.[8]

Quality changes also complicate the construction of price indexes. Almost everything undergoes quality changes over long periods. Automobile tires and electronic devices have become more durable and reliable. Today's supermarkets and restaurants contain a variety and quality of foods unimaginable in the era before cheap refrigeration and rapid transport. On the other hand, some labor-intensive services—such as mass transit and artisan's crafts—have declined in quality. Ideally, the CPI should include the cost of these qualitative changes by denominating goods in terms of the services they provide. Since an automobile tire provides miles of "safe" travel, perhaps a 40,000-mile radial tire should be counted as providing four times the consumer utility or satisfaction as a 10,000-mile tire of 40 years ago.

CPIs are necessarily limited in their coverage, meaning they do not track prices for all goods in all economic sectors. One reason is that CPIs are designed to track the price changes faced by a typical consumer. This limited focus means that the CPI leaves out unfinished goods used by producers, luxury goods, and many other categories, and it is thus not necessarily reflective of prices in the entire economy. Another reason is that the statistical sampling necessary to produce a timely CPI series intentionally leaves out some consumables.

The first three difficulties with the CPI all bias the measured inflation rate upward. In other words, the actual inflation rate is likely to be less than the rate as measured by the CPI. The direction of any bias caused by limited coverage is not known. Still another bias exists because the CPI is not an instantaneous "snapshot" of prices but rather a mixture of old and new prices. Thus, during inflation the CPI understates the price level (setting aside all the other biases); during deflation the CPI overstates the price level.

Despite these problems, the CPI remains a useful and important barometer of inflation. Researchers may wish to revise or backdate the consumer price index using more sophisticated construction methods. For practical purposes, however, the CPI provides useful information to those aware of its limitations.

[8]The U.S. market basket was last revised in 1987.

Producer Price Index

Because of the desire to measure prices other than those paid by consumers and because of the problems with the CPI just noted, a number of other price measures have arisen. The producer price index (PPI), (formerly known as the wholesale price index), measures the change in prices paid by the producers of goods. The U.S. index is calculated from a survey of prices received by producers in agriculture, mining, manufacturing, electricity, and natural gas. Many market participants view the PPI as an early indicator of inflationary trends because its components exhibit price changes before the CPI.

The component goods that the PPI is based upon are changed more than the CPI because consumers have certain basic needs (such as food) that change little. For example, a PPI from the 1800s puts a heavy weight on steel rails, nails, and turpentine.[9] Although these commodities are still used today, they are far less important than they were a century ago. Since 1986, component goods of the index are determined by a semi-annual sampling of 40 to 50 industries.

GNP Deflator

There are two types of deflators: implicit and fixed-weight. The implicit GNP deflator is calculated by dividing the current-dollar GNP by the constant-dollar GNP.[10] This calculation method means that the index reflects both changes in prices and the composition of output.[11] Because these effects are interwoven, the fixed-weight deflator has substantial advantages as an inflation measure. The fixed-weight deflator uses the same formula as the implicit deflator, but the GNP value in the numerator is altered to reflect the same weights for its components as the denominator, so that it reflects only price changes.

---

[9] *Statistical History of the United States from Colonial Times to the Present,* Fairfield Publisher, Stamford, Conn., 1965, pp. 122–124 (series E 101–112).

[10] Gross domestic product (GDP) deflators are used in many countries. The GDP measures the value of final goods and services produced *within* a country. The gross national product (GNP) measures the value of final goods and services produced by a nation's economy, including production in facilities owned by the nation's residents outside as well as within the country.

[11] Note that the GNP deflators do not measure the price of imported goods (although they are influenced by them) while the CPI does.

The Long-Term Record of Inflation and Deflation

The United Kingdom

The English record of inflation from the 1200s to the present, summarized at the beginning of the chapter, is one of the longest data series recorded for any form of human behavior. The tremendous length of the series is attributable to England's having had one government (more or less) and one monetary system for the entire time.[12] The level of consumer prices in England from 1260 to 1976 is illustrated in Figure 12-3.

Prices were quite stable across amazingly long periods of time. The price index, set in the year 1600 equal to 1, almost always remained within the range of 0.1 to 0.4 for 2½ centuries, between the years 1260 and 1510. In the sixteenth century the price level quintupled. England's inflation index rose from a level of 0.2 in 1510 to 1.4 in 1597, settling around 1.0 during the stable Elizabethan years in the first part of the seventeenth century. Between

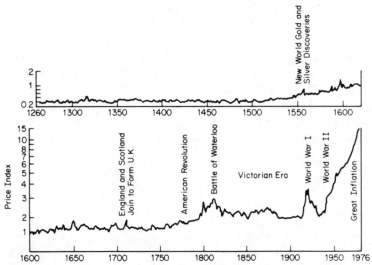

Figure 12-3. Seven hundred years of consumer prices: inflation in the United Kingdom, 1260–1976. (1600=1) (*Source: M. Jefferson, T. Mann, A.D. White, and W.W. Rostow,* Inflation, *Riverrun Press, New York, 1978, p. 75.*)

[12]The English or British Parliament (the government) has met continuously (except for 11 years) since 1295. The monarchical role (the state) has been subject to turbulence (War of the Roses, 1455–1485; Commonwealth, 1649; Restoration, 1660). The pound sterling has undergone few changes since medieval times. Originally defined as a quantity of silver (sterling), the gold sovereign, or pound as it is commonly understood, was unchanged (for all practical purposes) from 1560 to 1931.

1510 and 1610, inflation averaged a compound 1.6 percent per year, the highest long-run inflation rate between 1260 and 1914.

From about 1610 to 1750, the price level in England (later the United Kingdom) remained within the relatively narrow range of 0.8 to 2.0. After 1750, however, prices began to rise steadily, with the peak at the Battle of Waterloo. Wartime financing and the booming economy of the industrial revolution were associated with a doubling of the price level from 1.2 in 1750 to about 2.4 in the 1820–1870 period. Although this doubling of prices represents only a 1 percent compound rate of inflation, inflation rates in individual years were occasionally extreme in the modern sense, reaching 42 percent in 1799.

The Victorian Era was one of price stability. World War I brought on a rapid inflation of the kind associated with the financing of war expenditures. Afterward, prices fell sharply through the 1920s and the great depression of the 1930s. World War II caused another inflation of the classic type. After the end of the war in 1945, however, England entered the great inflation along with the rest of the world.

The United States

Year-by-year inflation rates for the United States beginning with the year 1720 are illustrated in Figure 12-4 and shown in Table 12-3. Prices were quite stable until the Revolutionary War began in 1775, causing rapid inflation. During the revolution, colonial bank notes were supplemented, and later supplanted, by the Continental currency, which was unbacked and authorized by the Continental Congress representing the rebellious 13 colonies. This currency soon became worthless—"not worth a Continental," in the

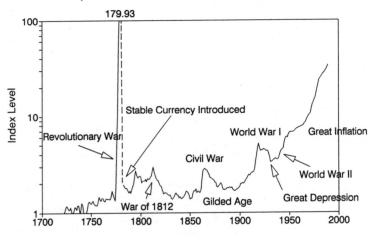

Figure 12-4. U.S. inflation index: 1720–1990. *(Source: Table 12-3.)*

Table 12-3. U.S. Price Index (1720–1990)

Year	Percent change	Price index	Year	Percent change	Price index	Year	Percent change	Price index
			1750	−7.00	1.31	1800	2.38	2.47
			1751	−0.18	1.31	1801	−1.96	2.42
			1752	−0.80	1.30	1802	−14.00	2.08
			1753	−1.79	1.27	1803	4.65	2.18
			1754	−0.73	1.27	1804	0.00	2.18
			1755	−1.65	1.24	1805	0.00	2.18
			1756	2.14	1.27	1806	4.44	2.28
			1757	−2.28	1.24	1807	−6.38	2.13
			1758	2.33	1.27	1808	9.09	2.32
			1759	14.05	1.45	1809	−2.08	2.28
			1760	0.56	1.46	1810	0.00	2.28
			1761	−3.58	1.41	1811	6.38	2.42
			1762	10.07	1.55	1812	2.00	2.47
			1763	2.25	1.58	1813	13.73	2.81
			1764	−12.46	1.39	1814	8.62	3.05
			1765	−0.84	1.37	1815	−12.70	2.66
			1766	5.32	1.45	1816	−7.27	2.47
			1767	−0.80	1.44	1817	−5.88	2.32
			1768	−3.23	1.39	1818	−4.17	2.23
1719		1.00	1769	−3.17	1.34	1819	0.00	2.23
1720	0.00	1.00	1770	4.92	1.41	1820	−8.70	2.03
1721	−8.82	0.91	1771	4.19	1.47	1821	−4.76	1.94
1722	3.82	0.95	1772	11.29	1.64	1822	0.00	1.94
1723	3.31	0.98	1773	−5.18	1.55	1823	−10.00	1.74
1724	5.46	1.03	1774	−4.64	1.48	1824	−8.33	1.60
1725	8.66	1.12	1775	−7.47	1.37	1825	3.03	1.65
1726	4.55	1.17	1776	38.46	1.90	1826	0.00	1.65
1727	−3.37	1.13	1777	205.19	5.78	1827	0.00	1.65
1728	−4.92	1.08	1778	81.47	10.50	1828	−2.94	1.60
1729	−0.32	1.07	1779	396.41	52.10	1829	−3.03	1.55
1730	5.95	1.14	1780	255.13	185.02	1830	0.00	1.55
1731	−11.12	1.01	1781	−51.77	89.23	1831	0.00	1.55
1732	−4.02	0.97	1782	−97.26	2.45	1832	−6.25	1.45
1733	7.66	1.04	1783	−14.68	2.09	1833	−3.33	1.40
1734	−3.11	1.01	1784	−5.37	1.97	1834	3.45	1.45
1735	0.69	1.02	1785	−6.83	1.84	1835	3.33	1.50
1736	−4.78	0.97	1786	0.10	1.84	1836	6.45	1.60
1737	8.97	1.06	1787	−1.14	1.82	1837	3.03	1.65
1738	0.00	1.06	1788	−6.26	1.71	1838	−5.88	1.55
1739	−9.77	0.95	1789	−3.49	1.65	1839	0.00	1.55
1740	6.20	1.01	1790	4.65	1.72	1840	−6.25	1.45
1741	28.98	1.31	1791	−5.56	1.63	1841	3.33	1.50
1742	−3.82	1.26	1792	10.59	1.80	1842	−4.29	1.44
1743	−11.73	1.11	1793	8.51	1.95	1843	0.19	1.44
1744	−4.92	1.05	1794	5.88	2.07	1844	2.43	1.47
1745	1.98	1.08	1795	21.30	2.51	1845	2.55	1.51
1746	7.55	1.16	1796	−11.45	2.80	1846	4.80	1.58
1747	10.93	1.28	1797	−10.27	2.51	1847	7.46	1.70
1748	12.75	1.45	1798	−6.87	2.34	1848	−0.47	1.70
1749	−2.57	1.41	1799	3.28	2.41	1849	−3.17	1.64

(Continued)

Table 12-3. U.S. Price Index (1720–1990) (Continued)

Year	Percent change	Price index	Year	Percent change	Price index	Year	Percent change	Price index
1850	−4.42	1.57	1900	2.42	1.84	1950	5.79	6.71
1851	−9.25	1.42	1901	4.28	1.92	1951	5.87	7.10
1852	1.32	1.44	1902	5.95	2.04	1952	0.88	7.17
1853	0.37	1.45	1903	0.00	2.04	1953	0.63	7.21
1854	12.99	1.64	1904	1.74	2.07	1954	−0.50	7.18
1855	5.25	1.72	1905	−0.13	2.07	1955	0.37	7.20
1856	−0.31	1.72	1906	2.89	2.13	1956	2.86	7.41
1857	5.32	1.81	1907	4.86	2.23	1957	3.02	7.63
1858	−9.06	1.64	1908	2.93	2.30	1958	1.76	7.77
1859	4.08	1.71	1909	4.98	2.41	1959	1.50	7.88
1860	−1.10	1.69	1910	5.08	2.53	1960	1.48	8.00
1861	−2.86	1.64	1911	−1.72	2.49	1961	0.67	8.05
1862	7.84	1.77	1912	1.42	2.53	1962	1.22	8.15
1863	21.21	2.15	1913	7.76	2.72	1963	1.65	8.29
1864	30.75	2.81	1914	1.35	2.76	1964	1.19	8.39
1865	3.35	2.90	1915	1.00	2.79	1965	1.92	8.55
1866	0.65	2.92	1916	7.57	3.00	1966	3.35	8.83
1867	−3.63	2.82	1917	17.43	3.52	1967	3.04	9.10
1868	0.68	2.84	1918	17.45	4.13	1968	4.72	9.53
1869	−6.14	2.66	1919	14.86	4.75	1969	6.11	10.12
1870	−5.42	2.52	1920	15.83	5.50	1970	5.49	10.67
1871	−6.05	2.36	1921	−10.67	4.91	1971	3.36	11.03
1872	−0.69	2.35	1922	−6.34	4.60	1972	3.41	11.41
1873	−1.85	2.31	1923	1.79	4.68	1973	8.80	12.41
1874	−1.89	2.26	1924	0.20	4.69	1974	12.20	13.92
1875	−2.29	2.21	1925	2.54	4.81	1975	7.01	14.90
1876	−3.94	2.12	1926	−1.49	4.74	1976	4.81	15.62
1877	−1.03	2.10	1927	−2.08	4.64	1977	6.77	16.67
1878	−9.84	1.89	1928	−0.97	4.60	1978	9.03	18.18
1879	−1.15	1.87	1929	0.20	4.61	1979	13.31	20.60
1880	3.63	1.94	1930	−6.03	4.33	1980	12.40	23.15
1881	3.51	2.01	1931	−9.52	3.92	1981	8.94	25.22
1882	3.12	2.07	1932	−10.30	3.51	1982	3.87	26.20
1883	−5.78	1.95	1933	0.51	3.53	1983	3.80	27.19
1884	−7.39	1.81	1934	2.03	3.60	1984	3.95	28.27
1885	−2.71	1.76	1935	2.99	3.71	1985	3.77	29.33
1886	1.08	1.78	1936	1.21	3.75	1986	1.13	29.66
1887	0.15	1.78	1937	3.10	3.87	1987	4.41	30.97
1888	3.21	1.84	1938	−2.78	3.76	1988	4.42	32.34
1889	0.44	1.85	1939	−0.48	3.75	1989	4.65	33.84
1890	0.00	1.85	1940	0.96	3.78	1990	6.11	35.91
1891	1.47	1.87	1941	9.72	4.15			
1892	1.47	1.87	1942	9.29	4.53			
1893	2.37	1.88	1943	3.16	4.68			
1894	−5.50	1.78	1944	2.11	4.78			
1895	−1.68	1.75	1945	2.25	4.88			
1896	−2.02	1.71	1946	18.17	5.77			
1897	1.59	1.74	1947	9.01	6.29			
1898	3.13	1.79	1948	2.71	6.46			
1899	0.30	1.80	1949	−1.80	6.34			

SOURCE: For 1720 to 1774, Anne Bezanson, Robert D. Gray, and Miriam Hussey, "Wholesale Prices in Philadelphia," part I, Industrial Research Study no. 29, Philadelphia, 1936, cited in *Historical Statistics of the United States*, Bureau of the Census, 1975, series E-97-111 (pp. 205–206). For 1801 to 1841 and 1914 to 1925, *Historical Statistics of the United States*, U.S. Bureau of the Census, Department of Commerce, Washington, D.C., various tables. For 1842 to 1913, *Review of Economics and Statistics*, February 1934, cited in *Historical Statistics of the United States*, Bureau of the Census, 1975, series E-184 (p. 212). For 1926 to 1990, *Stocks, Bonds, Bills, and Inflation 1991 Yearbook*™ (annually updates works by Roger G. Ibbotson and Rex A. Sinquefield), Ibbotson Associates, Inc., Chicago. For all other years, the information was collected by the authors from diverse sources.

phrase of the day. Introduction of a stable U.S. dollar in 1782 (replacing the colonial and ill-fated Continental currencies) brought prices back to their prewar level, producing a spurious 97 percent deflation rate for the year. Since the new currency was not convertible on a one-for-one basis with the old, those who held cash would not have realized a tremendous real gain. Therefore, the index line in Figure 12-4 is broken rather than shown as true deflation.

The nineteenth century, along with the early Federal period immediately preceding it, was a period of great price stability. Prices fluctuated in a two-to-one range from 1782 to 1915, exceeding even the British record of price stability. The severest inflation of this period occurred during the Civil War, when the inflation rate reached 31 percent, but prices fell quickly and steadily after the Civil War to a level equal to that of 1860.

The inflation index broke out of its 2-to-1 range in World War I, with sharp price increases in each year from 1916 to 1920. The economic boom of the roaring twenties then followed, with prices slowly *declining* over the period. (As the quantity of goods grew but the money supply did not, prices fell.) The great depression of the 1930s was associated with an extremely sharp contraction in the money supply and hence a deflation. Milton Friedman and Anna Schwartz have identified the money supply contraction as an important contributor to the severity of the depression.[13] Prices then began to rise, in response first to aggressive monetary expansion to fund New Deal measures in the 1930s and later to fund World War II in the 1940s. The 1950s and the first half of the 1960s exhibited price stability almost as impressive as that of Victorian Britain and America. But starting around 1966, as previously indicated, the United States too experienced the great inflation.

Hyperinflation

The record of inflation is incomplete without a consideration of *hyperinflation*, an unchecked and radical increase in the price level. While the United States and most industrial countries have not approached hyperinflation in the recent past, it is a constant reality for many third world countries and is a conceivable outcome in any economy based on unbacked money.

Two types of hyperinflation can be distinguished. The traditional kind is characterized by a gradual building from mere inflation to fabulously high rates of price increase, followed by a complete collapse of the monetary sys-

---

[13]Milton Friedman and Anna J. Schwartz, *A Monetary History of the United States, 1867–1960*, Princeton University Press, Princeton, N.J., 1963.

tem and a resulting currency reform. German inflation in 1923 typifies *traditional hyperinflation*, in that country, a cup of coffee reportedly doubled in price while being sipped. Such a hyperinflation ends when no one is willing to accept the currency as payment. The government is then forced into a true currency reform, which gives money a sound footing. In recent decades, a second type of hyperinflation has occurred in Israel and many Latin American states. We call it *managed hyperinflation* because double- or triple-digit inflation persists year after year, as governments avoid the move back to monetary discipline.

Traditional Hyperinflation

The first traditional hyperinflation to be carefully documented occurred after the French Revolution of 1789. Because the new popular regime was expected to provide prosperity through easy credit, the Revolutionary government issued *assignats*, or paper money supposedly backed by land, in ever-increasing quantities. But the land backing proved to be worthless, and free-market prices rose to astronomical levels. Meanwhile, the government, which became known for its Reign of Terror, prescribed death as the penalty for trading at prices other than low official prices. Ultimately, the French government repudiated the national debt, and a stable monetary policy was imposed under the dictatorship of Napoleon. This French hyperinflation set the pattern for future hyperinflations.[14]

A hundred and thirty years after the paper money inflation in France, neighboring Germany experienced a similar inflation. The two causes here were probably exorbitant war reparations and massive government debts incurred to finance World War I. German hyperinflation has been cited as a principal reason for the rise of Hitler and the totalitarian state, a connection popularized by the novelist Thomas Mann in *The Witches' Sabbath*.[15]

In Table 12-4, month-by-month German price levels in the period 1921–1923 are documented, along with month-by-month (and later week-by-week) price levels in post-World War II Hungary.[16] The 50-billion-fold rise in the German price index in the 28 months from July 1921 to November 1923 speaks for itself. This price spiral ended only when the German government repudiated its debts, stopped its reparation payments, and issued a new mark tied to gold.

---

[14]See Andrew D. White, "Fiat Money Inflation in France," in Michael Jefferson et al., *Inflation*, Riverrun Press, New York, 1978.

[15]Translated and reprinted in Michael Jefferson et al., *Inflation*, Riverrun Press, New York, 1978.

[16]David F. De Rosa, *Rates of Return on Common Stocks and Inflation: Theories and Tests*, doctoral dissertation, University of Chicago, 1978.

In Hungary after World War II, inflation reached even more preposterous proportions, with a 4 octillion to one rise in prices in a single year of furious money printing. (An octillion is 1 followed by 27 zeros.) Such numbers defy analysis.

Managed Hyperinflation

Managed hyperinflation has been a way of life in Israel since its founding and has become prevalent in many third world countries, especially in Latin America. In countries with managed hyperinflation, such as those in Table 12-5, very high rates of inflation have persisted without any meaningful currency reform. Token reforms, such as moving the decimal place and/or changing the name of the currency, do not affect the inflation rate. Nevertheless, this is done all the time, presumably so that people do not have to figure their transactions in billions. In a couple of generations, Brazil has gone from the reis to the milreis (1000 reis) to the cruziero (1000 milreis), the cruzado (10,000 cruzieros), and now the new cruzado (1000 old cruzados).

In economies with managed hyperinflation, consumers, investors, and institutions adjust to changing price levels. Ownership of short-term money market instruments is the investor's first line of defense against managed hyperinflations. Index-linked bonds, which have a payoff tied to a price index, have been popular in Argentina, Israel, Brazil, and other countries. Stocks and real estate are often held as inflation hedges, with varying success. Finally, tangible or consumable assets are bought in lieu of money-denominated assets. In Brazil, for example, a vintage automobile is often stored for years in a garage to preserve the owner's capital. Whatever the course of the new cruzado or the Brazilian economy, the car owner will receive a return in the form of transportation when this capital asset is used.

The spread of managed hyperinflation in recent years is astonishing. There are probably as many hyperinflations taking place today as in the remainder of recorded history. While tighter money and the drop in energy prices since the early 1980's has moderated inflation in most countries, some countries with managed hyperinflations continue to set new records for the speed of price increases.

Inflation and the Stock Market

Years ago, it was generally believed that inflation was good for the stock market. Corporations (it was held), as sellers of goods and services, would benefit from increases in the prices of the goods they sell every day. Meanwhile,

Table 12-4. Hyperinflation in Germany and Hungary

Germany: July 1921–Nov. 1923		Hungary: July 1945–July 1946	
Calendar month	Price index	Calendar month	Price index
July 1921	1.00	July 1945	1.00
August	1.34	August	1.63
September	1.45	September	3.61
October	1.72	October	23.15
November	2.39	November	123.61
December	2.44	December	395.03
January 1922	2.57	January 1946	688.86
February	2.87	February	4,151.30
March	3.80	March	17,837.27
April	4.44	April	340,860.58
May	4.52	May	107.30 million
June	4.92	June (1st week)	8.21 billion
July	7.03	June (2nd week)	9.09 billion
August	13.43	July (1st week)	29,202.42 trillion
September	20.07	July (2nd week)	108.82 quintillions
October	39.58	July (3rd week)	343,037.70 quintillions
November	80.70	July (4th week)	3,805,933.33 sextillions
December	103.51		
January 1923	194.76		
February	390.56		
March	341.47		
April	364.48		
May	571.33		
June	1,335.59		
July	5,229.86		
August	66,016.85		
September	1.70 millions		
October	496.20 millions		
November	50,769.20 millions		

SOURCE: For Hungary, David F. DeRosa, *Rates of Return on Common Stock and Inflation: Theories and Tests*, Ph.D. dissertation, University of Chicago, 1978. For Germany, Michael Jefferson et al., *Inflation*, Riverrun Press, New York, 1978.

they enter into long-term, fixed-price contracts with suppliers such as labor unions and sellers of raw materials. If this were literally true, unexpected inflation would boost corporate profits and stock prices.

This story cannot be true given the behavior of other agents in the economy. Corporations sell as well as buy goods according to long-term, fixed-price contracts; to the extent they do, they are hurt by unexpected inflation.

Table 12-5. Accelerating Inflation in Three High-Inflation Economies (1960–1990)

	Brazil		Israel		Mexico	
Period	Rate of change (%)	Index	Rate of change (%)	Index	Rate of change (%)	Index
1959		1		1		1
1960–1969	44.20	39	5.22	2	2.09	1
1970–1979	29.95	534	31.01	25	15.28	5
1980–1990	303.22	2,445,435,333	94.34	37,017	61.57	983

NOTE: Rate of change is the compound annual return for the period indicated.
SOURCE: *International Financial Statistics* (various issues), published by the International Monetary Fund, Washington, D.C.

Moreover, consumers resist price increases. Finally, noncorporate sellers of services, such as labor unions, have become aware of inflation risk and try to index their contracts to inflation. These factors combine to make inflation either damaging to corporations or, at best, neutral.

The regression results in Table 12-2 suggest a statistically weak negative relation between inflation rates and stock returns. Eugene Fama and William Schwert found a stronger negative relation.[17] Studying the special case of the 1923 hyperinflation in Germany, David DeRosa (see footnote 16) found that stocks, being claims to real economic assets, hedged inflation much better than any other financial instrument, but that stockholders would nevertheless have been better off had the hyperinflation not taken place.

Steven Leuthold, of the Leuthold Group in Minneapolis, suggested a framework in which the short-term effect of inflation on the stock market could be evaluated in a way that avoids some of the ambiguity of regression results.[18] Using this framework, we rank yearly equity returns by the year's inflation rate in the upper half of Table 12-6. Six rates of price change are identified:

1. Extraordinary deflation

2. Moderate deflation

3. Price stability

4. Moderate inflation

5. High inflation

6. Extraordinary inflation

[17]Eugene F. Fama and G. William Schwert, "Asset Returns and Inflation," *Journal of Financial Economics*, 1977.

[18]Steven C. Leuthold, *The Myths of Inflation and Investing*, Crain Books, 1980.

For each group, the average inflation-adjusted total return of the stock market is then calculated.

Price stability, moderate deflation, and extraordinary deflation all had salutary effects on stock prices and, consequently, on total real equity returns. During the years of moderate inflation, the stock market's returns were unexceptional. Stocks performed worse—in fact, real returns were negative—in periods of extraordinary inflation. Returns were only a little bit better in high inflation periods.

Inflation-adjusted returns are ranked by the rate of change in inflation in the lower half of Table 12-6. Four categories are identified:

1. Rapid deceleration

2. Low deceleration

3. Low acceleration

4. Rapid acceleration

The highest returns over the past two centuries occurred in the rapid deceleration years. Real returns were lowest when inflation accelerated rapidly. Results are similar for the postwar period.

In non-United States markets, changes in inflation are likewise observed to be negatively related to stock market performance. This is due primarily to the correlation of stock returns among countries and inflation rates among countries. In Japan, the two sharply negative years for the stock market, 1973 and 1990, occurred during rising inflation, whereas many of Japan's best stock market years, such as the middle 1980s, had falling rates. A similar pattern is discernible in the United Kingdom, Germany, and other countries.

While the results of this analysis are persuasive, they do not address the question of the long-run impact of inflation on stock market returns. The experience of the 1970s and 1980s suggests that stocks, like bonds, were damaged as inflation accelerated, then recovered as inflation decelerated. On net, the returns on the stock market over a cycle of accelerating and decelerating inflation were not notably higher or lower than returns over other long periods.

This observation is also found in the returns on stocks over the period from 1790 to 1990, shown in Table 12-6. Nominal stock returns were increased by the amount of inflation; real stock returns were about the same in the high-inflation period since 1945 as they were in the low-inflation periods before that date. Thus the negative relation between stocks and inflation is a short- or intermediate-run phenomenon. Over the very long run, stocks behave as claims to real economic assets, for which money (inflation) is a veil that does not affect value.

Table 12-6. Inflation Rate Changes and Equity Returns
1790–1990 and 1946–1990

	Long run: 1790–1990		Postwar years: 1946–1990	
	Number of years	Arithmetic mean real total return (%)	Number of years	Arithmetic mean real total return (%)
Inflation range				
Extraordinary deflation −4.00% and below	32	11.27	0	n/a
Moderate deflation −3.99% to -1.00%	24	12.90	1	22.01
Price stability −0.99% to 0.99%	35	12.53	5	23.02
Moderate inflation 1.00% to 3.99%	56	10.35	19	10.68
High inflation 4.00% to 7.99%	30	4.15	12	8.11
Extraordinary inflation 8.00% and above	24	−5.65	8	−7.82
Inflation rate changes from previous year				
Rapid deceleration Down 5.00% or more	34	11.74	4	10.37
Low deceleration Down 0.01% to 4.99%	64	10.86	18	16.92
Low acceleration Up 0.00% to 4.99%	72	6.90	20	1.79
Rapid acceleration Up 5.00% or more	31	2.69	3	−8.61
All years	201		45	
Arithmetic mean		8.55		7.91
Geometric mean		6.66		7.01

SOURCE: Tables 8-1, 8-2, 8-3, and 12-3

Conclusion

Sustained global inflation is a relatively recent phenomenon. In the past, inflation typically occurred only in countries that were fighting wars, undertaking rapid economic expansion, or importing gold. Inflation may have been minimal in the past because many currencies were tied to one or more monetary metals, which provide a long-term external discipline in the money creation process. The present era is unusual because inflation has persisted throughout the world, with little reason to believe that past price increases will be reversed through deflation. Inflation will probably remain a factor in contemporary society, primarily because governments spend more than they receive in taxes, forcing the governments to borrow. Monetization of this debt causes inflation.

When inflation rates are stable, inflation risk—the risk of a person's wealth changing because of a change in the inflation rate—is lessened. Except where wages and contracts are unconditionally indexed for inflation, persons who are compensated according to long-term, fixed-price contracts, such as bondholders and some wage earners, bear most of society's inflation risk and should be most interested in stabilizing inflation. These holders of monetary assets should also prefer lower inflation, since low inflation rates are almost always more stable than high rates. But it is the stability, not the level, of the inflation rate that counts the most, because if inflation is easily forecastable, economic agents can plan for it and mitigate its harmful effects.

Investors with financial as well as human capital should consider price-level changes when making decisions about assets in their portfolios. In evaluating the array of global assets, an adequate compensation for expected inflation is a critical part of expected returns.

13
Real Estate

Over the long run, real estate has provided returns competitive with those of stocks and bonds. Moreover, the low correlation of real estate returns with those of other assets has made real estate a valuable diversification tool. Finally, the degree of comovement between real estate returns and inflation means that it has served as an inflation hedge. This chapter provides a brief discussion of this complex investment.[1]

Characterization of the U.S. Market

The U.S. real estate market in 1990 was approximately the size of the U.S. stock and bond markets combined. Both individuals and institutions participate in this market, many holding real property for their own use. Over 60 percent of U.S. real estate market value is in owner-occupied single family homes. Although businesses most often rent space from investors, they may instead build or buy office buildings, retail stores, hotels, and factories for their own use.

The real estate market for investors includes office and apartment buildings, hotels, shopping centers, industrial property, and raw land. Real estate

---

[1]Portions of this chapter appeared in William N. Goetzmann and Roger G. Ibbotson, "The Performance of Real Estate as an Asset Class," *Journal of Applied Corporate Finance,* Fall 1990.

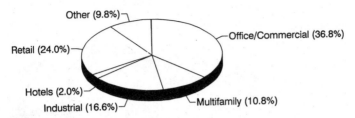

Figure 13-1. Institutional real estate holdings: 1991. (Note: Survey of top 50 managers ranked by tax-exempt assets.) *(Source:* Pensions and Investments *(September 16, 1991) copyright, Crain Communications, Inc. Reprinted with permission.)*

partnerships and institutional investors such as insurance companies and pension funds dominate the market for investment properties other than small apartment buildings. A 1991 survey of the 1000 largest pension funds found that 4.8 percent of defined benefit fund assets were invested in real estate equity and 1.1 percent in mortgages.[2] A similar study broke down institutional holdings by type of property. The percentages are given in Figure 13-1.

Real estate ownership has become more "securitized" through the use of partnerships, syndications, real estate investment trusts (REITs), and various mortgage-backed securities. Real estate securities have the advantage of being more homogeneous and somewhat more liquid than the properties themselves. Most, however, are not traded in organized markets, limiting liquidity and the availability of current price information.

Most residential real estate is held by owner-occupants or individual landlords and is out of reach of the institutional investor. Thus the residential market is not directly relevant to this chapter, which focuses on the "investable" commercial real estate sector. However, the data available to the researcher are both more abundant in scope and longer in historical time for residential real estate than for the commercial sector. We therefore use selected results from analysis of residential real estate to enhance our understanding of the real estate sectors with which institutional investors are concerned.

Sources of Data on Real Estate Returns

Real estate returns typically have been measured less accurately than other asset returns. In analyzing commercial real estate returns, we used three different price series:

[2]*Pensions & Investments,* January 21, 1991, p. 32.

1. The Real Estate Investment Trusts Index (hereafter referred to as REIT), a quarterly series that reports total returns to investment in a diversified portfolio of REITs[3]

2. A quarterly series of total returns based on the largest commingled real estate equity funds (CREFs) constructed by Evaluation Associates (henceforth, CREF)[4]

3. An index of annual returns since 1960 constructed by Roger G. Ibbotson and Laurence B. Siegel (I&S) that consists of unlevered properties[5]

Interestingly, the two principal sources of information about the aggregate performance of business real estate (REITs and CREFs) give conflicting signals. REITs (traded on the New York and American stock exchanges and on the NASDAQ) have higher returns and volatility than CREFs. In addition, the correlation between the return series for REITs and CREFs is low.

To supplement these data we use three residential real estate indicators:

1. The Home-Purchase Index (HOME) of the United States government, which is a monthly capital appreciation series based upon appraisals of a square foot of residential living space

2. A total return series estimated by the Harris Trust & Savings Bank, Chicago, over 1926 to 1986 (HARRIS) and updated by the authors over 1987–1989.

3. A hypothetical portfolio of residential properties with values based upon actual transactions

---

[3]Total return data for the equal-weighted equity REIT series is provided by the National Association of Real Estate Investment Trusts. The series is comprised of from 10 to 40 REITs holding more than 80 percent of their assets in real estate equity as opposed to mortgages. It is updated monthly and not subject to survivorship bias caused by the disappearance of REITs from the index.

[4]The CREF index is based upon approximately 33 of the largest CREFs in the United States, representing about $25 billion in assets. The income return is based upon the income accruing to the CREF shareholders. The appreciation return is based upon property appraisals.

[5]Roger G. Ibbotson and Laurence B. Siegel, "Real Estate Returns: A Comparison With Other Investments," *American Real Estate and Urban Economics Association (AREUEA) Journal,* Fall 1984. For the period 1960–1974, appreciation returns are based upon the Building Cost Index published by the Engineering News-Record. The returns are adjusted for depreciation at 2.5 percent per year; and net operating income is assumed to be a constant 3.5 percent per year, as estimated by Beryl W. Sprinkel and Robert J. Genetski, *Winning with Money,* Dow Jones-Irwin, Homewood, Ill., 1977. For the years 1975–1977, the income and appreciation returns of the First National Bank of Chicago Fund F are used, a commingled fund with a large portfolio of business properties. From 1978 to the present, the FRC Property Index is used. This index measures both capital appreciation and income returns on 900 large properties owned by 30 investment managers.

The third source was created by Karl E. Case and Robert J. Shiller (C&S).[6] The innovation of the C&S index is that it uses actual transactions, instead of appraisals or the stock market, for estimating the risk and return of real estate.

Because transactions occur only rarely, Case and Shiller found it impossible to use traditional index construction methods to produce a price series reflecting the true volatility of the underlying asset. To remedy this, they used a technique called repeat sales regression.[7] Their work has enabled investors to estimate the city-specific risk, and house-specific risk within a city, that is not captured by national aggregate data.[8]

Using the Case and Shiller data, we formed a composite index of residential real estate prices by weighting the four return series equally. As such, the C&S index provides a measure of capital appreciation returns to a very large portfolio of houses in four major markets over 16 years.[9]

For farm real estate, the United States Department of Agriculture (USDA) has been making semiannual appraisals of prices per acre in each U.S. county since 1913. The USDA also provides imputed rents, which allows for the estimation of total returns.[10] The farm real estate total return series (FARM) contrasts with the residential and commercial sectors in that it provides information about land prices only, ignoring the value of buildings.

Because of data collection problems, most real estate return series are much shorter than stock and bond return series. Fortunately, with the exception of the REIT series, all of our indexes extend through a variety of business

---

[6]Karl E. Case and Robert J. Shiller, "The Efficiency of the Market for Single Family Homes," *American Economic Review*, March 1989; "Prices of Single Family Homes Since 1970: Indexes for Four Cities," *New England Economic Review*, 1987; "Forecasting Prices and Excess Returns in the Housing Market," *AREUEA Journal*, Vol. 18, no. 3, 1991. Their portfolio of properties is composed of 40,000 homes which sold at least twice over the period 1970–1986 in four major urban housing markets: San Francisco, Atlanta, Denver, and Chicago.

[7]Repeat sales regression is a statistical technique that uses transaction prices only for properties that have traded two or more times over the period studied, so that actual return is captured, and makes adjustments with the intention that the volatility of the estimated return is as close as possible to the volatility of the underlying asset.

[8]To illustrate, while overall United States nominal returns to property were high throughout the 1980s, most sectors of the Houston housing market had low or negative returns (exhibiting geographic risk). Furthermore, while most of New England showed strong positive returns until the end of the decade, individual properties, depending on location and condition, may have appreciated or depreciated more than the average (exhibiting property-specific risk).

[9]Because no attempt was made to incorporate income (rental) returns into the series, it is not strictly comparable to the commercial series or the Harris residential series.

[10]In their 1984 *AREUEA Journal* article, Ibbotson and Siegel converted the USDA index of farm prices into a composite index (FARM) of farm acreage total returns using USDA imputed rent estimates.

conditions, including boom and recession, high and low interest and inflation rates, and other events that may affect real estate prices. Thus, despite their limited timespan, the data are sufficient to draw some useful conclusions about the long-term historical risks and returns of real estate investment.

Real Estate Returns
Compared to Other Assets

In Figure 13-2, cumulative wealth indexes of returns on five capital assets, including a composite total return index of commercial, residential, and farm real estate, are shown. The return performance of real estate over the last 65 years has been second only to that of common stocks. This observation requires some caveats, most importantly that only residential real estate returns are available for the first one-third of the period (1926–1947).

Depending on the series used, one can get a very different view of the risk and return in real estate. Table 13-1 contains summary statistics of annual returns for various classes of real estate, other assets, and inflation. Note that when compiling the table, we had access to data only through 1989. More recent real estate returns have been notably poor and their inclusion would somewhat alter real estate's risk-return profile. We believe, however, that inclusion of these years would not alter real estate's relative standing with respect to other asset classes over the long run.

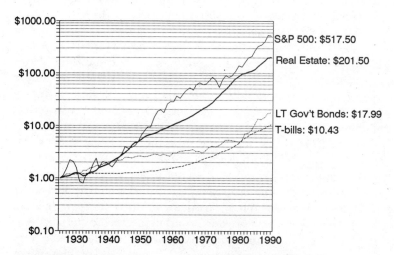

Figure 13-2. Wealth indexes of asset classes: growth of $1 invested at year-end 1925. (*Source:* I/IDEAS U.S. Capital Markets *and* Stocks, Bonds, Bills, and Inflation *data modules, Ibbotson Associates, Inc., Chicago, 1991.*)

Table 13-1. Summary Statistics of Annual Returns for United States
Real Estate, Stocks, Bonds, Bills, and Inflation

Series	Period	Compound annual return (%)	Arithmetic mean return (%)	Standard deviation (%)	Serial correlation
CREF (commercial)	1969–87	10.8	10.9	2.6	.43
REIT (commercial)	1972–87	14.2	15.7	15.4	.11
I&S (commercial)	1960–89	8.7	8.8	4.9	.73
C&S (residential)	1970–86	8.5	8.6	3.0	.17
HOME (residential)	1947–89	9.8	9.9	4.7	.54
HARRIS (residential)	1926–89	8.5	8.7	5.4	.55
FARM (farmland)	1947–89	9.9	10.2	7.8	.64
S&P 500	1947–89	12.3	13.5	16.7	−.10
Long-term govt. bonds	1947–89	4.6	5.0	10.0	.16
U. S. Treasury bills	1947–89	4.9	4.9	3.3	.86
Inflation	1947–89	4.2	4.3	3.5	.66

SOURCE: The CREF, REIT, and C&S summary statistics are from William N. Goetzmann and
Roger G. Ibbotson, "The Performance of Real Estate as an Asset Class," *Journal of Applied
Corporate Finance*, Fall 1990. All other series are from *I/IDEAS United States Capital Markets* data
module, Ibbotson Associates, Inc., Chicago, 1991.

Measures of Commercial Real Estate Return

We mentioned before that REIT and CREF returns give conflicting signals
about commercial real estate. This is illustrated in Table 13-1 where both
the REIT return and standard deviation are much higher than those for the
CREF series. These differences may be explained in part by the fact that
REITs and CREFs trade in two very different markets. Because REIT shares
trade on an exchange, any new information or prevailing opinion about the
future value of the assets is rapidly impounded into the share price by
investors and arbitrageurs. Thus, their returns should continuously reflect
the market's appraisal of the value of the real estate held.

In practice, the REIT series stands out from the other real estate series
with a risk-and-return profile strongly similar to that of the stock market and
has a low correlation with other measures of real estate return. This suggests
that either REITs are priced inappropriately by the market or the alternative
real estate indexes are unreliable. We lean toward the former view.
Although mispriced REITs may provide an arbitrage (if the mispricing is
expected to be corrected or if investors could force liquidation of the portfolio), such arbitrages are not unknown in the stock market: closed-end
mutual funds that hold only extremely liquid stocks are the best-known
example of securities that are priced inappropriately for long periods.

CREF shares are directly purchased from and sold to a fund. The price of CREF shares is estimated for the purpose of trading the shares by aggregating professional appraisals of individual properties in the portfolio. Probably because CREF appreciation returns are based on appraisals and not easily affected by the forces of arbitrage and speculation, they tend to be much more stable and predictable.

Despite these large differences, both series represent risks and returns that actually were experienced by various classes of investors in commercial real estate. All investors have access to the REIT market, and the equity REIT index can be viewed as a fair approximation of actual investor returns since 1972. Although most CREF shares lack the liquidity of stocks, tax-exempt institutional investors are usually able to purchase and redeem shares in commingled funds based upon the appraised appreciation series. Thus, their total returns are represented more or less accurately by the CREF indexes, even if their risks cannot be measured from weekly or monthly price fluctuations.

The Risk of Real Estate

With the exception of the REIT series, all real estate series had relatively little variability from year to year. These low standard deviations must be viewed with caution, however, because of "smoothing" in the appraisal process used to construct most of the indexes. In addition, the low standard deviation of the C&S series, which is transaction-based, is not confirmed by the other transaction-based series (the REIT series). Finally, the high serial correlations indicate a risk not fully revealed by the standard deviations.

Serial Correlation

The high serial correlation of reported real estate returns may be an artificial result caused by appraisal smoothing (see below). On the other hand, the serial correlation of inflation-adjusted, or real, returns for real estate is much closer to zero. This suggests that the high serial correlation of nominal real estate returns observed is largely caused by the high serial correlation of inflation, rather than by appraisal smoothing.

Appraisal Smoothing and Other Issues

The reported return on a real estate portfolio, when estimated by appraisals, may be less volatile than the underlying or true return because of smoothing. One difficulty with the appraisal process is a lack of agreement within the community of appraisers as to what appraisers are supposed to measure—price on value. Some believe the goal of the appraisal process is to provide an alternative measure of market price where explicit bid-ask quotes are not available. Others believe the appraiser is estimating a property's fundamental value. Since we are analyzing rates of return, the appropriate focus for the appraiser in this context is on price.

Appraisals are usually based on three approaches: discounted cash flows, replacement cost, and transaction prices of comparable properties. The present value of future discounted cash flows only approximates market price because of difficulty in estimating the cash flows and discount rate. The replacement cost and comparable sales methods smooth returns because they depend on previous price data—in the first case, costs and in the second, transactions—from various past time periods to estimate current market prices. In a real estate portfolio, returns are further smoothed because not all properties in a portfolio are appraised simultaneously. When all portfolio property returns are averaged, the result is an amalgamation of past and current returns.

Despite these problems, appraisal-based pricing is not necessarily misleading. A case can be made that the smoothed series is closer to the evolution of property prices. By basing the estimated price upon the price an "orderly" sale might bring, the appraisal explicitly ignores liquidity risk in estimating the fair market price of a property.[11]

This reasoning implies that real estate capital appreciation returns have both an orderly sale component and a liquidity risk component.[12] Some analysts have suggested that liquidity risk contributes twice as much to total risk as does the orderly sale component.[13]

In addition to smoothing, the C&S series may be biased. The reason is that to the extent that home sellers prefer to wait rather than sell at discounts to purchase price or perceived fair value, the C&S series overweights rising markets and underweights falling markets.

---

[11]Most stocks, bonds, and cash equivalents are liquid, that is, instantaneously marketable, or convertible into cash, with relatively low search and transaction costs. Reported returns for these assets, based on price quotations, are therefore very close to realizable returns. Real estate, however, cannot be sold instantaneously at the quoted or appraised priced. We call this *liquidity risk*.

[12]The orderly sale component is seen to be smooth when examining transaction prices because it includes only homes that are sold when the buyer wishes to sell. If home sellers are reluctant to recognize a loss (because they are unable to pay off the mortgage with the proceeds of a sale at a large loss, or for other reasons), then they would be less likely to sell their homes in periods of low prices.

[13]See Stephen A. Ross and Randall C. Zisler, "Managing Real Estate Portfolios, Part 3," *Goldman Sachs Real Estate Research*, November 1987.

Scott L. Lummer, Mark W. Riepe, and Laurence B. Siegel took a different approach to estimating the risk of a real estate portfolio.[14] They assumed that the true risk is related to return, and that the very long-run rate of return on real estate is likely to be accurate even if the volatility is seriously misestimated. In fact, over the 1890 to 1986 period, the compound annual return barely changes (as compared with the very different returns of stocks and bonds), even if both the starting and ending values are off by 2-to-1 errors in opposite directions. Their analysis of returns over this period implied a standard deviation of real estate annual returns of 11.7 percent—startlingly different from the C&S estimate of 3 percent, but between that of stocks and bonds.

Correlation of Real Estate Returns with Other Assets

Table 13-2 presents correlations of annual returns between the various real estate series and with other asset classes and inflation. Not surprisingly, the two commercial series (CREF and I&S) are strongly positively correlated, as are the two residential series shown (C&S and HOME). The table does suggest, however, that different classes of real estate are affected differently by general economic forces. Farm real estate has practically no correlation with commercial real estate, and commercial and residential real estate are only weakly correlated with each other. Only residential and farm real estate have a significant positive correlation.

In short, real estate returns appear to be driven by economic forces different from those influencing stock and bond returns. As a consequence, real estate investment provides an alternative to investors looking for ways to hedge against changes in the stock and bond markets. Even if real estate returns were lower and the standard deviation higher than indicated by the data, real estate would still occupy a significant percentage of many investors' optimal policy mixes because of its very low correlation with stocks and bonds.

The top panel of Figure 13-3 is a graph of yearly commercial real estate total returns, portrayed in both nominal and real terms. The bottom panel of the figure shows long-term government bond yields and inflation rates over the same period. Both nominal and real returns on real estate declined from the early 1980s to the early 1990s, a period over which bond yields and

---

[14]Scott L. Lummer, Mark W. Riepe, and Laurence B. Siegel, "Taming Your Optimizer," in Robert A. Klein and Jess Lederman, eds., *Advances in Asset Allocation*, forthcoming, 1993.

Table 13-2. Correlations of Annual Real Estate Returns with the Returns on Other Asset Classes and Inflation

	I&S	CREF	HOME	C&S	FARM	S&P	Long-term gov't. bonds	T-bills	Inflation
I&S	1.00								
CREF	.79	1.00							
HOME	.52	.12	1.00						
C&S	.26	.16	.82	1.00					
FARM	.06	−.06	.51	.49	1.00				
S&P	.16	.25	−.13	−.20	−.10	1.00			
Long-term gov't. bonds	−.04	.01	−.22	−.54	−.44	.11	1.00		
T-bills	.53	.42	.13	−.56	−.32	−.07	.48	1.00	
Inflation	.70	.35	.77	.56	.49	−.02	−.17	.26	1.00

NOTE: Correlation coefficients for each pair of assets and inflation use the maximum number of annual observations. The period for which each series is available is given in Table 13-1.

SOURCE: William N. Goetzmann and Roger G. Ibbotson, "The Performance of Real Estate as an Asset Class," *Journal of Applied Corporate Finance*, Fall 1990.

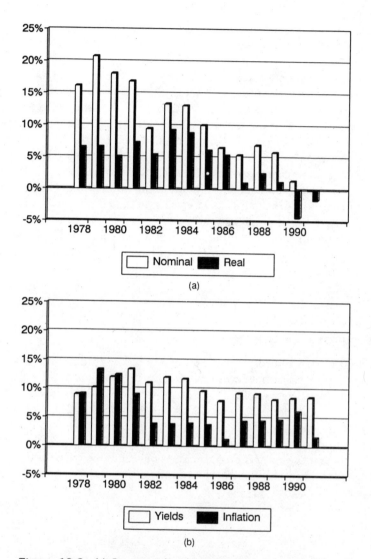

Figure 13-3. (a) Commercial real estate returns (nominal and real), 1978–1991. (b) Long-term government bond yields and inflation: 1978–1991. *(Source: I/IDEAS U.S. Capital Markets and Stocks, Bonds, Bills, and Inflation data modules, Ibbotson Associates, Inc., Chicago, 1991.)*

inflation also fell in tandem. This graph suggests that there is a loose relation between real returns on real estate and (either or both) interest and inflation rates.[15]

To probe this relation further, we regressed quarterly real and nominal real estate returns (from the I&S series) on long-term government bond capital appreciation returns and inflation rates over the period from the first quarter of 1978 to the second quarter of 1991.[16] The regression specifying the nominal return on real estate as the dependent variable shows a significant positive coefficient on inflation. Regressions using real returns on real estate, however, show no significant coefficient for either bond returns or inflation. These results suggest that nominal returns on commercial real estate impound current inflation rates but that inflation has little discernible effect on commercial real estate prices measured in constant dollars. The relation between bond yields and real estate returns, visible in Figure 13-3, appears to be an artifact of the relation between inflation and real estate returns.

Predicting Future
Real Estate Returns

If an asset is fairly priced, then its returns should be commensurate with the risks and other costs that investors perceive. In Chapter 3, we called for a new equilibrium theory (NET) in which the expected or required return on an asset is related not only to its risk as measured by the CAPM or APT but to the costs—such as information costs, transaction costs, and taxes—that investors incur to hold the asset. Using this NET framework, we examine the effects that the various characteristics of real estate have on the before-cost, before-tax returns that investors demand.[17]

[15]The relation must be regarded as loose because the sample period contains only one event in the variables studied (they all declined). In statistical terms, the sample period contains only one independent observation, from which confident conclusions cannot be drawn.

[16]We regressed real estate returns on bond capital appreciation returns, rather than yields, so that both independent variables would be in form of quarterly rates of change of a price level.

[17]The CAPM and APT (see Chapter 3) have limited usefulness in determining real estate returns because their underlying assumption of perfect arbitrage conditions are not even approximated in the real estate market. The nonrisk characteristics of real estate may be more important than those factors pertaining to risk.

Factors That Increase Required
Real Estate Returns Before Costs

The effects of general market movements and inflation on real estate were discussed earlier. Other factors that increase the required return (equivalent to the equilibrium expected return) to real estate before costs include residual risk and real estate heterogeneity.

Residual risk exists because most properties are large relative to the wealth of typical investors, even large institutions, and parcels are not easily divided, resulting in a less than perfectly diversified portfolio. Most asset pricing models ignore residual risk, but the market appears to demand some premium for assuming it.[18] The heterogeneity of real estate parcels increases the cost of acquiring information about them. Since this cost must be borne by real estate investors, it makes for higher required returns. In addition, investors expect to be compensated for real estate's high transaction costs.

Factors That Decrease Required
Real Estate Returns Before Costs

Various characteristics of real estate that dictate lower required returns have already been mentioned; these include the potential to diversify away the risk of other assets and some evidence of low volatility.

Another factor is control. Because of real estate's large unit cost, investors often control entire properties and are able to affect the return through management decisions. The control attribute is valued differently across investors, but generally control is desirable and results in higher prices, which translate to lower required returns.

Finally, real estate ownership has conferred tax benefits in some historical periods. Since these benefits are desired by most investors, they lower the before-cost required return.

An Empirical Investigation

As previously mentioned, reported real estate prices are less susceptible to the forces of arbitrage and rapid information processing than are stock prices. Since only properly anticipated prices (those that instantly incorporate all available information) fluctuate randomly, one might expect

---

[18]Through securitization, real estate parcels become divisible at a lower cost and greater diversification can be achieved. However, some of the diversification benefits are consumed by the cost of securitization, which is paid by the investor (that is, the cost is embedded in the price of the real estate-backed security).

Table 13-3. Autoregressive Behavior of U.S. Commercial
Real Estate Returns

Regression 1:   CREF nominal quarterly returns, 1969–1987

$CREF_t =$ α + $\beta_1(CREF_{t-1})$ + $\beta_2(CREF_{t-2})$ + $\beta_3(CREF_{t-3})$ + $\beta_4(CREF_{t-4})$

Coefficient	.007	.16	.36	−.05	.28
t-statistic	(2.11)	(1.47)	(3.34)	(−.47)	(3.25)

Adjusted R^2: .39, Durbin-Watson: 2.06

Regression 2:   CREF nominal annual returns, 1969–1987

$CREF_t =$ α + $\beta_1(CREF_{t-1})$ + $\beta_2(CREF_{t-2})$ + $\beta_3(CREF_{t-3})$ + $\beta_4(CREF_{t-4})$

Coefficient	.040	.77	.27	−.11	−.29
t-statistic	(1.45)	(2.90)	(.86)	(−.36)	(−1.49)

Adjusted R^2: .50, Durbin-Watson: 1.85

SOURCE: William N. Goetzmann and Roger G. Ibbotson, "The Performance of Real Estate as an Asset Class," *Journal of Applied Corporate Finance*, Spring 1990.

reported real estate prices, which do not incorporate all information immediately, to show some nonrandom behavior. In other words, it is likely that measured real estate portfolio returns are somewhat predictable. A direct manifestation of such predictability would be the significant first-order serial correlation of real estate returns already presented in Table 13-1; we now probe more deeply into this issue.

CREF Returns

Table 13-3 reports the results of higher-order autoregressions designed to measure the *persistence* of commercial real estate returns, that is, the extent to which current returns have been correlated with past returns. The results of Goetzmann and Ibbotson's regression 1 in Table 13-3 suggest that current returns on the CREF index are significantly related to CREF returns both 6 months and 1 year past.

To test whether such autocorrelation reflects the high autocorrelation of inflation rates, Goetzmann and Ibbotson ran a second regression (not reported in Table 13-3) substituting real for nominal returns in regression 1 and obtained similar results.

To test the proposition that the strength of autocorrelations could arise from the "staggered" appraisal process used by CREFs, Goetzmann and Ibbotson ran a regression using annual instead of quarterly returns.[19] The

[19]Typically, a fund uses an outside appraiser once a year for each property and then updates the appraisal internally each quarter. Consequently, the strength of year-to-year autocorrelation may reflect a tendency of outside appraisers to rely upon their most recent past estimates to assess current returns.

staggered appraisal method would tend to smooth returns within a single year, but not across years. Regression 2 in Table 13-3 supports the hypothesis that the trends are only short-term, or due to staggered appraisals, because the autocorrelation of annual returns after the first year is insignificant.

The Relation Between REITs and CREFs

We have previously mentioned that REITs and CREFs have not been strongly correlated (at least not contemporaneously). Perhaps then REITs provide a forecast by stock market participants of property values that will later be reflected in the appraisal-based CREFs.

To test this proposition, Goetzmann and Ibbotson regressed CREF returns on past REIT returns. Table 13-4 reports that there appears to be at most a weak relation between past quarterly REIT returns and current quarterly CREF returns. Between past annual REIT returns and current annual CREF returns, there is no discernible relation. In short, we find little evidence of the ability of REITs to predict the CREF series. Thus, if stock market prices for real estate portfolios are forecasting the future performance of commingled real estate funds, there is no compelling statistical evidence of it.[20]

Geographic Diversification

United States

Table 13-5 provides summary statistics on commercial real estate performance by region and on residential real estate by city for the four cities studied by Case and Shiller. Table 13-6 contains correlation matrices of those returns. Different regions have experienced differences in the risk and return of both commercial and residential real estate. There is some evidence that the economic fortunes of different regions may be countercyclical. For example, commercial property returns in the Midwest have been negatively correlated to those in the South and West. Likewise, residential appreciation returns in Chicago were negatively correlated to those in Atlanta. This is a bit surprising in light of the high correlation between real estate and inflation.

---

[20]One study does find that returns to the Frank Russell Company (FRC) index are predicted by the preceding year's REIT returns. See Joseph Gyourko and Donald B. Keim, "The Risk and Return Characteristics of Stock Market Based Real Estate Indexes," working paper, The Wharton School, 1990.

Table 13-4. Relation Between CREF Returns and REIT Returns

Regression 1: CREF nominal quarterly returns with lagged REIT nominal quarterly returns, 1972–1987

$$\text{CREF}_t = \alpha + \beta_1(\text{CREF}_{t-1}) + \beta_2(\text{CREF}_{t-2}) + \beta_3(\text{CREF}_{t-3}) + \beta_4(\text{CREF}_{t-4}) + \beta_5(\text{CREF}_{t-5}) + \beta_6(\text{CREF}_{t-6})$$

	α	β_1	β_2	β_3	β_4	β_5	β_6
Coefficient	.03	.01	.00	.04	.03	.09	.01
t-statistic	(12.60)	(0.33)	(0.09)	(2.45)	(1.91)	(0.52)	(0.85)

Adjusted R^2: .09, Durbin-Watson: 1.13

Regression 2: CREF nominal annual returns with lagged REIT nominal annual returns, 1972–1987

$$\text{CREF}_t = \alpha + \beta_1(\text{REIT}_{t-1}) + \beta_2(\text{REIT}_{t-2}) + \beta_3(\text{REIT}_{t-3}) + \beta_4(\text{REIT}_{t-4})$$

	α	β_1	β_2	β_3	β_4
Coefficient	.01	.22	.18	.11	.06
t-statistic	(0.05)	(0.88)	(1.13)	(0.66)	(0.62)

Adjusted R^2: .30, Durbin-Watson: 0.47

SOURCE: William N. Goetzmann and Roger G. Ibbotson, "The Performance of Real Estate as an Asset Class," *Journal of Applied Corporate Finance*, Spring 1990.

Table 13-5. Summary Statistics of Real Estate by Region
Using Annualized Quarterly Returns

Real estate category	Period	Series	Compound annual return (%)	Arithmetic return (%)	Standard deviation (%)	Serial correlation
Commercial	1978–1988	East	16.7	16.9	6.7	.35
		Midwest	11.7	11.7	3.9	−.18
		South	9.3	9.3	8.2	.34
		West	13.0	13.2	6.2	.53
Residential	1970–1986	Atlanta	6.4	6.6	5.3	.13
		Chicago	6.9	7.0	5.2	.67
		Dallas	9.4	9.5	6.6	.41
		San Francisco	11.1	11.4	7.8	.57

SOURCE: William N. Goetzmann and Roger G. Ibbotson, "The Performance of Real Estate as an Asset Class," *Journal of Applied Corporate Finance*, Spring 1990. The commercial data are from the Frank Russell Company as reported in Paul Firstenberg, Stephen A. Ross, and Randall Zisler, "Real Estate: The Whole Story," *The Journal of Portfolio Management*, Spring 1988. The residential data is from Karl E. Case and Robert J. Shiller, "Prices of Single Family Homes Since 1970: New Indexes for Four Cities," National Bureau of Economic Research, Inc., Working Paper Series No. 2393, 1987.

Table 13-6. Correlation of Real Estate Returns by Region
Using Annualized Quarterly Returns

	Commercial (1978–1988)			
	East	Midwest	South	West
East	1.00			
Midwest	.01	1.00		
South	.33	− .03	1.00	
West	.39	− .05	.57	1.00

	Residential (1970–1986)			
	Chicago	Atlanta	Dallas	San Francisco
Chicago	1.00			
Atlanta	− .05	1.00		
Dallas	.15	.07	1.00	
San Francisco	.13	.25	.16	1.00

SOURCE: William N. Goetzmann and Roger G. Ibbotson, "The Performance of Real Estate as an Asset Class," *Journal of Applied Corporate Finance*, Spring 1990. The commercial data are from the Frank Russell Company as reported in Paul Firstenberg, Stephen A. Ross, and Randall Zisler, "Real Estate: The Whole Story," *The Journal of Portfolio Management*, Spring 1988. The residential data is from Karl E. Case and Robert J. Shiller, "Prices of Single Family Homes Since 1970: New Indexes for Four Cities," National Bureau of Economic Research, Inc., Working Paper Series No. 2393, 1987.

Although there appears to be a large potential reduction in risk through geographic diversification, distance does not guarantee low correlation, or proximity a high correlation. Property values in a city's central business district may, for example, move in a direction opposite from values in nearby suburbs, and widely separated properties can be heavily influenced by the same economic factors.

Non-U.S. Real Estate

In principle, investors should consider adding foreign real estate to a portfolio for the same reasons that they should consider adding foreign stocks and bonds: the potential for diversification and superior returns.

As in the United States, an investor may participate in the foreign real estate market directly (through actual ownership of properties) or indirectly (through ownership of real estate-backed securities). The former market is subject to various restrictions and extra costs imposed on foreign investors. The latter market is less developed than its U.S. counterpart. Both barriers are diminishing in importance.

Table 13-7 indicates the recent favorite foreign countries for investment by real estate investors around the world. Note the frequency with which the preferred countries have cultural or geographic links with the country of the investor. Some of the criteria for selecting a country in which to invest are safety from expropriation, tax minimization, and sufficient liquidity.[21]

Typically, when discussing the safety of an investment, one is referring to the volatility of the returns on the asset itself. As we noted in Chapter 8 in relation to foreign stocks, safety has other dimensions when applied to foreign investing. Property rights may not be honored. For example, governments may seize the property of foreign investors. For nonportable assets such as real estate, this creates a risk not inherent in the asset and some transnational real estate owners use legal means to cloak their foreign identity to avoid this risk. Another related risk is that the investor may be granted limited property rights. Some property may be held by foreign investors only for their own use; the investor "owns" the property in a sense, but is deprived of some of the capital flows (rents) that the asset produces. If repatriation of proceeds from the sale of the property is restricted, additional losses can occur.

Taxes on real estate investment, too, differ among countries, particularly for foreign investors. Investors contemplating holding real estate outside their home country should be aware of ever-changing local statutes, tax treatment, and political and business conditions.

[21]For a more comprehensive discussion of these issues see M.A. Hines, *Guide to International Real Estate Investment*, Quorum, New York, 1988.

Table 13-7. Countries Preferred for Investments by Prospective Real Estate Investors

Investor's home country	First choice	Second choice	Investors do not seriously consider
Australia	New Zealand	United States, United Kingdom	S.E. Asia, Latin America, Africa
Canada	United States	United Kingdom, Australia	Any other country
France	United States, Western Europe	China, African Gold Coast	Any other country
Germany	United States, Western Europe	South Africa	—
Hong Kong	United States	China, Australia, Singapore, Canada	—
India	United States	—	—
Japan	United States, China	Australia	Any other country
Netherlands	United States, United Kingdom	Western Europe	—
Singapore	Indonesia, Malaysia	Australia	—
Sweden	Norway, Denmark	United Kingdom, Western Europe	—
Switzerland	Western Europe, United States	—	Eastern Europe, Africa, Middle East, Asia

SOURCE: Mary Alice Hines, *Guide to International Real Estate Investment* (Quorum Books, an imprint of Greenwood Publishing Group, Westport, Conn., 1988), p. 9. Reprinted with permission; all rights reserved.

One reason for the frequent appearance of the United States on the favorite country list in Table 13-7 is the unsurpassed liquidity and marketability of its real estate and the liberal treatment of capital flows. A country like Japan, while having a great deal of liquidity and marketability in most of its capital markets, is less attractive to non-Japanese investors when it comes to real estate.

Conclusion

Real estate is a complex investment vehicle requiring a book-length treatment. Nevertheless, some conclusions can be drawn. There is compelling evidence to recommend including real estate as a normal component of an investment portfolio. Over the long term, real estate should provide returns competitive with those on stocks and bonds, and its low correlation with other assets makes it valuable for diversification purposes. Real estate has also been a superior inflation hedge.

Real estate does have its drawbacks. Property-specific risks, high management and information costs, and liquidity risk can make a real estate investment an expensive proposition. Even for investors with a comparative advantage in the real estate sector, the cyclicality of the market presents a danger, especially when transactions are leveraged.

Above all, remember that, as every prospectus says, past results are not a guarantee of future performance. In 1978, California house prices were rising at a rate of 3 percent a month. Twelve years later they were falling at the same rate. This variability makes it difficult to form accurate forecasts of future trends. The spectacular returns of U.S. real estate over much of the last 3 decades are the result of favorable tax treatment and high, unanticipated inflation. With less inflation, lower tax rates, and a new tax code, these returns have fallen sharply in the early 1990s and are likely to be more moderate in the future.

14
Venture Capital

The term *venture capital* typically, but not always accurately, connotes high technology, rapid growth, creative ideas, hard-driving entrepreneurs, and the amassing of substantial financial gains. To create a venture capital-backed company, an entrepreneur with a high potential concept or product is combined with capital supplied by a venture capitalist who usually also acts as a counselor, strategist, adviser, and confidant to the entrepreneur. When successful (which applies to a minority of cases), this combination has produced dramatic returns for both the entrepreneur and the venture investor.

More precisely, venture capital is the process of investing private equity capital in companies with excellent growth prospects at the earliest stage of their development and working with these companies to build them into successes over time. It is a process that involves teamwork and close cooperation between the venture capital investor and the entrepreneurial management group of the company. The primary objective for venture capitalists is achieving a high rate of investment return to compensate for the large risk of failure associated with many venture-backed companies. Although the line between venture capital and other investment activities has become somewhat blurred in the last few years, venture capital is distinct from large leveraged buyouts, large management buyouts, small business investment company (SBIC) loans, corporation lending, or economic development.

A Brief History of Venture Capital

Venture capital has been primarily an American phenomenon. Before World War II, venture investments were undertaken by wealthy individuals who had an interest in a particular industry. It was not a very disciplined process. Following World War II, the process of venture investing became more formalized, primarily as the result of three individuals: General Georges F. Doriot, a French-born professor at Harvard Business School and two wealthy men, John Hay Whitney and Laurance S. Rockefeller. All three had a certain amount of idealism about the efforts that they undertook.

General Doriot had been teaching a very popular course in entrepreneurship at Harvard and, in 1946, was named President of American Research and Development Corporation. This gave him the opportunity to apply his ideas about building businesses in response to real world opportunities. General Doriot believed in focusing primarily on the individual entrepreneur. He felt that it was important that the individual be more than very bright; he or she also had to be extremely resourceful. He did not believe that profits should be the objective of venture investing. "Our aim is to build up creative men and their companies, and capital gains are a reward, not a goal."[1] Pursuing this aim, General Doriot funded a portfolio of successful venture companies, the most important being Digital Equipment Corporation, which yielded returns of $350 million on an initial investment of $70,000.

Jock Whitney was one of the wealthiest men in America when he set aside $10 million to create J. H. Whitney & Company just after World War II. It was Whitney who, in a lunch conversation with his longtime associate Benno Schmidt, concluded that Schmidt's suggested term *venture capital* best described the activity they had undertaken. Whitney also set out the partnership format which has become the standard organizational structure for venture capital firms. Whitney was more interested in the creativity that went into the development of new business entities than he was in profits. He helped found a number of significant business successes in the 1940s, 1950s, and 1960s, including Minutemaid frozen orange juice.[2] J. H. Whitney continues today as one of the leading venture capital firms in the country.

Laurance Rockefeller had a strong interest in science and technology and shared with General Doriot and Jock Whitney an idealistic view of venture capital. "What we want to do is the opposite of the old system of holding back capital until a field or an idea is proved completely safe. We are undertaking

---

[1]John W. Wilson, *The New Venturers*, Addison-Wesley, 1985, p. 20.

[2]Ibid., pp. 17, 18.

pioneering projects that with proper backing will encourage sound scientific and economic progress in new fields—fields that hold the promise of tremendous future development."[3] Using private family money he started a number of successful companies in the technology and aviation areas.

Venture capital was moved forward to a new level by the creation of the Small Business Investment Company loan program in 1958. This gave government support to the setting up of SBICs, a number of which became venture capital companies. The SBIC program did not, however, provide the ideal form of capital for small, early-stage companies, because most of their investments had to be in the form of debt instruments. The SBICs did provide fruitful training grounds for future venture capitalists.

The next two important steps in the development of the American venture capital industry came in 1978. First, the Department of Labor clarified the Employment Retirement Income Security Act of 1974 (ERISA) in such a way as to allow pension funds to put a portion of their assets in riskier investments that offered higher expected rates of return, as long as they provided diversification to the total pension fund. Second, Congress passed the Investment Incentive Act, which lowered the capital gains tax and set the stage for resurgence of venture capital following the significant slump in activity during the mid-1970s. Beginning in the late 1970s, substantial amounts of institutional money were invested in venture partnerships. The period from 1978 through 1983 was also a period of very high realized returns on venture capital investments made in earlier years, and this encouraged even more investment in the mid-1980s. Dollars committed to venture firms continued to grow and peaked at $4.3 billion in 1987. Average annual industry returns began dropping off in the year 1983–1984, and returns for venture capital started since then have, for the most part, been in the single digits.

A Global Perspective on Venture Capital

While venture capital has been primarily an American phenomenon, there has been significant growth in the 1980s (albeit from a very small base) in what is called venture capital outside the United States. This began first in the United Kingdom in the late 1970s, then spread to France and other Continental European countries in the 1980s. By the middle-to-late 1980s the expansion had spread to the Pacific rim countries.

---

[3]   Ibid., p. 15.

Each country's venture capital has its unique characteristics that are shaped by the laws, cultures, entrepreneurial climates, and securities markets of the country. In Europe, for example, leveraged buyouts and management buyouts—not strictly characterized as venture capital—have dominated. In Japan, the venture investments are primarily equity, but they are made in more mature private companies that would probably be publicly traded if they were in the United States. In Southeast Asia, much of the venture investing has been in franchising and in tourist and consumer-related businesses, not in high-technology companies. But what all these efforts do share in common is that they are risky investments, and they are called "venture capital" in the international arena.

The relative size of the global venture capital market estimated as of mid-1990 is shown in Table 14-1 in U.S. dollar terms. Currently, the European and Asian venture capital markets are each roughly half the size of the U.S. market.

While high quality data on the venture capital industry are difficult to get in the United States, they are almost unobtainable outside the United States. Performance data and track records for European and Asian firms are either nonexistent or too recent to be meaningful. Compounding the lack of information, the risk of venture investing outside the United States is further heightened by currency exposure, different tax structures, and very difficult legal and accounting systems, not to mention the distances involved. Most American investors have chosen not to invest in venture capital outside the United States. There are a growing number, however, who are beginning to make small investments in international venture firms to

Table 14-1. Composition of the World Venture Capital Market (1990, Midyear)

Region	Number of firms	Money under management ($ billion)
United States	600	31.0
Asia (including Australia and New Zealand)	335	19.5
Europe	300	16.1
Canada	70	2.8
Total	1,305	$69.4

SOURCE: Venture Economics, Inc., Boston, Mass. and *Asian Venture Capital Journal*, Hong Kong.

further diversify their portfolios and to improve their understandings of non-U.S. venture capital conditions.

Structures of Venture Capital Investments

Partnership Investments

Following Jock Whitney's original format, the typical vehicle for institutions and individuals to invest in venture capital continues to be a limited partnership, with the venture capitalist being the general partner and the investors (pension plans, institutions, and individuals) being the limited partners. Often a single venture capital firm will manage several limited partnerships that have been formed at intervals of 3 to 5 years. Each partnership typically invests in 20 to 40 individual venture-backed companies. These partnerships usually have a 10-year life with two or three 1-year extensions possible. Customary management fees for the general partners are 2.5 percent of committed capital per annum and a share of the profits on the investments, usually 20 percent. There are now more than 600 venture capital firms in the United States, each of which serves as general partner for one or more limited partnerships.

The entrepreneur who starts the company invests mostly time and effort or "sweat equity" in building a successful company. The entrepreneur's share of ownership in the company will decline as the company grows and requires more venture capital investment, but the value of that piece of the company should grow significantly as the company progresses.

Direct Investments

A few large institutions that have been involved in venture capital for a number of years have also made direct venture capital investments in venture-backed companies. Because of the high specific risk of each individual investment and the time and resource commitment required to make successful investments, direct investments by large institutions, however, are not common and this activity has declined in recent years. Some large corporations have chosen to set up direct venture capital investment programs to get a "window on technology," or support corporate development objectives, as well as achieve a superior return. In the last 15 years, many of these have yielded disappointing results.

Characteristics of the Venture Capital Asset Class

Long Time Horizon

Building a successful company usually takes at least 5 to 7 years. As mentioned earlier, the term of a venture capital partnership is typically 10 to 12 years. The routes to liquidity in venture capital are: (1) an initial public offering (IPO) or (2) the sale of the venture-backed company, but the median age of both venture-backed IPOs and venture-backed company sales is 5 years.

Returns from venture capital investments tend to follow a "J" curve, whereby returns are flat to negative for the first 3 or 4 years, and the high returns associated with venture capital are only achieved over a 5- to 12-year period. A representative pattern of cumulative returns is shown in Figure 14-1.

There are several reasons for this pattern. First, some of the early-stage investments will fail relatively quickly. A product development effort will not be successful, a competitor will produce a product more quickly, a market will not develop, or a management team will fail in its implementation. These events can happen quickly in an early-stage company. Second, venture capital fees are based on the total size of the fund, but the funds are drawn down and invested over a 4- or 5-year period. So in the early years, a

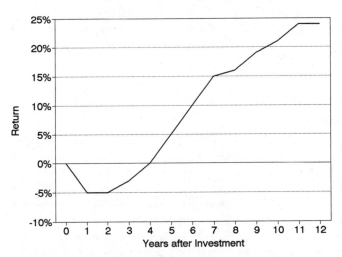

Figure 14-1. Pattern of year-by-year returns on a hypothetical successful venture capital investment. *(Source: Venture Economics, Inc., Boston, Mass.)*

fee of 2.5 percent of the total fund can be 10 to 20 percent of the dollars actually invested. Finally, successful companies take a substantial period of time to build. Investments are generally carried at cost until there is an arm's length transaction in the market, which places a higher value on the company's stock. If the company is well funded in the beginning, or if existing investors continue to fund a successful company without bringing in any new investors, a well-performing company can be carried at cost for a significant period of time. In short, in the early stages of a venture partnership both losses and fees tend to depress early returns.

Lack of Liquidity

Because venture capital investments are made in private companies, the investments are illiquid until the company goes public or is sold and the proceeds are distributed to the limited partners. This illiquidity is inherent in the nature of the securities that venture capitalists purchase and in the stages of development that a typical partnership must go through. The partnership usually has a four-stage cycle over its 12-year life. The first few years—years 1 to 3—are a period of intense investment activity. Most of the companies that will determine the ultimate success of the partnership are brought into the portfolio during this period. Years 4 to 6 are a growth period in which follow-on investments are made in the potentially successful companies already in the portfolio; also, a few new investments are added. This is the time when the general partners decide which ventures to cut and which to continue to support. There are usually few positive returns in this period and several complete write-offs. Years 7 to 9 are a harvest period, when the general partners' focus is primarily on exit strategies for the successful portfolio companies. Cash management during this stage is very important in determining returns. Finally, in the maturity period, years 9 to 12, the sole focus of the general partners is liquidation of their positions in the remaining companies in the portfolio.

High Risk

Within a given portfolio of venture capital investments the returns will vary widely. A few will return many times the initial investment, others will fail completely, and many will simply struggle and become part of what is commonly known as "the living dead." Based on Venture Economics' analysis of venture investing for the past 20 years, approximately 40 percent of all venture investments are losers. Thirty percent become the living dead, where there is a chance of recouping principal but little, if any, appreciation is likely. Twenty percent of the investments generate returns of 2 to 5 times the

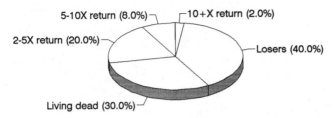

Figure 14-2. Distribution of returns on original investment in venture capital. *(Source: "The Venture Capital Industry: Opportunities and Considerations for Investors," Venture Economics, Inc., Boston, Mass., 1987.)*

original investment. Eight percent have returns of 5 to 10 times the original investment, and only 2 percent of all venture investments end up having returns of 10 times the initial investment or more.[4] This clearly means that portfolio diversification is the key to managing the high specific risk of each individual venture investment (see Figure 14-2).

The Valuation of Venture Partnerships and Performance Measurement

The securities held by venture capital partnerships are private. Therefore, the market value of a venture portfolio is not easily determined. The venture capital community has set up guidelines or conventions to aid in the valuation of portfolio companies. The most common guideline is that investments are carried at cost until there is either a new arm's length transaction at a different share price involving a new sophisticated investor, or the performance of the company changes significantly. Typically, each partnership has a valuation committee that approves the valuations on each of the portfolio companies before they are sent to the limited partners. In addition, partnerships are audited each year by an independent auditor. Accounting firms are beginning to take a more informed interest in venture capital portfolio valuations.

In recent years the industry has moved to a "vintage year" approach for measuring returns. This approach examines how all funds started in a given year are performing to date. An example of the return matrix is shown in Table 14-2. Given the partnership nature of venture capital investing and the long-term commitment that is involved, this kind of performance com-

---

[4]"The Venture Capital Industry: Opportunities and Considerations for Investors," Venture Economics, Inc., 1987.

Table 14-2. Capital-Weighted Internal Rates of Return to Limited Partners in Percent
By Vintage Year, or Year of Initial Investment in Partnerships

Vintage year	Calendar year										
	1980	1981	1982	1983	1984	1985	1986	1987	1988	1989	1990
1976 to 1979	30.9	26.4	27.1	32.2	24.8	22.0	21.2	20.3	19.2	18.9	17.4
1980		13.2	20.0	37.0	25.0	21.0	20.8	19.9	19.7	19.1	18.5
1981			8.2	27.4	13.4	7.9	7.5	9.5	8.7	8.7	7.8
1982				12.0	5.5	0.3	2.0	1.7	2.4	2.6	2.5
1983					3.7	2.5	5.0	6.2	6.5	7.0	5.2
1984						-3.9	1.3	3.5	2.6	3.6	1.8
1985							2.5	2.9	5.0	4.8	3.7
1986								1.3	1.4	3.3	2.3
1987									-3.5	1.7	1.0
1988										-4.0	-1.4
1989											-7.1

NOTE: The numbers shown for vintage years 1987, 1988, and 1989 are interim performance measurements and are not indicators of the long-term results of these funds. All returns are cumulative since inception through calendar year.

SOURCE: Venture Economics, Inc., Boston, Mass.

parison is probably the most appropriate industry standard or index, but for these comparisons to be meaningful the industry must continue its efforts to standardize portfolio company valuation guidelines.

Why Invest in Venture Capital?

High Returns

Venture capital has historically achieved high rates of return. But venture capital performance has also varied greatly. The capital-weighted internal rate of return to limited partners in the funds started in 1980 was 18.5 percent through 1990. On the other hand, the returns for funds formed in 1984 look like they will be single digit. This wide variation in returns over time emphasizes the importance of diversifying across time as well as industry and stage of investment.

The range of returns for venture capital partnerships for any given year is also quite broad. For example, an investor investing in the late 1970s could have received a compound return over the life of the portfolio as high as 71 percent or as low as 8.5 percent. No partnership established before 1982 had a negative rate of return on final liquidation, although several partnerships established since then will, in fact, have negative rates of return. Over the period 1959 through 1990, venture capital has achieved the highest rate of return for any U.S. asset class. It also has the highest risk as measured by the standard deviation of returns. Table 4-2 provides estimates of the long-run equilibrium return and risk characteristics of venture capital as well as other global asset classes.

Diversification

Table 14-3 contains the estimated long-run, equilibrium correlations of venture capital returns with the returns of other asset classes. The table illustrates that venture capital returns have a desirable low correlation with the returns in other asset classes. The high expected return and the low correlation with other asset classes suggest that an appropriate investment in the venture capital class can lead to a higher risk-adjusted rate of return for a well-diversified portfolio.

Table 14-3. Estimated Equilibrium Correlations of
Annual Returns on Venture Capital with Other Asset Classes

	Correlation with venture capital
U.S. equity	.35
Non-U.S. equity	.15
Dollar bonds	.15
Nondollar bonds	.10
Real estate	.25
Cash equivalents	−.10

SOURCE: Brinson Partners, Inc.

Current Venture Capital Trends

Decline in Dollars Committed

As Figure 14-3 shows, dollars committed to venture capital grew rapidly from the late 1970s through 1987. Since then there has been a steep decline with only $1.8 billion being committed to venture capital in 1990, with the decline continuing in 1991.

The rapid growth in funds committed to venture capital in the early 1980s was caused by a surge in returns of funds liquidating during that period and the overheated IPO market for technology companies. Following a dip in commitments in 1985, funds committed to private venture capital partnerships grew to a new high in 1987. These new dollars came from pension funds, including many public pension funds that entered the venture arena for the first time, as shown in Table 14-4.

Growth in Pension Fund Investment

As Table 14-4 shows, pension fund investment in venture capital has grown from 15 percent of total venture capital investment in 1978 to 53 percent in 1990. Public pension fund growth has been dramatic in the last half of the 1980s and now comprises almost a quarter of the total venture investment. Since 1978, individuals have significantly reduced their investment in venture capital as a percent of the total dollars raised.

Broadening of Geographic Focus

The venture capital industry began primarily as a local phenomenon, centering on Boston's Route 128 in the 1970s and Silicon Valley in the San Francisco Bay area in the 1980s. These investments were focused primarily on high-technology businesses. But as the scope of venture investment

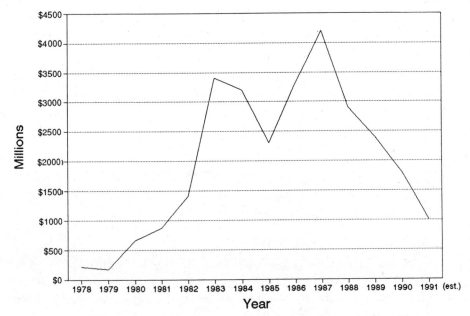

Figure 14-3. Dollars committed to venture capital private partnerships in the United States annually: 1978–1991. *(Source: Venture Economics, Inc., Boston, Mass.)*

broadened in the 1980s so has the geographic coverage of the industry, as indicated in Table 14-5. In addition, a number of state governments have either undertaken venture capital programs themselves or supported the establishment of private venture firms in the state, believing that venture capital programs will encourage economic development of their states.

Broadening of Focus by Industry

In the 1970s and early 1980s venture capital was synonymous with high-technology. Much of this high technology was computer or semiconductor related. In the last 6 to 8 years the industry focus has broadened to include low-tech businesses, retail businesses, and service-oriented businesses as shown in Table 14-6. This broadening has occurred primarily because returns in the high-tech area (particularly computer hardware, semiconductors, and electronics businesses) were disappointing in the last half of the 1980s. Venture capitalists used the increased dollars available to them to finance too many start-up companies to exploit a given high-tech market opportunity. As a result, intense competition developed among venture-backed companies and many of them failed. The disk drive industry is the classic example of this phenomenon.

Table 14-4. Source of Capital Commitments to Venture Funds
As a Percent of Total (Private Independent)

	1978	1988	1990
Public pension plans	—	20	22
Corporate pension plans	15	27	31
Non-U.S. investors	18	13	7
Corporations	10	12	7
Insurance companies	16	9	9
Endowments	9	11	13
Individuals	32	8	11

SOURCE: Venture Economics, Inc., Boston, Mass.

As the industries in which venture investments are made have broadened, venture capital firms have increasingly specialized in particular industries. Often individual general partners will concentrate on one or two industries. In several cases, specialized funds have been formed to focus on specific industries, for example, biotechnology, advanced materials, or defense electronics.

The Future of Venture Investing

Certainly, future returns for the venture industry are hard to predict. However, there do seem to be several reasons why the returns will not be as high as the 35 percent annual returns that were achieved by some firms in the late 1970s and early 1980s. First, the venture industry itself has become much more competitive and is a more efficient market than it was then. Second, there are many more experienced professionals involved in the industry than there were in the late 1970s and early 1980s; this has created not only successful companies but wealthy individuals who also now provide

Table 14-5. Geographic Distribution of U.S.
Venture Capital Investment
As a Percent of Total

	1984	1986	1988	1990
West Coast	48	40	42	41
Northeast	24	29	25	27
Southwest/Rockies	12	12	9	11
Midwest/Plains	8	8	8	8
Southeast	5	7	9	6
Mid-Atlantic	3	4	7	7

SOURCE: Venture Economics, Inc., Boston, Mass.

Table 14-6. Distribution of Venture Capital Investment by Industry
As a Percent of Dollar Amount Invested

	1984	1986	1988	1990
Technology, communications	15	16	14	15
Computer hardware, software, peripherals	40	29	23	27
Other electronics	13	13	9	7
Subtotal	68	58	46	49
Medical	10	16	21	24
Industrial products, automation	5	4	5	4
Consumer	7	9	13	10
Other	10	13	15	13
Total	100	100	100	100

SOURCE: Venture Economics, Inc., Boston, Mass.

capital and guidance to venture-backed companies. On the whole, one should expect that long-term returns in the venture industry will be significantly above public equity market returns because of the risk and the illiquidity of venture investments. But those long-run returns will probably be more in the annual range of 15 to 20 percent than in the 25 to 35 percent range achieved in the late 1970s and early 1980s.

In 1991, the initial public offering market was receptive to venture-backed public offerings. In the first 11 months of that year, 104 venture-backed companies had initial public offerings, raising a total of $3.7 billion. The receptive public markets and the significant decline in dollars committed to venture capital partnerships have made most venture capitalists more optimistic about future returns in the industry than they have been any time since 1983. Several trends begun in the 1980s will probably continue. First, the globalization of venture capital should continue if venture capital investments outside the United States turn out to yield satisfactory returns given their riskiness. Second, the broadening of venture capital investment within the United States by industry and by geography should continue as venture capital investors seek to find investment opportunities that yield high returns. Finally, from an asset allocation point of view, venture capital should continue to play an important, although small, role in the fully diversified global portfolio.

15

Gold, Silver, Commodities, and Tangible Assets

An ounce of gold could buy a good quality men's suit in the time of Shakespeare, that of Beethoven, in 1929, and today. No other financial or physical asset has been as reliable a store of value over long periods of time. While financial assets are the focus of most investors' attention, nonfinancial assets form the greater part of world wealth and have been more stable in value during periods of financial and social turbulence.[1] Nonfinancial assets include, but are not limited to, gold, silver, agricultural and industrial commodities, and valuable personal property such as art and antiques. Table 15-1 contains Salomon Brothers' estimates of compound annual returns on the financial and nonfinancial assets over the recent past.

Gold and Silver

For centuries, countries used metals as currency. With an ounce of copper, a beggar could buy a morsel of food; with an ounce of silver, commoners could purchase household necessities; and with an ounce of gold, a family could rent a cottage with a thatched roof. The portability, durability, and

---

[1]While the distinction between financial and nonfinancial assets is necessarily arbitrary, a classification can be made. Goods with intrinsic value in use (sometimes called "goods in the real economy") are nonfinancial. Claims against such goods are financial assets. Real estate spans both the real and financial economies, because properties have value in use while deeds to properties—the good traded in the market—represent claims against actual real estate.

Table 15-1. Returns on Tangibles versus Returns on Financial Assets
June 1970–June 1991

June 1970–June 1980		June 1981–June 1991	
Asset class	Compound annual return (%)	Asset class	Compound annual return (%)
Oil	34.7	Stocks	16.0
Gold	31.6	Old masters	15.8
U.S. coins	27.7	Bonds	15.2
Silver	23.7	T-bills	8.8
Stamps	21.8	Chinese ceramics	8.1
Diamonds	15.3	Housing	4.4
U.S. farmland	14.0	CPI	4.3
Old masters	13.1	Foreign exchange	3.6
Housing	10.2	Stamps	−0.7
CPI	7.7	U.S. farmland	−1.8
T-bills	7.7	Gold	−2.9
Foreign exchange	7.3	Oil	−5.9
Stocks	6.1		

SOURCE: "Stock Research: Investment Policy," Salomon Brothers, New York, June 6, 1985; June 10, 1991. All rights reserved. Used with permission.

divisibility of monetary metals helped to make these metals a store of value and a medium of exchange throughout the world.

Over long periods of time, gold and silver have had real returns near zero. Their effectiveness as a long-run inflation hedge, and as insurance against economic and political upheavals, make them worthy of inclusion in a discussion of global asset markets.

Gold Supply and Demand

The supply of gold relative to other metals is stable compared with the demand for it—for adornment, industrial uses, dentistry, speculation, investment, and as a store of value. About 3 percent of the world's wealth is held in the form of gold.

The distribution of world gold ownership is portrayed in Figure 15-1. Private holdings (private investment plus decorative) constitute half of the ownership, a fact which suggests that the gold market is relatively liquid. Governments and agencies account for 34 percent of gold ownership. The remaining gold is either in industrial use or lost. Theft is responsible for only a small fraction of that which is lost because it is eventually traded for goods and goes back on the market. Most lost gold is buried and unrecovered, or lost at sea. Treasure hunters are slowly placing this wealth back in private hands.

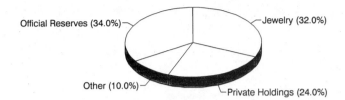

Official Reserves (34.0%)
Jewelry (32.0%)
Other (10.0%)
Private Holdings (24.0%)

Figure 15-1. Distribution of world gold supply: 1990, 106,000 metric tons. *(Source: Gold Fields Mineral Services, World Gold Council.)*

Gold, Silver, and Inflation

For centuries, gold and silver *were* money. A gold or silver *standard* exists when a country's currency and its banking and international trading structures are based to some degree on gold or silver. Governments either used the metals directly as coins or defined their currencies in terms of weights of gold and/or silver. When these metals are equivalent to money, the money prices of gold and silver by definition do not change.

If gold and silver are money, what does it mean to measure returns from investing in monetary metals? When a metal like gold is monetized, it becomes the unit of account by which investment returns are measured. For instance, when the United States was on a gold standard, a $20 gold piece was legally worth $20. Thus, a monetized metal, considered as an investment asset, always has a return of zero relative to the currency.

Fiat money is unbacked money, such as the paper currency now used in every country, that is not convertible into metal at a prespecified official rate. When a fiat currency prevails and when gold and silver trade freely, returns from metals are computed like those on any other investment. If gold rises in price from $400 to $480 an ounce, it is meaningful to say that the investment provided a 20 percent return. Thus, when a monetary system has employed fiat currencies, gold returns can be computed using market prices.

Inflation-adjusted returns on gold and silver indicate the value of gold and silver in terms of consumer goods. Monetary metals are often viewed as prototype commodities—that is, commodities which track or reflect the price changes of consumer or producer market baskets. (Commodities are treated more generally later in this chapter.) Inflation-adjusted returns on these metals, then, indicate the divergence between the price of gold and that of consumer goods. When the price of gold tracks the prices of consumer goods exactly, the inflation-adjusted return on gold is zero. When gold and consumer goods diverge, as they did in the 1970s, when gold raced ahead of inflation, or in the 1980s, when it fell behind, the inflation-adjusted return on gold may be highly positive or negative. As we will show, inflation-adjusted returns on gold are extremely close to zero when measured over long periods. This result suggests that gold is in fact a store of value or a prototype commodity.

Gold and Silver Prices

United Kingdom.   Today gold sells at 90 times the price of silver, but this was not always the case. A visitor to Egypt in the time of the Pharaohs would have observed price parity between the two.[2] In the Anglo-American world, silver substantially predates gold as a monetary metal. It is believed that King Penda (circa 600 A.D.) of Mercia, in present-day England, first began minting silver pennies of which 240 constituted a physical pound. By the 1100s, these silver pennies were being called "sterling." The pound sterling was thus originally equivalent in value to a pound of sterling silver. This relationship has not held up well, with a pound (12 troy ounces) of fine silver costing over 27 British monetary pounds in 1991.

Gold prices from 1343 to 1799 are presented in Table 15-2, and prices for the nineteenth and twentieth centuries are shown in Table 15-3.[3] Gold coins first circulated widely in England in the eighteenth century. By defining a gold guinea of a specific weight to be worth 21 shillings in 1717, Britain—acting under the powerful influence of the philosopher John Locke—adopted a gold standard as official policy. From 1717 to 1759, the price of gold (per ounce) hovered around £3.88. Then, because of the political uncertainty caused by the Napoleonic Wars, commoners began to withdraw gold guineas from banks and hoard them. Consequently, the government ordered the Bank of England to stop redeeming bank deposits in gold, temporarily lifting the gold standard. By 1814, at the climax of the Napoleonic Wars, the price of gold had escalated to £5.50.

After the war's end, the United Kingdom returned to a gold standard. In 1820, Sir Robert Peel, invoking Locke's ghost, persuaded Parliament to fix the price of gold at "the ancient standard of £3.8938 per ounce, a magic price for gold from which England ought never to stray and to which, if she did, she must always return as soon as possible."[4]

---

[2] *The Economist,* March 2, 1991, p. 78.

[3] Even under systems where paper money was backed by gold or silver, investors often could trade gold and silver freely, at prices different from the official price. In these periods, returns are measured using market rather than official prices. When market prices are lacking, official prices are employed to complete the data series.

[4] Peel had many virtues as a Prime Minister, but a long memory was not one of them. The £3.88–£3.89 standard was certainly not more ancient than 1717 and was violated between 1760 and 1772.

Table 15-2. U.K. Gold Prices from 1343 to 1799

Period	£/ troy ounce	Period	£/ troy ounce	Period	£/ troy ounce
1343	1.24	1549	3.00	1763	4.02
1344	1.14	1560–1589	2.72	1764	3.95
1345	1.15	1590–1599	2.71	1765	3.90
1346	1.20	1600	2.71	1766	3.96
1351	1.30	1601–1603	2.74	1767	3.98
1355	1.31	1604–1610	2.96	1768	3.97
1412	1.47	1611	3.21	1769	4.01
1464	1.64	1612–1618	3.28	1770	4.02
1465	1.92	1619–1662	3.31	1771	3.99
1467	1.95	1663–1695	3.69	1772	4.00
1471	1.98	1696–1698	4.06	1773	3.89
1492	2.00	1699	3.96	1774–1781	3.88
1526	2.25	1700–1716	3.96	1782	3.89
1544	2.40	1717–1759	3.88	1783	3.85
1545	2.50	1760	3.95	1784–1785	3.89
1546	2.60	1761	4.00	1786–1796	3.88
1547	2.90	1762	3.99	1798–1799	3.89

SOURCE: Data from 1343 to 1549 are from Sir Albert E. Feavearyear, *The Pound Sterling* (1st edition), Humphrey Milford, Oxford University Press, London, 1931 (by permission of Oxford University Press). Quoted in shillings and converted by the authors to pounds using 20 shillings per pound. U.K. prices from 1560 to 1799 are reconstructed by the authors from indexes in Roy W. Jastram, *The Golden Constant*, copyright © John Wiley & Sons, Inc., 1977. Reprinted by permission of John Wiley & Sons, Inc. Jastram constructed his indexes using free-market prices, Bank of England buying prices, and Mint prices, in that order of preference.

And stray she did not. For almost a century, from 1820 until 1919, gold's price did not deviate from £3.89 by as much as 1 percent. After the inflation during World War I, gold's price peaked at £5.18. The British quickly returned to Lockean tradition and restored the price of £3.8938 with the Gold Standard Act of 1925. (The 1926 gold price is the first in Table 15-3 to reflect the Act.) England's actions in both 1820 and 1925 lend credence to the philosopher John Maynard Keynes's statement that "practical men, who believe themselves to be quite exempt from any intellectual influences, are usually the slaves to some defunct economist."[5] When Britain went off the gold standard in 1931, gold's price rose slowly at first and then at an unprecedented speed, from £12.43 in 1950 to over £280 in 1982. The price of gold then fell to about £200 by 1991.

[5]John Maynard Keynes, *The General Theory of Employment, Interest, and Money*, Harcourt, Brace, Jovanovich, New York, 1936.

United States. American gold prices for the nineteenth and twentieth centuries are also shown on Table 15-3. With the Coinage Act of 1791, the newly constituted United States adopted a bimetallic standard, with gold and silver prices officially linked in a 15:1 ratio. Gold prices in U.S. dollars were stable for the next 7 decades.

When the Civil War began in 1861, the United States introduced paper money, the Union's notoriously unstable greenback. With the war's inflation, gold prices doubled to $42.02, but by 1878, gold had fallen back to its prewar level of $20. When in 1897 the U.S. Treasury again required banks to exchange paper currency for monetary metal, gold was the only coin that could be freely minted. Thus, the United States operated on a *de facto* gold standard until the Gold Standard Act of 1900 gave gold official or *de jure* recognition.

During the Depression, the United States made owning gold illegal, prohibited gold exports, and stopped exchanging dollars for gold. Between 1934 and 1971, the dollar was loosely defined in gold, at a price determined by the U.S. Treasury.

Since the gold standard was abolished in 1971, the dollar price of gold has fluctuated wildly, rising to unprecedented levels in this period of high inflation. From an official price of $35 at the beginning of 1968, gold escalated to a market price of more than $800 per ounce for a few days in 1980, and bookmakers took bets on when the first gold quote of $1000 an ounce would occur. Gold never did reach $1000 and was quoted at $350 per ounce in August 1992.

Like gold, silver prices rose with other tangible assets in the Great Inflation of the late 1970s and rocketed upward in 1979–1980. Table 15-4 presents silver prices (in dollars) in the United States from 1792 to 1990. Silver's year-end peak was $28 per ounce in 1979. For a few days in January 1980, however, silver sold above $50 per ounce as widespread speculation dominated the market. Like gold, silver prices had dropped substantially, to $4 per ounce by August 1992.

Real Returns on Gold and Silver

Gold and silver prices must be restated in terms of their purchasing power to determine the inflation protection that they have provided. The Stanford University economist Roy W. Jastram constructed an index with the real (inflation-adjusted) price of gold in 1930 set equal to 1. Real returns on gold (in British pounds) are graphed in Figure 15-2.

The most remarkable feature of these graphs is the constancy of gold's value. Over long periods, the real gold price indexes for both countries are quite stable. In Britain, the compound real return from gold over 4 centuries was 0.1 percent per year, and 0.7 percent per year in the United States over two centuries. Gold, like other cash instruments, has had a real return

Table 15-3. U.S. and U.K. Gold Prices from 1800 to 1990

Period	£/ounce	$/ounce	Period	£/ounce	$/ounce
1800	4.25	19.39	1921	5.18	20.67
1801	4.30	19.39	1922	4.90	20.84
1802	4.15	19.39	1923	4.28	20.67
1803–1808	4.00	19.39	1924	4.14	20.67
1809	4.53	19.39	1925	4.29	20.67
1810	4.60	19.39	1926–1930	3.89	20.67
1811	5.00	19.39	1931	4.24	20.67
1812	5.40	19.39	1932	5.41	20.67
1813	5.40	19.39	1933	5.72	20.67
1814	5.50	19.39	1934	6.31	35.00
1815	5.25	19.39	1935	6.51	35.00
1816	4.00	19.39	1936	6.43	35.00
1817	3.92	19.39	1937	6.45	35.00
1818	4.07	19.39	1938	6.53	35.00
1819	4.05	19.39	1939	7.10	35.00
1820	3.89	19.39	1940–1949	8.60	35.00
1821	3.89	19.39	1950–1959	12.43	35.00
1822–1824	3.87	19.39	1960	12.45	35.00
1825	3.89	19.39	1961–1967	12.43	35.00
1826–1828	3.87	19.39	1968	16.31	39.27
1829–1833	3.89	19.39	1969	16.37	35.45
1834	3.89	20.05	1970	14.75	37.65
1835–1861	3.89	20.67	1971	15.78	43.85
1862	3.89	23.42	1972	24.26	65.20
1863	3.89	30.01	1973	40.46	114.55
1864	3.89	42.02	1974	64.65	186.75
1865	3.89	32.51	1975	72.58	140.35
1866	3.89	29.12	1976	66.11	134.75
1867	3.89	28.57	1977	86.54	164.95
1868	3.89	28.88	1978	111.08	226.00
1869	3.89	27.49	1979	230.22	512.00
1870	3.89	23.75	1980	247.17	589.50
1871	3.89	23.09	1981	209.64	400.00
1872	3.89	23.23	1982	283.00	456.90
1873	3.89	23.52	1983	262.98	381.50
1874	3.89	22.99	1984	267.19	309.00
1875	3.89	23.75	1985	226.24	326.80
1876	3.89	23.05	1986	265.11	390.90
1877	3.89	21.66	1987	258.67	484.10
1878	3.89	20.84	1988	226.85	410.25
1879–1919	3.89	20.67	1989	246.93	398.60
1920	4.13	20.67	1990	202.58	391.00

SOURCES: U.K. prices from 1560 to 1976 are reconstructed by the authors from indexes in Roy W. Jastram, *The Golden Constant,* copyright © John Wiley & Sons, Inc., 1977. Reprinted by permission of John Wiley & Sons, Inc. Jastram constructed his indexes using free-market prices, Bank of England buying prices, and Mint prices, in that order of preference. Prices from 1977 to 1990 are from *I/IDEAS* U.S. Capital Markets data module, Ibbotson Associates, Inc., Chicago, 1991.

Table 15-4. Silver Prices in U.S. Dollars per Ounce
(1792–1990, Year-end)

Period	$/ounce	Period	$/ounce	Period	$/ounce	Period	$/ounce
1792–1833	1.29	1890	1.05	1924	0.67	1958	0.89
1834–1836	1.21	1891	0.99	1925	0.69	1959	0.91
1837–1859	1.29	1892	0.98	1926	0.62	1960	0.91
		1893	0.78	1927	0.56	1961	1.03
1860	1.35	1894	0.63	1928	0.58	1962	1.20
1861	1.33	1895	0.65	1929	0.53	1963	1.29
1862	1.35	1896	0.67			1964	1.29
1863	1.34	1897	0.60	1930	0.38	1965	1.29
1864	1.34	1898	0.58	1931	0.29	1966	1.29
1865	1.34	1899	0.60	1932	0.28	1967	2.06
1866	1.34			1933	0.35	1968	1.96
1867	1.33	1900	0.61	1934	0.50	1969	1.80
1868	1.33	1901	0.59	1935	0.64		
1869	1.32	1902	0.52	1936	0.45	1970	1.63
		1903	0.54	1937	0.45	1971	1.38
1870	1.33	1904	0.57	1938	0.43	1972	2.04
1871	1.32	1905	0.60	1939	0.39	1973	3.28
1872	1.32	1906	0.67			1974	4.37
1873	1.30	1907	0.65	1940	0.35	1975	4.16
1874	1.28	1908	0.53	1941	0.35	1976	4.37
1875	1.24	1909	0.52	1942	0.38	1977	4.78
1876	1.16			1943	0.45	1978	6.07
1877	1.20	1910	0.53	1944	0.45	1979	28.00
1878	1.15	1911	0.53	1945	0.52		
1879	1.12	1912	0.61	1946	0.80	1980	15.65
		1913	0.60	1947	0.72	1981	8.25
1880	1.15	1914	0.55	1948	0.74	1982	10.90
1881	1.13	1915	0.50	1949	0.72	1983	8.95
1882	1.14	1916	0.66			1984	6.36
1883	1.11	1917	0.81	1950	0.74	1985	5.83
1884	1.11	1918	0.97	1951	0.89	1986	5.37
1885	1.06	1919	1.11	1952	0.85	1987	6.70
1886	1.00			1953	0.85	1988	6.02
1887	0.98	1920	1.01	1954	0.85	1989	5.18
1888	0.94	1921	0.63	1955	0.89		
1889	0.94	1922	0.68	1956	0.91	1990	4.18
		1923	0.65	1957	0.91		

NOTE: Prices are year-end except where not available. The prices from 1792 to 1859 were derived by the authors by converting gold to silver prices using the ratios established by Congress on April 2, 1792 of 15:1, on June 28, 1834 of 16.002:1, and on January 18, 1837 of 15.988:1.

SOURCES: The data from 1860 to 1975 is from Beryl W. Sprinkel and Robert J. Genetski, *Winning with Money*, Dow Jones-Irwin, Homewood, Ill., 1977. Prices since 1975 are the Handy and Harman closing prices for the year, as reported by the *Wall Street Journal.*

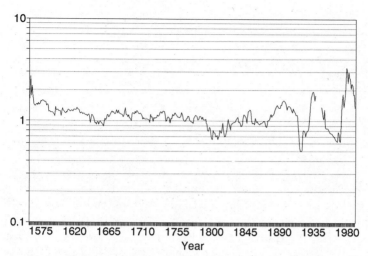

Figure 15-2. U.K. real gold price index: 1560–1990, (1930=1.00). *(Source: Roy W. Jastram,* The Golden Constant, *copyright © John Wiley & Sons, Inc., 1977. Reprinted by permission of John Wiley & Sons, Inc. Data since 1976 are from I/IDEAS U.S. Capital Markets data module, Ibbotson Associates, Inc., Chicago, 1991.)*

near zero and may be expected to in the future. In other words, gold prices and commodity price indexes have tracked one another over the long run. Gold can thus be viewed as a prototype commodity, whose price represents commodity prices in general.

The long-run stability of gold returns is not necessarily mirrored over the short run. An investor who bought an ounce of gold at year-end 1971 realized a nominal compound annual return of 33.6 percent (23.0 percent in real terms) by 1980. However, from year-end 1980 to year-end 1990, the nominal compound annual return was −4.0 percent (−8.1 percent in real terms).

Investment Characteristics of Gold and Silver

With real long-run returns near zero, gold and silver are unlikely to be held for their return. Allowing for acquisition, storage, and insurance, they may have negative real returns.

Although some investors regard gold as simply another form of cash, gold is far riskier than short-term bills over the short run. When choosing between gold and interest-bearing paper as a short-term defensive instrument, paper is the proper choice.

Why, then, do some investors hold gold and silver? There are three reasons: to insure against catastrophes, to diversify, and to hold assets that are part of the world market wealth portfolio.

Gold and Silver as Insurance Assets.   More than other assets, gold and silver provide insurance against such catastrophic changes as economic collapse or hyperinflation, since these metals tend to become money during periods of crisis, constituting a portable store of value and medium of exchange in hard times.

Because both gold and silver usually gain in value during inflationary periods, they are held as an inflation hedge. Over the long run, the purchasing power of gold has been remarkably constant, but recently its price has been unstable. Thus, gold and silver are inflation hedges, but not perfectly dependable ones.

To insure against hyperinflation and economic collapse, gold is a suitable medium. One might hold a small amount of gold to insure that, if other economic institutions fail, beneficiaries would have some residual wealth.

It should not trouble the investor that an insurance asset has a zero or negative expected real rate of return. All insurance assets do. Car insurance, for example, has a return of −100 percent in every period in which the insured car performs well. When the car is wrecked, the return on that period's premium is spectacularly positive. The expectation that the car insurance will have a negative return on average does not deter the car owner from buying the insurance, because the "return" on the car and the return on the insurance move in opposite directions.

Diversification Benefits.   Low correlations with other assets make a given asset a powerful diversification tool to potentially reduce portfolio risk. The correlations of gold with the major investment assets have been low, especially when one includes the 1979 to 1980 inflationary episode. This suggests that when traditional assets perform poorly, gold fares well. Silver has a similar track record, but has had higher, and thus less favorable, correlations with all assets except real estate. Statistically, then, gold may be expected to reduce portfolio risk.

Gold and Silver as a Share of World Assets.   Gold and silver are a significant part of the world's wealth. In 1960, gold alone accounted for 3.7 percent of investable global assets. By 1980, when metal prices reached historical highs, gold and silver made up an astonishing 14 percent of the world's investable assets, exceeding the depressed value of U.S. equities. By the end of 1990, with great increases in world stock and bond values, gold and silver's proportion has dropped to about 3.0 percent of investable assets.[6]

---

[6]I/IDEAS World Capital Markets data module, Ibbotson Associates, Inc., Chicago, 1991. Data from all dates (1960, 1980, 1990) may include gold held by corporations, or used as collateral for government bonds; thus some monetary metals may be double-counted in assessing the wealth of the world.

The silver market is very thin compared to the gold market. During the January 1980 silver bubble, the price of silver was almost four times higher than its price a year earlier. In contrast, when large and small investors caught gold fever in 1979 and 1980 and bid up the price of gold, the peak price was only twice as high as the price that prevailed a year earlier. Large institutions could easily have a powerful impact on prices in relatively thin markets like that for silver, making it a more speculative play.

As we noted in Chapter 3, investors under certain conditions find it optimal to hold a portfolio composed of proportionate shares of all the assets in the world. From this perspective, gold, and to a lesser extent silver, are worthy of consideration as investments.

Commodities

Commodities trading is one of the oldest forms of commerce. Forward and futures contracts have traded on a privately negotiated or over-the-counter basis for thousands of years, while exchange-traded futures trading dates back to 1848 in the United States (grain futures at the Chicago Board of Trade) and the 1600s in Japan (rice futures). Today, the advanced development of futures exchanges enables institutional investors to trade any number of different commodities in large quantities.

A recurring theme throughout this book is the importance of diversification. Like gold, silver, and other inflation hedges, commodities have low correlations with other assets, especially bonds. Because commodity futures are claims to real assets while bonds are claims to money payments, commodity futures and bonds tend to react in opposite directions to changes in inflation. Thus, commodity returns have a distinctly negative correlation with bond returns.

Some investigators regard commodity futures as potentially a better diversifier than gold. The Ohio State University agricultural economist Scott Irwin and the Mexican businessman Diego Landa found that when a portfolio of real estate, commodity futures, gold, stocks, and bonds is subjected to mean-variance optimization, gold drops out.[7]

Investors desiring commodity exposure have passive and active vehicles for obtaining it. The CRB index futures contract, based on the Commodity Research Bureau's index, is a passive, diversified commodity investment and is traded on the New York Futures Exchange. This index is an equal-weighted composite of futures prices for 21 commodities. In late 1992, the Chicago Mercantile Exchange introduced a futures contract based on the Goldman Sachs Commodity Index. If the contract attains substantial liquidity, it would

---

[7]Scott H. Irwin and Diego Landa, "Real Estate, Futures, and Gold as Portfolio Assets," *The Journal of Portfolio Management,* Fall 1987.

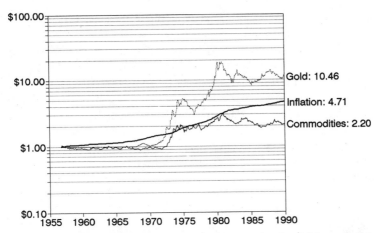

Figure 15-3. Commodities, gold, and inflation: growth of $1 invested in September 1956. *(Source: for commodities, CRB Futures Chart Service, weekly publication of Commodity Research Bureau, a Knight-Ridder Business Information Service, 75 Wall Street, 22nd floor, New York, NY 10005; for inflation, Table 12-3; for gold, Table 15-2.)*

offer a more representative exposure to commodities than the CRB contract. Investors desiring an active exposure can place funds with one or more commodity trading advisors (CTAs). CTAs are active asset managers who restrict their transactions to commodity futures contracts.

To study the returns on commodity futures, we looked at the CRB index, which has a long history.[8] Figure 15-3 shows the growth of a dollar invested in the CRB index,[9] gold, and consumer goods (inflation) from 1956 to 1990. Gold had the highest return, but was much more volatile than the CRB index; the CRB tracked inflation fairly well, but underperformed it, yielding a negative real return over the period.

---

[8]These results originally appeared in Laurence B. Siegel, "Commodity Index Futures as an Asset Class," presented at the New York Institute of Finance, June 21, 1990, and reprinted as an Ibbotson Associates working paper, 1990. As of this writing, a reconstruction of the back history of the Goldman Sachs Commodity Index has recently become available and deserves a similar analysis.

[9]Spot prices of the CRB index were used to construct Figure 15-3 because the futures contracts on the index did not exist over much of the period. The spot CRB index is not traded, but has been shown to be a reasonable proxy for the purpose of measuring what returns on a hypothetical CRB futures contract would have been over the whole period.

Tangible Assets

Tangibles are assets that can be touched and moved and that are functional or useful; in economic terms, they have consumption value. Tangibles, in the broadest sense, include everything of value other than financial claims such as stocks and bonds. The most widely held tangible assets are consumer durables: automobiles, appliances, electronics, and the like. The tangibles most appropriately regarded as investments, however, are gold, silver, and commodities (covered previously in this chapter); real estate (covered in Chapter 13); gems; and works of art.

Tangibles as Investments

Tangible assets have two kinds of returns: monetary, usually in the form of capital appreciation realized at the end of the asset's holding period; and nonpecuniary, the pleasure or utility of owning and using the asset. Tangibles most often held for investment are those on which investors expect monetary returns and which trade in relatively liquid markets. Tangibles are distinguished from other investment-grade assets by their limited marketability, high maintenance costs, and high information costs, all of which affect their expected monetary returns.

Limited Marketability.   The indivisibility of tangibles decreases their marketability. An institution can sell some of its IBM shares without altering the value of the remaining shares, but a Stradivarius violin must be sold in one piece to realize maximum value.

The high transaction costs for both buyers and sellers also reduce the marketability of tangibles. These transaction costs include:

- *High search costs.* Because tangibles are often unique, matching buyer and seller takes time, which results in high brokerage commissions and/or dealer fees. If the search is too lengthy, the seller may be forced to lower his price; if the search is too short, the buyer might pay too much.

- *High fees.* By fees we mean not only direct costs such as sales commissions but also the information costs incurred to verify an asset's authenticity, quality, and in some cases provenance (the names and reputations of the previous owners).

High Maintenance Costs.   Many tangibles, like works of art, require special handling to prevent damage that can seriously erode value. As a further precaution, insurance is frequently purchased.

High Information Costs. Tangibles expose the investor to information costs that can approach extreme levels. Two authentic paintings by the same artist, appearing to the casual eye to be of comparable quality, may have a 10-to-1 price difference. Information about the value of a tangible asset is a complex combination of expertise concerning the asset itself, comparable assets, and the set of individual tastes that govern the market for the asset and its comparables. The investor's cost to acquire this information, so as to transact advantageously, can be a major decrement to the asset's return, if purchased. Because investors typically also acquire information about assets not purchased, the information cost per dollar invested is even higher than it first appears.

Heterogeneous Expectations. The value of tangibles such as art contains a larger subjective component than almost any other asset. The inherent subjectivity implies large discrepancies in valuation among investors. This valuation discrepancy will result in price fluctuation as the subjective components change over time.[10]

Total Expected Returns from Tangibles

An asset's total return is composed of the change in price of the asset over time and the income earned from the asset while held, plus any nonpecuniary return. Unless they are rented out, most tangible assets yield no cash income. The *net* financial (investment) return from a tangible asset is equal to its capital appreciation minus the owner's information, transaction, and maintenance costs.

The particular characteristics of a tangible asset affect its price. For example, if an asset's maintenance or transaction costs are high, the demand for that asset will be lower, thus lowering the price of acquiring the asset and

---

[10]For a fuller discussion of the implications of the valuation gap see William N. Goetzmann, "Accounting for Taste: An Analysis of Art Returns over Three Centuries," Columbia University working paper, March 1990. The amount of an artwork's value that is attributable solely to subjective components has implications for whether or not high bidders at art auctions are subject to a winner's curse. The winner's curse is the likelihood that the highest bidder at an auction for an item that has some common valuation paid too much for it. If the value of a work of art is completely subjective and no common valuation exists, then, by definition, there is no winner's curse. If the value of a work of art has a common component then a winner's curse should appear, unless rational bidders are aware of the curse and uniformly lower their bids to avoid the curse. Goetzmann empirically examines this issue and finds no winner's curse, but points out that his statistical tests are unable to distinguish between the absence of a winner's curse and rational action taken by bidders to avoid overbidding in the presence of the curse.

raising its expected return before investor-specific costs. In other words, if investors are required to take on the higher costs of holding the asset, then they will demand a higher monetary return on their investment. The next section examines the historical returns in the art market. While works of art make up only one segment of a large and complex market for tangible assets, they are the segment for which prices are well-documented over a long period of time.

Historical Art Returns

Whereas durable goods have functional value, artistic works have value that is mostly subjective and aesthetic. Why else would Van Gogh's *Irises* sell for $53.9 million in 1988 while other good paintings by other reputable artists of the same period sell in the thousands of dollars? Fashion, economic conditions, and buyer's wealth levels all influence the price, as do the work's intrinsic characteristics, such as its quality, authorship, rarity, and condition.

Although much of the return on art comes from aesthetic enjoyment, it can also provide a monetary return. Art return indexes exist, but are likely to be biased upward. Paintings that have fallen in price are much less likely to be put up for sale, and are less likely to be negotiated through top dealers like Christie's or Sotheby's, where accurate prices would be recorded and incorporated into indexes. Thus, returns tend to be computed using paintings that have mostly risen in value, producing an obvious upward bias relative to the average return of all artwork.

With these caveats, the Sotheby index of art prices had a compound annual return of 15.4 percent from year-end 1975 to year-end 1990 as compared to 13.9 percent for the S&P 500. (Individual components of the Sotheby index had greatly varying returns.) To get a much longer perspective on art as an investment, the Columbia University economist William Goetzmann examined 3329 repeat sales transactions to construct an art price index covering the years 1714 to 1986. Figure 15-4 reports the growth of £1 invested at year-end 1713. Table 15-5 reports art and equity returns and inflation for this same period, which are given in both nominal and real terms.

Figure 15-4 reveals four great bull markets: 1730–1770, 1780–1820, 1840–1870, and 1940–1986. The bulk of the appreciation for the entire period occurred in the last 50 years. The 1780–1820 and 1940–1986 markets were associated with high inflation. There have also been four great bear markets: 1714–1730, 1820–1840, 1870–1880, and 1920–1940. All of

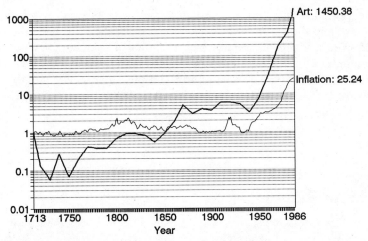

Figure 15-4. Goetzmann art index: growth of £1 invested in 1714. *(Source: William N. Goetzmann, Accounting for Taste: An Analysis of Art Returns over Three Centuries, Columbia University working paper, 1990.)*

these periods were associated with economic recessions or depressions.[11] For the entire period, the annual rate of return is 3.2 percent with a stunning annual standard deviation of 56.5 percent. This high volatility is even more striking given the diversified nature of Goetzmann's portfolio.

Table 15-5. Art Returns, Equity Returns, and Inflation (1714–1986)

In Percent

Period	Art		Equity		Inflation
	Nominal	Real	Nominal	Real	
1714–1750	−6.96	−6.72	0.75	1.02	−0.27
1751–1800	4.70	2.93	−0.04	−1.73	1.71
1801–1850	0.55	1.94	0.72	2.11	−1.36
1851–1900	2.84	2.94	1.60	1.69	−0.09
1901–1950	1.48	−0.33	5.24	2.67	1.82
1951–1986	15.67	8.49	14.68	7.33	6.62

NOTE: Equity returns represent capital gains only from 1714 to 1918.

SOURCES: William N. Goetzmann, "Accounting for Taste: An Analysis of Art Returns over Three Centuries," Columbia University working paper, March 1990. Equity returns from 1919 to 1986 are from Peter Thompson, Jeffrey Thompson, Bryan Allworthy, and David Roden, *BZW Equity-Gilt Study,* Barclays de Zoete Wedd, London, 1989.

[11]Britain, the source of many of the painting sales in Goetzmann's sample, experienced a weak economy in the 1920s. The huge initial decline starting in 1714 was contemporaneous with a sharp drop in the London stock market (see Chapter 8).

The risk-reward combination that art provides should not be viewed in isolation. Much like the other assets studied in this chapter, art might be expected to have low correlations with other assets, making it an effective tool for diversification. To test this proposition, Goetzmann calculated correlations of his art index with British inflation, Bank of England short-term rates, and capital appreciation returns from the London Stock Exchange for the 270-year period.[12] The correlations are 0.28 with inflation, 0.53 with short-term Bank of England rates, and 0.67 with the capital appreciation returns on stocks. The fairly strong relation to stocks may indicate that art returns are linked to changes in individual wealth. The unexpected finding is that the correlation with inflation is low relative to other instruments used as inflation hedges.

Conclusion

The disadvantages of tangibles include their lack of short-term liquidity and high volatility. Changes in taste, supply shocks, and general economic changes such as a recession or a financial-assets boom can make investments in tangibles very risky.

In determining value, both the objective and subjective components of price are best understood by experts within the field who can gauge quality, authenticity, and the market's subjective opinion. The result is that nonspecialized investors are at a disadvantage.

The physicality of tangibles also decreases their attractiveness as an investment. High maintenance costs are sometimes incurred to avoid deterioration. Tangibles also should be insured against theft and damage. Furthermore, when tangibles are moved across international boundaries, import and export tariffs may also reduce their returns. Finally, unlike income from many financial investments, the nonpecuniary income from some tangible assets cannot generally be reinvested to compound their returns. Despite all of these problems, tangibles are often used to provide diversification and inflation protection. Institutional investors may wish to hold portions of their portfolios in precious metals and/or financial instruments providing exposure to commodity price fluctuations.

In evaluating tangibles, investors should not confuse investment with consumption. As a result of their special characteristics, tangibles with substantial nonpecuniary returns, such as art, should be bought by investors who receive special pleasure from them. Since such assets are priced by peo-

---

[12]British data were used because the bulk of art transactions occurred in the United Kingdom. Because dividend yield data on British stocks are not reliable before 1919, total returns cannot be calculated.

ple who like them the most, this nonpecuniary income is part of the return. An investor who does not receive as much nonpecuniary return will have overpaid for the asset. For these reasons, tangibles with high nonpecuniary returns are not generally appropriate for institutional investors.

PART 6

Conclusion

16

What the Future Holds

The search for investment value is an appraisal of the future. Quite literally, investors care only about the future. The value of a security today is the present value of all future cash flows that it is expected to generate. In this purely mathematical sense, the past is irrelevant. Investors should study the past only to the extent that it provides insight into patterns and relations that *have* characterized capital markets and might be expected to do so in the future. Even though the past is not a prescient description of the future, a solid understanding of what forces shaped the past, combined with an understanding of the extent to which those same forces are expected to be important in the future, provides a useful starting point for determining what the future holds.

The Dynamic Marketplace

The only certainty is change itself. This view dominates contemporary thought, perhaps to the detriment of appreciating the past. Nevertheless, the unrelenting advances in technology, finance, and science, if not also in human nature, have made change the norm.

Capitalism is the enabling mechanism of that change. About 60 years ago, the economist Joseph Schumpeter wrote of capitalism's "creative destruction," which he defined as the unsentimental tearing down of nonadaptive traditions and their sudden replacement by new ideas and methods. We observe this creative destruction every year, as new businesses are born while old ones die; in every generation, whole industries, as well as technologies, appear and disappear.

In Table 16-1, the largest U.S. industries are ranked by the number of persons employed for 20-year periods from 1880 to 1980. In 1880, fiber product industries—cotton, wool, men's clothing, and lumber—were the top four in importance. By 1920, railroad car manufacturers employed the most people and automobiles made their first appearance on the list. By 1940 railroads and men's clothing dropped from the list, and steel and automobiles held the top two spots. In 1960 aircraft and newspapers first appeared; in 1980 communications and plastics made the list.

Table 16-1. The Rise and Fall of Industries (1880–1980)

Persons Employed, in Thousands

1880		1900		1920	
Cotton goods	185.5	Machine and foundry	350.3	Railroad car shops	484.4
Woolen goods	161.6	Cotton goods	302.9	Machine and foundry	482.8
Men's clothing	160.8	Lumber	283.3	Lumber	481.0
Lumber	148.0	Iron and steel	220.5	Cotton goods	431.0
Machine and foundry	145.4	Men's clothing	191.0	Iron and steel	375.1
Iron and steel	141.0	Railroad car shops	173.7	Shipbuilding	344.0
Boots and shoes	133.8	Printing and publishing	163.0	Electrical equipment	212.4
Brick and tile	66.4	Boots and shoes	143.0	Boots and shoes	211.0
Furniture	59.3	Carpentry	124.0	Automobile	210.6
Printing and publishing	58.5	Masonry	110.6	Men's clothing	175.2

1940		1960		1980	
Autos	397.5	Autos	694.5	Autos	714.3
Steel	368.9	Aircraft	679.2	Aircraft	580.5
Cotton goods	312.2	Steel	620.2	Communications	566.1
Lumber	285.2	Newspaper and		Electrical components	498.6
Footwear	218.0	periodicals	374.3	Newspaper and	
Bakery goods	201.5	Women's clothing	364.1	periodicals	491.8
Wool	140.0	Lumber	349.3	Steel	489.9
Meatpacking	120.0	Structural metal	328.4	Plastics	470.1
Paper products	110.6	Meat products	306.9	Structural metals	464.6
Canned food	98.0	Bakery goods	306.0	Women's clothing	456.4
		Commercial printing	302.2	Commercial printing	414.6

SOURCE: "Sunrise, Sunset," Manhattan Institute for Policy Research.

In the near future we anticipate the communications industry to retain its significance. The outlook for U.S. cars and steel manufacturers is less sanguine. Overall, if the past is any guide, the leading employer in the year 2020 is probably not on the list and may not even exist today.

But what about the pace of change? We have just been through an industrial revolution, the third in 250 years (see Chapter 1). The recent revolution in the use of computers and other electronic devices to perform everyday tasks has been as profound as any major historical shift. Can such a pace of change possibly be expected to continue?

Having identified capitalism as the enabling mechanism of change, we believe the pace of change may actually continue to accelerate. As of this writing, vast areas of the formerly communist and developing world are experimenting with capitalism. The Eastern European discovery of Adam Smith's ideas garners the most attention, but the rigid central control that has hampered growth in noncommunist Latin American and other developing economies for decades is also being eroded. Mexico is an example of an economy that is currently booming in response to decentralization of control. As capitalist experiments become more successful in these countries, the many changes they cause (for better and worse, but largely better) will be made manifest. The seeds of change will be planted not only by residents of Western Europe, Japan, and the United States, but by the people of the entire world.

Global Integration: The Next Phase

Because the world economy is in a continual state of flux, its capital market prices are not likely to fully reflect all technological and social developments. Over the very long run this represents an opportunity to achieve better-than-market returns for investors who correctly anticipate developments. In 1851, at the Crystal Palace exhibition in London, Prince Albert of Britain said that because of the technologies displayed, humanity would someday live under one roof. By 1903 inventions that would unify the world—the automobile, airplane, and telephone—had all been invented. In another 50 years, such inventions were fully integrated into everyday life. Had Prince Albert's insight been turned into a long-run investment strategy, the returns would have been phenomenal.

While virtually all countries are becoming more globally integrated (to date, the increase in the multinational character of corporations is the primary indicator), the degree of movement toward global integration has not been uniform across countries. Most of the integration has served to link the developed world. Although much remains to be done on this front (with human capital, the world's most valuable resource, being still deeply segmented even within countries), most future integration will come from developing countries and the formerly communist areas of Eastern Europe.

It is not enough to say that integration will continue because it has occurred in the past. One must identify the force behind increasing integration and determine whether that force will be a factor in the future. We believe that force, reduced to its elemental form, is the basic human drive for self-improvement, which is greatly facilitated by free markets where ideas, goods, and services can be exchanged. If people believe they are better off with the option to exchange goods, capital, and effort, they will do what is necessary to overcome the basic illogic, or economic inefficiency, of borders that create barriers to such exchange.

As borders become more permeable and transportation costs decline, the world economy will become more efficient because labor, capital, and other resources will migrate more quickly and cheaply to the places where they receive the highest wages and rents. Such migration greatly lessens the inequality of compensation among people of comparable skill as well as among nonhuman capital assets with comparable attributes.

The continued breakdown of borders has important implications in the six areas discussed below.

Standards of Living

Gaps between rich and poor populations will narrow, not widen. The richest countries have already achieved near zero population growth and their economic growth rates have fallen to sedate if not sleepy levels. Meanwhile, some poor countries have fabulously high economic growth rates, like those observed in the United States and Europe a century ago. The sustained 12 percent annual growth rate of southern coastal China is probably not achievable in most economies, but it represents the kind of growth that can sometimes be achieved by a dynamic emerging economy. As this process continues, standards of living are likely to become gradually more uniform throughout the world.

The future may not appear as sanguine for the low-skilled residents of developed nations. The continued breakdown of borders makes it easier for firms in developed nations to relocate manufacturing plants to countries with inexpensive labor. While this relocation is frequently a boon for the country receiving the new plant, this process may temporarily disrupt the employment situations of low-skilled residents of developed nations.

Business

Most large companies are multinational and are becoming more so. This trend is likely to continue. When profit opportunities in chocolate exist abroad, Nestlé has no incentive to limit its sales to Switzerland, or even to Europe. Also, business in the future is likely to be subject to less regulation and taxation. Political entities that impose excessive burdens will be seen as uncompetitive. Finally, unprocessed data from throughout the world will be cheap and abundant, but sorting and interpreting—that is, converting data to information—will be a key business activity.

Capital Markets

Capital markets of the future will almost certainly encompass new types of investment opportunities. Less restrictive borders mean more integrated markets. Already, borders have a very limited meaning in the foreign exchange markets where a push of a button can send a trillion yen across the globe. As more securities become continuously traded, the character of capital markets will be altered. The exchanges in New York, London, Tokyo, Singapore, and other cities may become practically perfect substitutes for one another as investors execute where the terms are most favorable at the moment. Exchanges as physical entities may disintegrate. A farfetched but not wholly unrealistic possibility is that even the most tradition-laden capital market institutions, the New York and London stock exchanges, will disband within a generation or two as securities traders execute transactions via computer from their cottages on Cape Cod and from poolside in Puerto Vallarta.

The nature of corporate financing is also subject to change in a borderless world. Increased capital market integration means that investment opportunities will be available to corporations that will demand more capital to finance these endeavors and investors will more freely supply capital across borders. One implication of this trend is that costs of capital will become more equal among countries.

Investment Portfolios

As the business environment becomes more global so will investment portfolios. Investors will have to hold a global portfolio in order to achieve significant diversification of risk. This will be facilitated by the increasing flow of information on foreign securities. This process is already underway as the number of internationally oriented mutual funds proliferates, creating intense demand for cross-country standardization of information on companies.

Language

For educated and scholarly people, mathematics and data have always stood as a kind of universal language. These languages are now being adopted by a much broader segment of society. Just as a knowledge of Latin was required as evidence of competence in Western cultures during the nineteenth century, a rudimentary understanding of computers and mathematics is required today and a deeper understanding will be necessary tomorrow.

Even more widespread is a knowledge of English. No language in history has ever been more widely used than English, and in a more integrated world its influence will only continue to increase.

Culture

In a broader sense, Prince Albert's vision of humanity under one roof will become more of a reality. This phenomenon is, of course, already underway. McDonald's hamburgers and Coca-Cola are consumed worldwide, to name just two examples. But there is a deeper level at which the world is becoming more integrated. The values of each culture are being disseminated to other cultures, creating more commonalities among people. The dissemination of values is imparted more by the consumption of cultural products, such as music, literature, television, and movies than by formal learning. Radio programs that feature an Italian opera singer, a British rock band, and an American jazz quartet probably have more impact on other countries than philosophical writing about the values of these cultures. In addition, the dissemination of cultural values is more the result of multinational corporations than academia or government, since business is typically the medium for distributing cultural products.

Conclusion

Investors face an increasingly complex environment. This is good news and bad; complexity means that investors will have to work harder and be smarter to understand the environment in which they operate. However, those who anticipate the future with even a moderate degree of accuracy can profit handsomely.

Optimists perceive the future to be a cornucopia, affording riches to those who simply participate. They remember that a dollar invested in U.S. equities in 1789 would have grown by now to over $9 million. They now see a landscape of investment choices a thousand times broader than the most visionary capitalist of 1789 could have imagined. Since nothing suggests that the reward for taking risk has changed dramatically, the wealth expansion since 1789 ought to be repeatable, give or take a few orders of magnitude.

Pessimists have a very different view of the future. They consider the possibility that most of the economic growth that will take place already has. Although poor people and poor countries aspire to become rich, there is no natural law saying that they will succeed or that an investor can automatically share in such success should it occur. Pessimists would note that a single tempest in the market, or a bad investment decision, could wipe out one's hard-earned capital. The crash of 1929 to 1932, the 1950 to 1981 collapse in bond prices, and various price crashes in real estate, gold, and oil provide plenty of examples in the United States alone. Finally, they remember the many foreign markets where capital was wiped out by war or revolution, and they conclude that investing is a dangerous business indeed.

The resolution of these contradictory visions lies in realizing that diversification and knowledge provide investors with both safety and gains. By diversifying among asset classes, investors obtain protection against events like the U.S. stock market crash from 1929 to 1932; over that period, bonds went up slightly. By diversifying internationally, investors are much more likely to pick at least one winner: even though the crash of 1929 was multinational, the accompanying depression was over by 1931 in the United Kingdom, with shares passing their 1929 highs by 1936.

Knowledge is equally beneficial. Safety is achieved by understanding all of the risks of an investment, not just the most obvious ones. Investors can then distinguish real bargains from apparent ones with hidden risks. Gains are available to investors who can perceive value that is not discerned by the market. Since most capital markets are partially inefficient, investors who are both skilled at interpreting information and willing to risk their capital on the results are the ones who can earn the highest returns.

The investment landscape of the future will encompass the globe. To fail to consider securities that are not in one's home country deprives a portfolio of much potential gain and potential for risk reduction. A common factor that will characterize most successful investment policies in the future will be that they involve global investing.

Index

Note: The letters t, f, and n following a page number indicate table, figure, and footnote, respectively.

About the Authors

Roger G. Ibbotson, Ph.D., is Professor of Finance at the Yale School of Management and President of Ibbotson Associates, a Chicago-based consulting firm specializing in finance, investments, and economics.

Gary P. Brinson, CFA, is President of Brinson Partners, Inc., a Chicago-based institutional investment management firm with offices in London and Tokyo that specializes in global capital markets.